CHICAGO 1890

THE SKYSCRAPER AND THE MODERN CITY

Joanna Merwood-Salisbury

THE UNIVERSITY OF CHICAGO PRESS | CHICAGO AND LONDON

JOANNA MERWOOD-SALISBURY is assistant professor in
the Department of Architecture, Interior Design, and Lighting
at Parsons The New School for Design, New York City.

The University of Chicago Press, Chicago 60637
The University of Chicago Press, Ltd., London
© 2009 by The University of Chicago
All rights reserved. Published 2009
Printed in the United States of America

18 17 16 15 14 13 12 11 10 09   1 2 3 4 5

ISBN-13: 978-0-226-52078-0 (cloth)
ISBN-10: 0-226-52078-1 (cloth)

Library of Congress Cataloging-in-Publication Data

Merwood-Salisbury, Joanna.
  Chicago 1890 : the skyscraper and the modern city /
    Joanna Merwood-Salisbury.
      p. cm.—(Chicago architecture and urbanism)
  Includes bibliographical references and index.
  ISBN-13: 978-0-226-52078-0 (hardcover : alk. paper)
  ISBN-10: 0-226-52078-1 (hardcover : alk. paper)
  1. Skyscrapers—Illinois—Chicago. 2. Architecture
and society—Illinois—Chicago—History—19th century.
  3. Chicago (Ill.)—Buildings, structures, etc. I. Title.
  NA6232.M46 2009
  720'.4830977311—dc22
                              2008026986

♾ The paper used in this publication meets the minimum
requirements of the American National Standard for
Information Sciences—Permanence of Paper for Printed
Library Materials, ANSI Z39.48-1992.

This book is for Ned.

CONTENTS

ILLUSTRATIONS

ACKNOWLEDGMENTS

This book would not exist without four gifted teachers, whose work has set the highest standard for a new generation of scholars: Beatriz Colomina, Mark Wigley, Georges Teyssot, and Alessandra Ponte. I am deeply grateful for all the guidance they have given me. The bulk of the research was undertaken while I was teaching at the University of Illinois at Chicago. My thanks go to David Sokol for giving me the opportunity to be there, and to Carl Ray Miller, Deborah Fausch, and Ellen T. Baird for their hospitality. I would also like to thank my colleagues at Parsons The New School for Design, especially Kent Kleinman and Peter Wheelwright, for their ongoing support.

Bob Bruegmann and David Van Zanten, editors of the Chicago Architecture and Urbanism series at the University of Chicago Press, have been more than generous with their encouragement and practical help over a number of years. At the Press, Susan Bielstein, Anthony Burton, and Sandra Hazel have guided me through the editing and publication process expertly and efficiently. I would also like to thank Sophie Hartley, who located many of the images, and Naomi Linzer, for compiling the index.

The production of the book was supported by grants from the Graham Foundation for Advanced Studies in the Fine Arts and the Parsons The New School for Design Faculty Development Fund.

Many people offered valuable insight on drafts, talks, and papers as this project grew into a book, including Stan Allen, Anthony Alofsin, Edward Eigen, Kevin Harrington, Reinhold Martin, Lisa Pincus, Mark Rakatansky, Katerina Rüedi Ray, Felicity Scott, Andy Shanken, and Lauren Weingarden. I am especially indebted to a wonderful group of friends for the advice they provided along the way, particularly Mark Campbell, Gabrielle Esperdy, Michael Lobel, Marcos Sánchez, and David Smiley. Much of my thinking and writing has been shaped by discussions with Jonathan Massey and Tom Weaver. The best parts of this book are due to them. Finally, I remain grateful for the love and support of my family: Mary Atwool, Brent Southgate, Laura Southgate, and my husband, Ned Salisbury.

INTRODUCTION

In 1890 Chicago reached the peak of an unprecedented real estate boom. The wholesale quarter to the south and the light-manufacturing district on the Near West Side were rapidly expanding. Further out, suburban lots increased in value as commuter rail lines extended residential areas in all directions. However, the defining icon of the boom was not at the periphery of the city but in the center, where twelve- and even sixteen-story buildings eclipsed the five- and six-story structures built only a few years earlier. These tall office buildings were concentrated in three areas: along LaSalle Street, the financial hub; at the southern end of the growing business district along Dearborn Street; and around State and Washington streets, in the heart of the shopping district. Together these buildings confirmed an argument for unrestricted urban growth made by Chicago architects and businessmen: the city would expand where and when it needed to, upward and outward without regulation or control. In 1890 the tall office building was the future of the American city.

Yet these buildings were not just portents of a magnificent and prosperous future but also records of a tumultuous past. Between 1880 and 1890, Chicago solidified its position as the premier city in the Midwest. These years were rocked by terrific turmoil as the young city grappled with an unstable industrial economy fueled by the dramatic growth of almost unrestricted trade, which was serviced by wave upon wave of immigrants. Despite boosterish claims to the contrary, Chicago suffered under almost unbearable pressure in these years: pressure that the economy would not hold; pressure that the city would destroy itself by growing too fast; pressure of imminent political revolution. With their designs for tall office buildings, architects and real estate developers provided not only an economic mechanism for unrestricted urban growth but also aesthetic and programmatic solutions to these social and political problems.

This book is about those solutions. It reconstructs the urgent debates about the form and function of the Chicago skyscraper that appeared in specialist architectural journals, real estate and building trades magazines, and newspapers and magazines with a mass readership (fig. 0.01). Chronologically it is bounded on one end by the appearance of the first tall office buildings in the city around 1882, when Chicago architects began to construct a narrative of this building type as the natural and organic product of its environment, the symbol of the strength, independence, and prosperity of the American West. It is bounded on the other end by the growing disillusionment with the type following the financial crash of 1893, when huge amounts of office space lay unoccupied and unwanted. Under the influence of the City Beautiful movement at the turn of the century, the tall office building began to seem like an expensive folly, an unwelcome symbol of individual hubris. Consequently, the "heroic skyscraper," less than twenty years old, fell out of favor around this time.

THE CHICAGO TRIBUNE: SUNDAY, MAY 8, 1892—FORTY-FOUR PAGES.

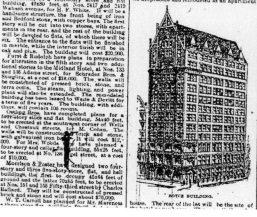

0.01 "Chicago's New Office Buildings: Structures Commenced or Open to the Public during the Current Month," *Chicago Daily Tribune*, May 8, 1892, p. 39. This article illustrates some of the tall office buildings constructed in Chicago during 1891–92: Northern Hotel, Monadnock, Columbus Memorial, Venetian, Boyce Building, Unity Building, and Title and Trust Building.

Louis Sullivan, the most celebrated Chicago architect of this period, famously described this short-lived cycle in his *Autobiography of an Idea* (1924). Sullivan claimed that the first generation of American skyscrapers was born in Chicago about the time he began practicing there in the 1870s; that these buildings achieved their peak with his own designs for the Wainwright and Guaranty buildings in the early 1890s; and that they then fell into decline under the poisonous influence of the 1893 World's Columbian Exposition. In the twentieth century many critics and historians repeated this story, building a genealogy of American architecture with Chicago at its center. This genealogy privileges the work of Sullivan and his colleague John Wellborn Root as the spontaneous eruption of a native American style, a powerful strain of early modernism inspired by the Boston architect H. H. Richardson, one that died an untimely death at the hands of Root's partner Daniel Burnham, and barely survived into the twentieth century via the work of Sullivan's pupil Frank Lloyd Wright and his colleagues in the Prairie School.[1]

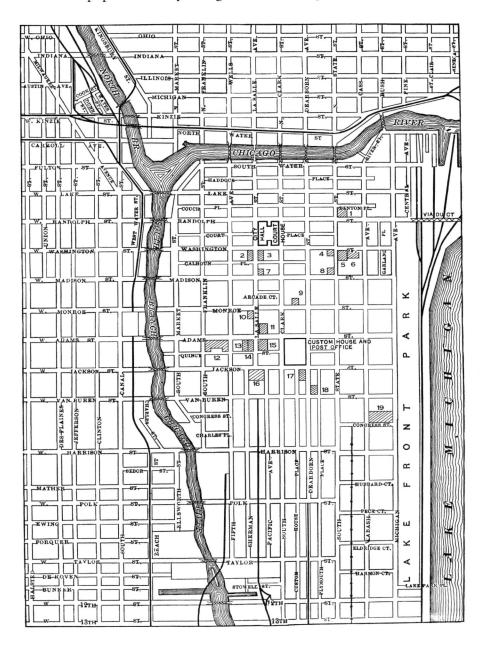

0.02 Map of downtown Chicago Loop, ca. 1890; based on *Rand McNally's Bird's-Eye Views and Guide to Chicago* (Chicago, 1898): (*1*) Burnham and Root, Masonic Temple, 1890–92; (*2*) Adler and Sullivan, Chicago Stock Exchange, 1893–94; (*3*) Baumann and Huehl, Chamber of Commerce, 1888–90; (*4*) D. H. Burnham and Co., Reliance, 1889–95; (*5*) W. W. Boyington, Columbus Memorial, 1891–93; (*6*) Holabird and Roche, Venetian, 1891–92; (*7*) Holabird and Roche, Tacoma, 1887–89; (*8*) Holabird and Roche, Champlain, 1893–94; (*9*) Burnham and Root, Montauk, 1881–82; (*10*) Burnham and Root, Woman's Temple, 1890–92; (*11*) William Le Baron Jenney, Home Insurance, 1883–85; (*12*) H. H. Richardson, Marshall Field Wholesale Store, 1885–86; (*13*) Burnham and Root, Rand McNally, 1888–90; (*14*) Burnham and Root, Insurance Exchange, 1884–85; (*15*) Burnham and Root, Rookery, 1885–86; (*16*) W. W. Boyington, Chicago Board of Trade, 1883–85; (*17*) Burnham and Root, Monadnock, 1885–92; (*18*) D. H. Burnham and Co., Fisher, 1895–96; (*19*) Adler and Sullivan, Auditorium, 1887–89.

In this way, then, this book treads over well-established territory, following as it does the transition from the tall office building as an individual symbol of regional strength and capitalist power (represented by Sullivan), to the skyscraper as an integral part of a larger urban system with national aspirations (represented by Burnham). However, my interest is not in the formal or technological development of the type (there will be no diagrams), or in architecture considered as an autonomous artistic discipline (the genealogical aspect of architectural history holds little interest for me). Instead, I want to examine these architectural artifacts through the lens of their own time, in their social and urban contexts. My interest lies in placing the design and reception of these buildings within the dominant concerns of their era. In the case of Chicago in 1890, this means paying attention to the frontier philosophy through which self-described "westerners" constructed their own history; the ethnic and class conflicts that consumed all aspects of urban life; and the growing fears about the health of the city. Though there are many ways one might approach this topic, I have chosen to focus on the *Inland Architect*, the professional journal of Chicago architects published between 1883 and 1908, treating it as a medium for the expression of ideas about the skyscraper. I will give particular emphasis to three of the buildings so important to contemporary critics: the Monadnock (1889; fig. 0.03), the Masonic Temple (1892; fig. 0.04), and the Reliance Building (1895; fig. 0.05), tracing in them the emergence of new forms of aesthetic expression and new urban solutions.

As Sarah Bradford Landau and Carl Condit have written in their definitive history of the tall office building in New York City, "The skyscraper building type owes its existence and much of its character more to the desire for money and prestige, to advances in technology, and to adventures in real estate speculation than to abstract ideals or theories of style or aesthetics."[2] This is undeniably true. Focusing principally on the rise of steel-framed construction and the way in which architects gave it formal expression, Condit published the canonical history of the early Chicago skyscraper in 1964.[3] More recently, Carol Willis has revealed the ways in which its design was determined by real estate practice and by building regulations.[4] Pushing further the connections between urban form and the capitalist economic system in nineteenth-century American cities, Mario Manieri-Elia has described the landscape of the downtown Loop as the creation of forces of capital acting almost unchecked in the context of the laissez-faire economy.[5] Yet the businessmen involved in the construction of this urban landscape, new architectural patrons, did not see the buildings they commissioned as entirely technical and economic machines. As Daniel Bluestone has shown, the speculators who founded Chicago in the 1830s had their own aesthetic and cultural aspirations. Fifty years later, their successors believed that the skyscraper should express not only the power and wealth of their metropolis but also their own taste, refinement, and civic-mindedness. Bluestone and others have illustrated the role of clients, patrons, and civic groups in the formation of Chicago's skyscrapers, understanding their design as a collective and collaborative enterprise with social and cultural purposes, as well as commercial ones.[6]

Recent scholarship has reinserted the first generation of Chicago skyscrapers into the concerns of the late nineteenth century rather than seeing them as prefigurations of the concerns of the twentieth. It has shown that Chicago architects, real estate developers, and private patrons were not pure pragmatists or intellectual innocents but active participants in an attempt to reconcile new programs

0.03 *(opposite)* Burnham and Root, the Monadnock (1885–92), southwest corner of Jackson and Dearborn streets. Photograph by Webster Brothers, ca. 1940. Used by permission from the Chicago History Museum; ICHi-23481.

0.04 *(left)* Burnham and Root, Masonic Temple (1890–92), northeast corner of State and Randolph streets. Photograph ca. 1901. Courtesy of the Library of Congress; LC-USZ62-123683.

0.05 *(opposite)* Burnham and Root / D. H. Burnham and Co., Reliance Building (1889–95), southwest corner of State and Washington streets. Photograph by J. W. Taylor. Historic American Building Survey, ILL, 16-CHIG, 30-2. Courtesy of the Library of Congress.

RELIANCE · BLD.

Lapp & Flershe...

and technologies with traditional architectural forms and traditions. With varying methodological approaches, scholars have drawn attention to the intellectual and social aims of particular Chicago architects, especially William Le Baron Jenney, Daniel Burnham, John Wellborn Root, William Holabird, Martin Roche, Dankmar Adler, and Louis Sullivan.[7] Some of their most radical buildings, such as the Home Insurance (1884), the Tacoma (1889), and the Manhattan (1890), garnered national and international attention not only because of their height but also because of their apparent lack of design. Critics from the East Coast and from Europe thought these buildings were ugly, existing only for profit with no thought as to beauty. In response, Chicago architects were motivated to find a place for themselves and their work within architectural history.

These creators of the metropolis spent endless hours debating how the tall office building should look, and what its urban impact would be.[8] Countering criticism that the skyscraper was nothing but the raw product of commerce, they described it as a regional type, nature's newest and best creation. As the environmental historian William Cronon has shown, the narrative of Chicago as an "organic" landscape was not particular to architecture—it was central to the formation of the city in the mid-nineteenth century. The organic narrative masked the fact that the city was in essence a machine at the center of a vast regional garden, organizing and processing the agricultural products of the Midwest for distribution to the East Coast and abroad.[9] At meetings of their professional organization, the Western Association of Architects, local architects talked of the evolution of European styles into a new American style derived not from historic precedent but from simple needs. For them, truly organic architecture was symbolic of the fecundity of the West, and of the strength and resourcefulness of the western people.

The discourse of architecture in Chicago was informed not only by abstract philosophies such as organicism but also by local events. As the historian Carl Smith has shown, between the 1870s and '90s the rapid growth of the industrial city was interrupted by fierce conflict.[10] Violent strikes and demonstrations over wages and labor conditions were met with brutal responses on the part of business leaders, the police, and the local militia. These disputes involved not only class divisions but ethnic divisions as well, since the laborers toiling to build the new city were largely recent immigrants, first from Ireland, then from central, eastern, and northern Europe. Fueled by an uncompromising war of words in newspapers and broadsheets, these conflicts created an intense hostility between classes. For Chica-

goans, mindful of recent events in Germany, France, and Russia, the threat of social revolution was real. It was reflected in all areas of life, including architecture. As much as architects justified the skyscraper as the finest product of the city, socialists and anarchists denounced it as a symbol of class oppression and economic inequality. In his indispensable work on Louis Sullivan, Joseph Siry has demonstrated that one of the most revered Chicago skyscrapers, Adler and Sullivan's Auditorium Building (1889), was designed in direct response to these conflicts.[11] As this book shows, concern over class and ethnic conflict is the subtext for organic architecture in America, and it inflected the debate about the form and function of the tall office building in multiple and significant ways.

Around 1890 every description of the new urban landscape struggled to reconcile the philosophy of organicism with the realities of industrial production. Labor disputes were not an abstract concern for Chicago architects. At the very moment the skyscraper was born, the practice of design and construction was being turned upside down by the mechanization of traditional crafts and the bureaucratization of the building industry.[12] The industrialization of the building trades caused turmoil as architects, contractors, and craftsmen fought to master and control these confusing changes. It also led to a paradigm shift within architectural discourse. Suddenly the model of Gothic architecture, of slowly and carefully handcrafted building techniques, was no longer appropriate. Steel-framed towers rose on the horizon in a matter of weeks. New materials such as terra-cotta tile and plate glass were developed to clad them. In response, Chicago architects sought out different forms of aesthetic expression for the industrial age to replace the Gothic model that had dominated American building since the mid-nineteenth century.

Chicagoans were also forced to confront the environmental consequences of their transformation of the land. Despite the rhetoric of organicism, the built environment and the natural world did not always operate in harmony. As Harold Platt has shown, the founding of the industrial city meant radical changes to the region's natural ecology.[13] The land itself was raised to provide adequate foundation for roads and buildings. The Chicago River and Lake Michigan became highly polluted. Huge concentrations of people living in squalid slums led to cholera epidemics and death. The magnificent vista of Chicago was obscured by clouds of coal smoke pouring from the rooftop chimneys of each new building (fig. 0.06). These environmental changes necessitated new ways of thinking about architecture and urban design if the city—and its citizens—were to survive.

0.06 Bird's-eye view of Chicago, 1913. Photograph by J. W. Taylor. The rhetoric of organicism that dominated discussion of the growth of Chicago was not easy to reconcile with the realities of the industrial landscape. The design of the buildings constructed during the skyscraper boom of 1882–93 must be seen in the context of the heavily polluted atmospheric environment surrounding them. Courtesy of the Library of Congress; LC-USZ62-123294.

Taking these social and environmental factors into consideration means re-thinking the history of the Chicago skyscraper. The new building form did not have a singular meaning architecturally, economically, or socially. In investigating the complex and contradictory meanings of the skyscraper, much of my research derives from a systematic reading of the *Inland Architect and Builder* (Chicago, 1883–87) and the *Inland Architect and News Record* (Chicago, 1887–1908), the official organ of the Western Association of Architects, a partner to the East Coast–based American Institute of Architects. Founded in 1883 under the editorship of the journalist Robert Craik McLean, the *Inland Architect* provided the primary venue for criticism and debate on not only technical and professional issues but also aesthetic ones.[14] Through an investigation of essays published in the magazine, the first chapter lays out the intellectual basis of the debate. It pays particular attention to the narrative of organicism as a way to think about the development of architectural style, and also as a way to think about the relationships between the diverse ethnic groups in the city.

In the nineteenth century, the processes of urbanization and professionalization and the practice of tourism created larger and more diverse audiences for modern architecture. As industrialization transformed cities in Europe and created new cities in North America, an explosion of print media provided new venues in which to view and discuss these territorial changes.[15] Supplementing the discussion of the tall office building in the *Inland Architect*, I draw on contemporary criticism of Chicago architecture published in other professional magazines, including the *American Architect and Building News* (Boston, 1876–1908), the *Brickbuilder* (Boston, 1892–1916), and the *Architectural Record* (New York, 1891–); in journals aimed at real estate interests, such as the *Building Budget* (Chicago, 1885–90); and in periodicals aimed at middle-class readers, including *Atlantic Monthly* (Boston, 1857–1932), *Harper's Weekly* (New York, 1857–1976), and *Scribner's Magazine* (New York 1887–1939). Where possible I use images other than the much-reproduced iconic photographs that Peter Bacon Hales has described as "grand style urban photography."[16] These images purposefully convey an ideological message, presenting business buildings as a series of isolated monuments to progress rather than as constituent parts within a larger city. Instead, I use street views (often from stereo cards), newspaper illustrations, and cartoons to help place these familiar buildings back in their unfamiliar contemporary context: the crowded, messy, smoky, and sometimes dangerous streets of Chicago. Through these publications and images, I reconstruct the debate about the tall office building between those invested in the continued growth of Chicago (architects, real estate developers, their businessmen clients, and journalist "boosters") and those still ambivalent about it (visitors and cultural critics from more established northeastern cities and from abroad).

Louis Sullivan's lyrical essays describing the appearance of a new organic architecture symbolic of American democracy are the most famous writings to appear in the *Inland Architect*.[17] As they are usually reproduced outside the context of the magazine, it is sometimes easy to forget that Sullivan was not a lone voice but part of a wider intellectual conversation, and that his now familiar essays were written in response to particular events in the life of the city. Chapter 2 reexamines Sullivan's invention of an industrial ornament, placing his well-known philosophy of "democratic architecture" in the context of the Chicago building trades strikes of the 1880s. In investigating the ways in which his aesthetic and political goals grew out of the industrialization of traditional building practices, I draw on criticism of the skyscraper as a symbol of the industrial city under capitalism, as published in socialist and anarchist journals such as *The Alarm: A Socialist Weekly* (Chicago, 1884–86), publications that had a specialized readership of largely working-class immigrants.

As codesigner of the three buildings discussed here, the Monadnock, the Masonic Temple, and the Reliance Building, Sullivan's friend and contemporary John Wellborn Root is a central figure in the conceptualization of the tall office building around 1890. Although Root went to great lengths to synthesize European architectural theory with his own practice, and his writing was undoubtedly an inspiration for Sullivan, few scholars besides Donald Hoffman have paid attention to the connections between Root's written and built works.[18] Chapter 3 examines the design of the Monadnock through Root's writing on the tall office building. I am particularly interested in the ways in which Root thought about design in the local context of a busy urban environment. His solution, to focus on the tactile and chromatic qualities of industrial materials rather than on ornament, provides an interesting counterpoint to that of Sullivan.

Chapter 4 focuses on efforts to remake the skyscraper as a civic rather than a wholly commercial icon, by investigating Burnham and Root's Masonic Temple on State Street. In particular I examine conflicts between the conservative social aims of the clients, the Chicago Order of Freemasons, and the spectacular nature of the building as it was finally realized, the site of a variety of mass entertainments including tourism, shopping, and theatrical productions. Supplementing the modernist reading of the Chicago skyscraper as a prototypical glass tower, chapter 5 recovers a contemporary debate about the Reliance Building, also on State Street, in relation to ideas of climate and hygiene. Criticism of the Reliance presents us with a telling insight into the contemporary view of the industrial city as a new and potentially threatening environment, both literally and metaphorically. Chapter 6 describes the decline of the heroic skyscraper ideal in the face of the new urban agenda of the City Beautiful movement, epitomized by the 1893 World's Columbian Exposition and Burnham and Edward Bennett's 1909 *Plan of Chicago*. In this era Chicago architects turned to a new vision of urban design. Though tall buildings were still built, the unchecked skyscraper city no longer seemed appropriate as an urban solution. The skyscraper as laissez-faire expression of individual power and will was replaced with a unified civic image. A postscript discusses the ways in which early twentieth-century European architects and critics revived the idea of the heroic Chicago skyscraper as a stand-alone object, reinforcing the organicist agenda of the first generation of Chicago architects and setting the scene for the so-called Second Chicago School in the mid-twentieth century.[19]

The historian T. J. Jackson Lears has described the simultaneous uncertainty about and enthusiasm for material progress in late nineteenth-century American society. Locating a strain of "antimodernism" running alongside modernist rationalism, he gives as his goal the "illumination of the ambiguities surrounding notions of modernity" in relation to America's social and cultural life.[20] Through investigations of the discussion of the skyscraper in the *Inland Architect* magazine, and the various meanings attributed to the Monadnock, the Masonic Temple, and the Reliance Building, I hope to do the same in relation to the architectural discourse. The proliferation of claims made about these buildings denies the possibility of a singular reading, because they are in many ways more idiosyncratic than typological. Their rich indeterminacy is clearly counter to the modernist canon that demands objectivity. In their idiosyncrasy rather than their homogeneity, these buildings reveal the far-reaching perimeters and conflicting ideologies of the historical moment they are seen to define. It is only in viewing the Chicago skyscraper through the lens of its own time that we can see it as a contentious building type, one whose future technical, aesthetic, social, and urban importance was far from assured.

A NOTE ABOUT NOMENCLATURE

The definition of the "skyscraper" is ambiguous. Is it characterized by height, style, or structural technology?[21] For many years the building type had no commonly agreed-upon name. In his essay "A Great Architectural Problem" (1890), which specifically described his approach to the design of the tall office building, John Wellborn Root gave it no name at all. In the early 1880s most Chicagoans used the phrase "business block," though some persisted in using an even older nomenclature, "business house." Later, after it was assimilated into architecture proper, the new building type was described as the "commercial style." It was not until about ten years after its appearance in Chicago that the term *skyscraper* gained common currency. For example, in his 1892 guide to the city, John J. Flinn wrote of the "mammoth buildings known as 'sky scrapers.'"[22] In 1895 the *California Architect and Building News* wrote of "high buildings, or 'skyscrapers' as it is now the fashion to call them."[23] Yet this slang phrase was still somewhat pejorative, and seldom used by professional architects and critics. In 1896 Louis Sullivan, the man credited with perfecting the aesthetic form of the type, called it simply "the tall office building." In this book I use Sullivan's term to describe any tall commercial building constructed in Chicago before 1893. I use the term *skyscraper* only in describing debates about the type from the mid-1890s onward, when the word was more commonly used.

1 WESTERN ARCHITECTURE
THE TALL OFFICE BUILDING AS REGIONAL TYPE

CHAPTER

In the pages of the *Inland Architect*, the professional journal published between 1883 and 1908, Chicago architects described the tall office building as the natural result of European expansion, a regional type unique to the American West. In response to contemporary criticism of the new industrial city as a dangerous place, controlled by raw business interests, unchecked by cultural feeling, and fraught with social disruption, they constructed a counterimage of the West as a new ethnographic region; of Chicago as the organic product of human evolution; and of its commercial architecture as the natural outgrowth of the land, the only form possible according to the laws of adaptation and natural selection. Borrowing from European theory, they married an older tradition of organicism to new ideas of the regionally and racially specific evolution of architectural styles. This deterministic view was used to support the architects' interests and those of their patrons in the social and political battles dividing the city.

THE ARCHITECTURE PROFESSION IN CHICAGO

The *Inland Architect and Builder* (later titled the *Inland Architect and News Record*) packaged Chicago building design and the western region for national consumption. One of the first architectural journals published in the United States, it was established as a regional counter to the Boston-based *American Architect and Building News*.[1] Like its older counterpart, it focused on creating a separate identity for architects as a professional group, apart from builders, mechanics, and engineers. Both magazines differed from literary publications in which architecture was discussed as one of the fine arts. The *Inland Architect* emphasized the architect's practical expertise as well as his creative talent. It had an explicitly regionalist agenda, promoting the architecture of the so-called inland empire formed by the western states: Illinois, Indiana, Iowa, Michigan, Minnesota, Missouri, Ohio, and Wisconsin. (Although the American frontier had reached California by the 1880s, the inhabitants of these states still called themselves "westerners"). The magazine was not only a record of practice in the West, with Chicago as its acknowledged center, but also a venue for theoretical writing aimed at reconciling local architecture with a wider history.

Western architects simultaneously bemoaned and reveled in the freedom generated by provincialism. They upheld their lack of intellectual tradition as a positive attribute. The founders of the *Inland Architect* cast themselves as men of action, unencumbered by the morass of historicism choking Europe and the East Coast. The idea of the West as a pioneering place where the can-do spirit flourished assumed mythic proportions in late nineteenth-century American thought.[2] Pragmatism was quickly claimed as the primary characteristic of western architecture. "The originality of American architecture rests to a great degree upon the basis of studying the necessities of labor and life, and meeting them without hesitancy or prejudice," the young Chicago architect George W. Maher wrote in 1887.[3]

But the story of the western architect as a frontiersman was largely fictional. By 1880 Chicago was a rapidly growing city and home to a large number of architects with diverse and sophisticated educations. Architects trained in East Coast offices like those of Richard Morris Hunt and Frank Furness, or at the new American professional schools like the Massachusetts Institute of Technology, flocked to the western city in the wake of the great fire of 1871, sensing that the rebuilding work would not merely replace the existing frontier town, but be grand in its scope. Some had even studied in Paris at the École des Beaux-Arts or at the German polytechnics. The West was establishing its own institutions based on these models. Influenced by German pedagogy, the University of Illinois established its own program in architecture in 1873, and the University of Michigan was experimenting with one at the same time.[4] Despite this professional acculturation, the *Inland Architect* encouraged men thoroughly assimilated into the education and practices of architecture to construct a new and modern image of themselves as happily removed from the restrictions of architectural tradition, as both pragmatic and objective. Yet at the same time, the magazine appropriated and adapted European architectural writing for its own instrumental ends, disseminating European architectural theory (such as articles reprinted from the English *Builder* and translated from the French *La Semaine des Constructeurs*) to its readers, and demonstrating its own relevance to easterners and to Europeans. However fictitious, the self-constructed myth of western independence was extremely useful. The view of the Chicago architect as a builder, an engineer, and a creator but never as a writer or a theorist has remained remarkably dominant in histories of American architecture.

In the nineteenth century, critics from Europe and the East Coast condemned Chicago and its style of architecture as brutish, ugly, and uncultured. The urban landscape, so unlike anything that had been seen before, was created by economic and environmental conditions rather than by the creative efforts of architects, they claimed.[5] Much of this criticism was directed toward the vertical grouping of tall office buildings crowded into the narrow downtown area. An 1892 article in the *Builder* clearly articulates the belief that the skyscraper arose autonomously out of local conditions, and not by design. "The Chicago architect does not build high because he likes it, but because the problem presented to him forces him to do so," the anonymous author claimed. The new type was bizarre, in the writer's opinion. No one would purposely design buildings so "preposterously high."[6] In reaction to this negative criticism, the *Inland Architect* attempted to rewrite architectural history, placing these new forms firmly within the architectural tradition, not as a marginalized offshoot but as its culmination, its strongest and most progressive branch.

Chicago architects took the metaphor presented to them by outsiders, the idea that the urban landscape of the West was the spontaneous product of a new environment, and turned it on its head. They used the organic analogy not to criticize but to justify their buildings. Their work, they argued, though very different from that seen anywhere else, was the natural result of the evolution of European architectural forms adapted to a new place and to new social conditions. The metaphor of evolution was central to the writing in the *Inland Architect*. In the 1880s and '90s the editors published more than a dozen essays promoting the architecture developing in the West as a regionally specific style.[7]

Louis Sullivan, the young Bostonian who came to the city via Philadelphia in 1873, has long been credited with inventing the idea of organic architecture in Chicago. In his *Autobiography*, Sullivan described the early days he spent wandering the city, seeking employment and at the same time taking in his strange new home. He found it all "magnificent and wild: a crude extravaganza; an intoxicating rawness; a sense of big things to be done."[8] From the first years of the town's existence in the early decades of the nineteenth century, visitors from the East had been interpreting this crudeness and rawness as a nascent state of becoming. As the environmental historian William Cronon has pointed out, the idea of Chicago as the site of the future midwestern metropolis was vital to its expansion from the time it was little more than a fortified military encampment and a few traders' cabins.[9] From the 1830s boosters and real estate speculators used the language of organicism to sell the idea of the site's potential. Yet the organic analogy masked an unpalatable truth about the city's real origins. The land on which it was built had been taken from Native American tribes under a series of treaties brokered and broken in the first decade of the nineteenth century.[10] One of the first cities to have an entirely industrial history, Chicago depended for its founding and growth not on its beneficent environment but on the mechanization of agriculture, the industrialization of meatpacking, the invention of rail, postal, and telegraph networks, and the founding of large-scale corporations. Despite Sullivan's romantic prose, the site of the first tall office buildings was not the open prairie but the highly artificial commercial and industrial landscape of the downtown Loop, and dependent as much on the flow of its capital as the flow of its river.

THE "CITY IN A GARDEN"

Chicago was the westernmost town planned along a new trade and settlement route running north from New York City, up the Hudson River to Albany, and west across the Great Lakes.[11] In 1825, when the Erie Canal opened, New York and the other northeastern cities were connected to the emerging agricultural markets in the western states, and a new avenue for trade was created. Three years earlier, the federal government authorized the Illinois and Michigan Canal Commission to survey land between Lake Michigan and the Mississippi River with a view to building a canal. Part of this survey involved platting a town at the mouth of the Chicago River, next to the site of an existing military fort.[12] The canal established a connection between the east, west, south, and north, with the imaginary town as its nexus. Drawn up in 1830, the plan was made up of a few straight lines representing streets and lot lines, and a few curving ones representing a lake and a forked river. It was in effect an agreement between the Canal Company and prospective buyers of the lots: the Canal Company would bring business to the area in the form of river traffic, and the new landowners would provide capital to build the canal.

The Chicago grid was simpler than that of other American grid-plan cities (fig. 1.01). No topographical accommodation was thought necessary for the low-lying and all but flat site, and consequently there was little deviation in the absolute homogeneity of lots. Although some large areas were set aside for unspecified Canal

Company use, the plat had no central town square and no hierarchy of larger and smaller roads. The lots for sale were basically square, about 360 feet by 320 feet, and bisected by an alley running either north-south or east-west. The shores of Lake Michigan received little attention in early town planning. The lake was the backyard of the city. In contrast, the Chicago River was the lifeblood of the town, its principal "street" and its main reason for being. Driven by land speculation, the city grew rapidly. When it was incorporated in 1837, it had reached 10 square miles in area and housed a population of about four thousand people. The already brisk growth accelerated further when the railroad was introduced in the 1850s. By the 1870s the city was threaded by train tracks servicing a livestock economy that linked Chicago with the Great Plains to the south and west, and New York, Philadelphia, and Boston to the east. If there was a town center it was the enormous Union Stock Yard constructed on the South Side in 1865. By 1880 Chicago was no longer a remote outpost but the center of a huge transportation web linking it to other national and global cities. Its destiny as the midwestern metropolis was fulfilled.

The first commercial buildings in Chicago were warehouses erected along the north and south banks of the Main Branch of the Chicago River, built for the storage and trade of meat, grain, and lumber as well as goods from the East Coast (fig. 1.02). Cast iron– and stone-fronted stores, where samples of these goods were on display, occupied the streets to the south of the river. By the late 1860s, as rail traffic began to take over from river traffic, the land around the river became polluted with waste. The city expanded southward to encompass a seven-by-five-block area bounded by the Chicago River to the north and west and Lake Michigan to the east, a district that came to be known as "the Loop." The development of this area was greatly facilitated by a catastrophic fire in October 1871 that burned for three days, destroying an area 4 miles long and more than half a mile wide (fig. 1.03). After the fire, new city ordinances required all construction in the burned-over district to be fireproof, effectively banishing wooden houses to the edges, and creating a functionally segregated city with commerce in the center and residential dwellings around the periphery.[13] In the years after the fire the Loop grew in the manner of classic American "downtowns." This central urban area was devoted to commercial businesses, including banks, insurance agencies, law and medical offices, newspapers, department stores, shops, hotels, and restaurants, as well as government agencies. These enterprises were housed in a new architectural type: the office building, a four- to five-story structure, with stores on the ground floor and offices above.

The industrialization of agriculture in the Great Plains required centralized management by large corporations. In Chicago, as in other large American cities, office buildings were constructed to house the businesses that marshaled regional resources. These businesses controlled the flow of goods and capital through the western plains, and the office building was their physical manifestation. Its height allowed for the dense occupation of a small urban area, and its volume allowed multiple businesses, both small and large, to thrive. While some office buildings were built to be occupied by a single company, the vast majority were not. Soon businesses were created whose sole job was to construct buildings to rent out to other businesses. Banks, newspapers, and insurance agencies led the demand for rental office space, followed by manufacturing companies, which could now separate their business offices from their factories because telegraph and telephones

1.01 Joshua Hathaway Jr., "Chicago with the School Section Wabansia and Kinzie's Addition. Compiled from the Four Original Surveys as Filed in the Cook County Clerk's Office," 1834. This map was commissioned by John H. Kinzie, one of the first settlers, to advertise land he had for sale. It shows the concentration of early settlement around the two branches of the Chicago River. The dark dotted line indicates the limits of the city when it was first platted in 1830. Used by permission from the Chicago History Museum; ICHi-05614.

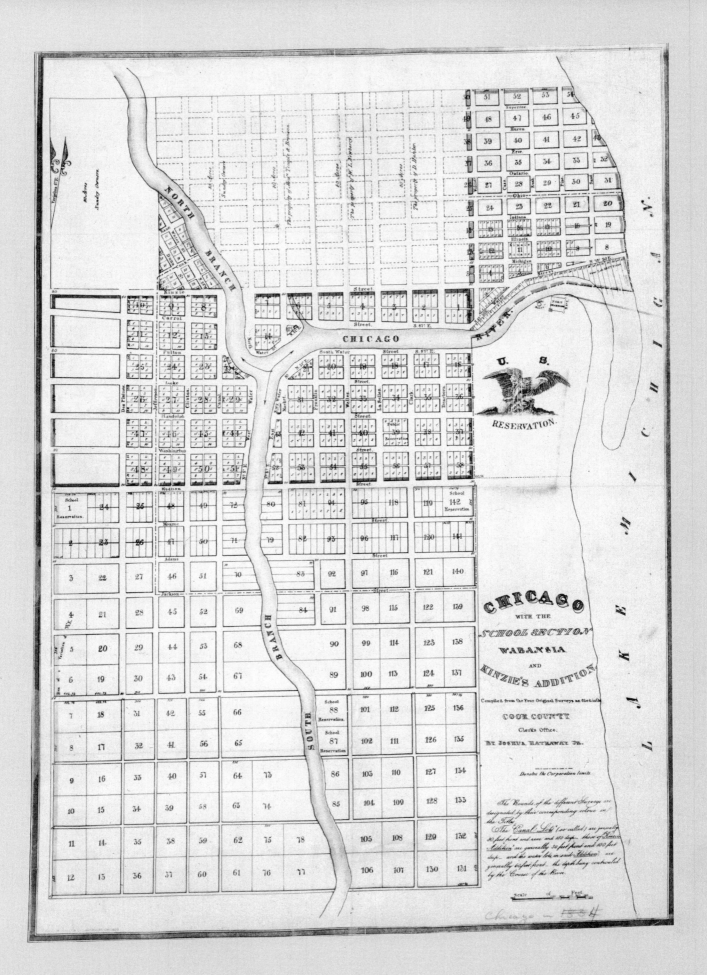

1.02 *(right)* "South Water St., Chicago, Ill., the Busiest Street in the World," ca. 1899. The earliest commercial buildings in Chicago were low wood and masonry structures concentrated around the Main Branch of the Chicago River. Courtesy of the Library of Congress; LC-USZ62-95802.

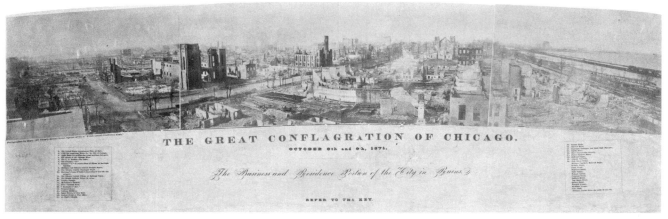

1.03 *(above)* "The Great Conflagration of Chicago. October 8th and 9th, 1871. The Business and Residence Portions of the City in Ruins." Photograph by William Shaw. This view looks north up Wabash Street and Michigan Avenue from around Congress Street (Adler and Sullivan later built the Auditorium Building nearby). The devastation caused by the fire led to the functional segregation of the city into a central business district and residential areas to the north, west, and south. Courtesy of the Library of Congress; LC-USZC4-9440.

allowed rapid communication between the two.[14] Any company could afford to rent a small office space in such a building, and the proximity of these offices facilitated communication between them.

As Chicago architects quickly realized, and as Carol Willis has shown, the rules dictating the construction and exterior form of these buildings were highly codified by interior requirements, especially the developers' desire for offices of standard dimensions and the tenants' need for well-lit interiors.[15] These rules amounted to real estate formulas that varied little from building to building. Office space was a commodity in much the same way that the original Chicago lots were. Considering that these lots were nearly identical in size, the only variable was the amount of money each developer was willing to spend on amenities, and on making his building aesthetically pleasing.

The tall office building was the product of fantastic gains in property values in the Loop during the 1880s, when building owners instructed their architects to build higher and higher in order to maximize their rents and their return on investment. Burnham and Root's Montauk Block on Monroe Street, completed in

1.04 Burnham and Root, Montauk Block (1881–82), Monroe Street between Dearborn and Clark streets. Photograph by J. W. Taylor. Rising high above its neighbors, the ten-story Montauk was designed to look like a unified block from its two street façades. As this photograph shows, the rear façades were significantly plainer. Used by permission from the Chicago History Museum; ICHi-38280.

1882 between Dearborn and Clark streets, is considered the first high-rise building in Chicago (fig. 1.04).[16] Buildings constructed in the Loop after the disastrous fire of 1871 were typically four to six stories high. At ten stories, the Montauk represented a dramatic jump in height from those around it. As Carl Condit and Robert Bruegmann have pointed out, the Montauk was not the first building to be constructed or planned in a particular way. The technologies it employed— passenger elevators, isolated footings, metal framing, and fireproofing—had all been in use for some years, but it was the first to realize a new aesthetic.[17] Standing on a corner site, it was imagined as a tall, self-contained volume rather than as a flat façade sandwiched between two others. Its exterior was heavy and solid, not a thin cast-iron screen dominated by glass, as earlier shop fronts were. This massiveness lent dignity to the Montauk, and a sense of permanence and solidity in a city just recovering from a disaster and nervous about its architectural identity.

The Montauk encouraged landowners to build even higher and more magnificently. Real estate prices pushed the commercial district southward, further away from the Main Branch of the Chicago River. In the 1850s the commercial center lay along Lake Street. By the 1860s it was creeping south along State Street, prompted by speculative real estate investment. In 1882 this southward movement was accelerated by the completion of the monumental Chicago Board of Trade at LaSalle and Jackson streets. Designed by the venerable Chicago architect W. W. Boyington, the Board of Trade was built on a specially created site that effectively closed off LaSalle Street. Befitting its status as a monument terminating a grand urban vista, it was capped by an ornamental tower.[18] The construction of this important building was closely followed by a rise in property prices in the immediate vicinity, and the construction of the city's first very high buildings along the length of LaSalle Street (figs. 1.05 and 1.06). This street quickly became Chicago's premier location for financial business, and the tall buildings built along it represented the young city's growing power as the locus of trade in the Midwest. Complementing State Street, the primary shopping street, and preceding the conversion of Michigan Avenue to a cultural thoroughfare, LaSalle Street was home to the city's most important buildings—not only William Le Baron Jenney's famous Home Insurance Building (1884) and Burnham and Root's Rookery (1886) but also Holabird and Roche's Tacoma Building (1889), Baumann and Huehl's Chamber of Commerce Building (1890), and Adler and Sullivan's Stock Exchange Building (1894). These structures became iconic in the history of American architecture, where they are used to illustrate the rise of a new modern style developed according to the principle of organicism.[19]

Busy, bustling LaSalle Street was the site for Chicago's first self-consciously "organic" architecture. In 1922, just as many of the city's first generation of skyscrapers were being demolished to make way for shorter, more lucrative

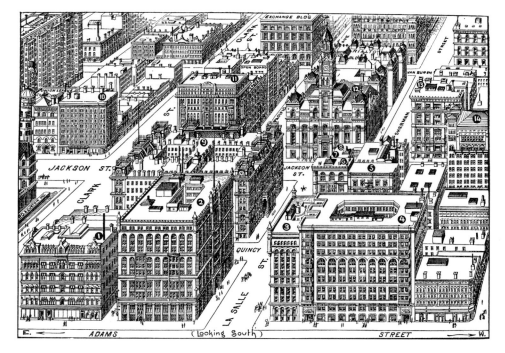

1.05 *(top)* "LaSalle Street, the Heart of the Financial District, North from Board of Trade, Chicago." Stereo card by H. C. White Co., ca. 1906. This northward-facing view from the Chicago Board of Trade on LaSalle Street shows the extent of the city's new financial district. The Illinois Trust and Savings Bank is on the immediate right; next to it is the Rookery. The Rand McNally building is across the street, on the left. Courtesy of the Library of Congress; LC-USZ62-76726.

1.06 *(bottom)* "Vicinity of the Board of Trade"; from *Rand McNally's Bird's-Eye Views and Guide to Chicago* (Chicago, 1898). The construction of the Chicago Board of Trade on a site terminating LaSalle Street at Jackson created a building boom in the immediate area. The Board of Trade is marked "12" in this illustration. Burnham and Root's Rookery is "2," their Rand McNally is "3," and the Insurance Exchange is "4."

buildings, the journalist Robert Craik McLean described LaSalle Street as the locus of the frontier spirit upon which Chicago had been founded. "It was on this Chicago street, named in memory of that great romantic pioneer the Chevalier de la Salle," he said, "that thirty years ago America's architectural romance found its abundant blossoming, and where its sequence is now written in its solid five blocks of imposing bank and office buildings."[20] For McLean these blocks were the aesthetic expressions of La Salle's pioneering spirit. Just as the French explorer forged a path west and south from Montreal down the Saint Lawrence and Mississippi rivers, contemporary Chicago architects were forging a path upward into the sky. The tall office building was the triumphant consequence of colonial exploration and expansion.

The Kansas City–based architect Henry Van Brunt summarized this idea in an 1889 essay, "Architecture in the West." The architecture being built in the eastern states was pretentious and doomed to failure, he argued, because it aspired to a level of style and sophistication "unnatural" to the United States. This sham architecture, the result of mutated development, would soon die out until, "like all other experiments in the evolution of forms, only the fittest remain."[21] As Van Brunt's choice of words makes evident, the discourse on western architecture drew heavily on nineteenth-century ideas of evolution. The tall office building was the result of a natural process, the acclimatization of European styles to the rugged conditions of the West.

THE INTELLECTUAL BASIS OF "WESTERN" ARCHITECTURE

The *Inland Architect* created a new category of "western" architecture synonymous with other "Romantic regionalisms" being constructed at the same time in Germany, England, and Scandinavia, each seeking an architectural identity in vernacular building forms.[22] Though the mythical landscape of the prairie that was so important to Frank Lloyd Wright and his followers in the early years of the twentieth century does not appear in the *Inland Architect*, a general idea of the West as an exceptional landscape with its own architectural forms has its roots in the magazine. In 1884 architects in the wider Chicago region founded the Western Association of Architects to promote this idea.[23] The *Inland Architect* was its official organ. Daniel Burnham, a partner with John Wellborn Root in Burnham and Root, one of the most successful architectural firms in Chicago during this period, was the first president of the WAA. One of the few architects actually raised in the city, and with an ambitious pioneering spirit of his own, he was well placed to promote the potential of the western territories.[24] At a banquet celebrating the launch of the WAA, Burnham suggested that the organization would establish a truly American style of architecture, one arising from the needs and wants of the people.[25] At the same banquet, McLean, editor of the *Inland Architect* at the time, offered a parable of the natural development of Chicago architecture, in which the first "inland architect" was not a man but a nest-building bird. The next "architects," he said, were beavers and muskrats, succeeded in turn by the American Indians.[26] Here, as in other narratives of the West, the Indian represented the link between the world of nature and the world of man. The implication, of course, was that the work of the present generation of architects was similarly natural and inevitable.

The English sociologist Herbert Spencer provided the model by which Chicagoans could understand their city as a natural environment, and architecture as an organic product.[27] In his address to the WAA, Burnham called Spencer "the famous scientist whose philosophy crowns the thought of this century."[28] Spencer was also one of Sullivan's heroes, and his influence was to remain strong in Chicago architectural circles into the early years of the twentieth century.[29] In his enormously popular *Principles of Sociology* (1874–96), Spencer claimed that natural law dictated not only the organic world but also human society. Individual bodies and the body politic shared common attributes, he argued. Each was continually growing, changing, and adapting to its environment. The supposed natural evolution of human society provided justification for all forms of human activity, from building to the founding of cities. Spencer himself applied his theory to architecture in an 1852 essay, "The Sources of Architectural Types," where he cited vernacular buildings as evidence of the harmony of organic and inorganic life.[30] (The Swiss cottage, whose steeply pitched roof echoes the adjacent mountain peaks and pine trees, particularly charmed him.)

In their descriptions of the character and philosophy of western architecture, Chicago architects and critics offered their own contribution to a larger nineteenth-century fascination with organicism.[31] Since the early nineteenth century, Americans had been obsessed with finding a basis for American art in the laws of nature rather than in established European traditions. This discussion was initially a literary one in the hands of writers from the New England transcendentalist movement, like Ralph Waldo Emerson and Henry David Thoreau.[32] Emerson's friend, the sculptor Horatio Greenough, first expressed this idea in relation to architecture in his essay "American Architecture" (1843).[33] For Greenough, the true American architecture was to be found in the adaptation of material and structure to need, not in the external application of fashionable styles. Arguing that everyday crafts such as shipbuilding and wagon making were the most beautiful and the most perfectly realized constructive arts the country had yet produced, he urged designers to look to nature as an example. He sought out what he called the "great principles of construction" in the zoomorphic development of animals. Throughout the second half of the nineteenth century, the belief in nature as the ultimate model for American architecture was reinforced by a number of less literary, more practical texts written by architect-craftsmen, all of whom emphasized the basis of design in the efficient and elegant use of materials and the fulfillment of functional requirements.[34]

Organicism, derived from both literary and professional discourses, formed the basis of the writing in the *Inland Architect*. In its very first issue published in 1883, the architect William Le Baron Jenney echoed Greenough when he wrote, "Nature in all her works has style, because, however varied her productions may be, they are always submitted to laws and invariable principles. We can spare nothing from a flower because in its organization every part has its function, and it is formed to carry out that function in the most beautiful manner."[35] Jenney was the elder statesman of Chicago architecture and an acknowledged authority because of his Parisian training and long experience.[36] The analogy he made between architecture and nature was essential to the writing of many of his sometime employees, including Daniel Burnham, who spread the word in his many speeches, and Louis Sullivan, whose poetic prose and elegant designs ultimately made him the most influential Chicago architect of the period. In 1887 Sullivan repeated the organic theme, claiming that, as in nature, every building contains "a single, germinal impulse or idea, which shall permeate the mass and its every detail with the same spirit."[37] Though he expressed his thoughts in an unusually lyrical way, Sullivan's voice was one among many.

Architectural organicism in the United States derived only from the sociology of Spencer and the Romantic philosophy of the transcendentalists but also from the writing of the English art critic John Ruskin.[38] Ruskin emphasized that the best and most truthful design was arrived at by strict emulation of nature, and he believed the Gothic style was the best approximation of natural principles (fig. 1.07). His lifelong interest was nature study, the scrupulous recording and description of clouds, rock formations, and mountains. Nature, as the work of God, was the only precedent for truly Christian art, he believed. "There are sometimes more valuable lessons to be learned in the school of nature than in that of Vitruvius," he wrote.[39] The analogy between the building and the living body is persistent throughout his writing. In *The Seven Lamps of Architecture* (1849) and *The Stones of Venice* (1851–53), he described the importance of "vitality" in architectural ornament.

Ruskin's writing became the bible for the founders of the American Institute of Architects when they met in New York in 1857. Peter B. Wight, Leopold Eidlitz, and Russell Sturgis spread the gospel of Ruskinism throughout the United States, building in his preferred style and disseminating his ideas in magazines like the *Crayon* (1855–61) and the *New Path* (1863–65).[40] Here they emphasized the importance of expression over imitation in design, arguing that man is infinitely creative, continually adapting himself and his artifacts to new environments in an organic manner. Echoing Ruskin, Eidlitz wrote in 1858, "Nature, the mother of Art, is the only guiding principle for the government of architects, at all times, in the bold pursuit of their calling."[41] Ruskin's ideas were popularized for a mass audience by the architect Andrew Jackson Downing in his treatises on landscape gardening and country house design, which presented a picturesque neo-Gothic style as the most natural one for suburban American dwellings.[42]

1.07 Illustration from John Ruskin, *The Stones of Venice* (1853). Photograph: Joseph Zehavi 2007. In his famous essay, "The Nature of Gothic," Ruskin explicitly connected eclectic Gothic ornament with life, energy, and vitality, and the regimented ornament of classical architecture with death. From the mid-nineteenth century, American architects believed the Gothic style best represented the rapid growth of a new nation. Used by permission from The Pierpont Morgan Library / Art Resource, NY.

Chicago architects were well versed in Ruskin's ideas through the influence of these journals and books, as well as through the writing of the architect and critic Peter B. Wight, a transplanted New Yorker and a leading contributor to the *New Path* in his younger days.[43] In "The Development of New Phases of the Fine Arts in America," an essay published in the *Inland Architect* in 1884, Wight promoted Gothic architecture, saying that it contained within it the true principles of construction, principles that could be adapted and expanded to the needs of the present time.[44] Wight spread this gospel to his many employees, including the young Root. In 1887 Root claimed that, as architectural style develops over time, "each architectural style will, in its turn, be taken and Americanized—that is, acclimatized and modified by local conditions."[45] The unprecedented new commercial buildings being constructed in Chicago were a test case for the evolution and adaptation of the Gothic. Looking back over the history of Chicago building in 1899, Wight concluded that the Gothic tradition promoted by Ruskin had finally achieved modern greatness in the tall office building.[46]

In this way Chicago architects placed the tall office building at the forefront of architectural development, presenting it as the natural evolution of the Gothic style adapted to meet the needs of western business. As we will see, a closer reading of the *Inland Architect* reveals that these theories of architectural evolution and adaptation were not neutral but allied to the mythology of the frontier, a narrative of progress used to justify territorial expansion. Chicago borrowed from Europe a way of understanding architecture not only in terms of organicism but also in terms of ethnography, seeing it as a physical manifestation of the westward march of European civilization. To consider architecture a result of its environment, Root claimed, "is as obvious as to say that a man's exterior form shall be the result of his interior structure, that his skin and hair shall be colored by the climate where he lives."[47] As this quotation implies, the idea of the evolution of western architecture was closely related to a belief in the evolution of a new American people.

ORGANIC ARCHITECTURE AND THE MYTHOLOGY OF THE FRONTIER

It is difficult to overstate the importance of ethnography in nineteenth-century histories of architecture. As Georges Teyssot has noted, the Victorian classification of architecture into types had little to do with the architectural typologies of the eighteenth century.[48] Instead, these types echo the racial classifications so popular at the time. The leading proponent of this form of architectural classification was the French architect Eugène-Emmanuel Viollet-le-Duc. His comparative analysis expanded on Abbé Laugier's eighteenth-century idea that the origins of architecture might be found in a primitive hut made up of tree branches. In his *Histoire de l'habitation humaine* (1875), Viollet multiplied Laugier's singular model to take into account different regional climates and racial identities.[49] To illustrate this point, he proposed "The History of Habitations," an exhibition for the 1889 Paris Exposition, illustrations of which were published in Chicago's *Building Budget*.[50] The French architect's suggestion that architectural evolution differed according to race and climate was captivating for an American audience, because this comparative approach allowed American architecture to be accommodated into

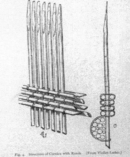

architectural history on a more or less equal footing with European styles.

In the first theoretical writing published in the *Inland Architect*, in 1883 William Le Baron Jenney (who may have heard Viollet-le-Duc lecture while studying in Paris during the 1850s) incorporated American architecture into Viollet-le-Duc's system of tectonic and ethnographic classification (figs. 1.08 and 1.09).[51] He presented the Native American "Wig Wam" alongside Sudanese houses and other versions of primitive dwellings as examples of architecture obeying the "great principle . . . that the form of the building grows out of the requirements modified by the material at hand, and the degree of civilization of the builders."[52] An unwieldy collage of fragments cribbed from Viollet-le-Duc and the Scottish architectural historian James Fergusson, Jenney's article, originally a set of lectures delivered at the University of Michigan, is based on the premise that architecture should be studied as a branch of ethnography. This ethnography was that of the nineteenth century, in which the four principal races were believed to be, in Jenney's words, "the Turanians, Semitics, Celts and Aryans."[53] Each had its own system of religion and government and also its own sensibility toward built form. The Turanians, ruled by despots and worshipping an animate world, exhibited a "lower state of civilization," he believed, but excelled at monumental architecture such as the pyramids. As a nomadic people, he continued, the Semitics had little appreciation for permanent architectural form; they emphasized surface decoration instead of structure. In turn, the Aryans were defined by their "practical

1.08 *(left)* Illustration from William Le Baron Jenney, "Architecture Part III," *Inland Architect and Builder* 1, no. 4 (May 1883): 49. Jenney compared a bamboo "Malay" hut found in the Philippines with an "Aryan" hut built from log and thatch. He quoted Viollet-le-Duc's opinion that the construction methods of the various races developed in the same way as language. Used by permission from Ryerson and Burnham Libraries, Art Institute of Chicago.

1.09 *(right)* William Le Baron Jenney, *Building of Primitive Egyptian House (from Viollet-le-Duc)*; from "Architecture Part VI," *Inland Architect and Builder* 2, no. 2 (September 1883): 105. Jenney agreed with Viollet-le-Duc that Egyptian reed construction was the basis of the Greek Doric order. This allowed him to argue that Western architecture originated in a marshy plain around a river, a similar climate to Chicago. Used by permission from Ryerson and Burnham Libraries, Art Institute of Chicago.

common sense" and the plainness and simplicity of their architecture. Jenney explicitly characterized the people of the United States as present-day Aryans, who are "again migrating westward and spreading themselves over the United States from the Gulf of Mexico to Canada and the Pacific to produce a new center of civilization."[54] For Jenney, as for Viollet-le-Duc, the history of architecture was the history of civilization, which was, in turn, the history of race and racial expansion.

While Viollet-le-Duc heavily influenced Jenney and other Chicago architects educated in Paris, German-speaking architects fell under the sway of the German architect Gottfried Semper, who espoused his own version of organicism. Like Viollet, Semper understood architectural origins and development in terms of region and race. In his *Four Elements of Architecture* (1851) and *Style in the Technical and Tectonic Arts* (1860–63), Semper drew on contemporary archaeological and ethnographic studies to argue for a strict relationship between handcrafts (which he described as the first architectural products), climate, race, and human development.[55] His emphasis on material and technique as the basis for style seemed particularly suited to Chicago, where new technologies were exhausting the possibilities of historic styles to represent them. The German-American architect and contractor Frederick Baumann disseminated Semper's writing among the architects of the city. During the 1880s and '90s he gave many lectures, and published a number of articles in the *Inland Architect* based on Semper's teaching.[56] Under Baumann's influence, Root and the German-born terra-cotta manufacturer Fritz Wagner translated Semper's 1869 essay "Über Baustile," which they titled "Development of Architectural Style."[57] The first translation of the German architect's work in America, it was published in the *Inland Architect* in serial parts from December 1889 to March 1890. It introduced Chicago readers to Semper's contention that building styles "are not invented, but develop in various departures from a few positive types, according to the laws of natural breeding, of transmission and adoption. Thus the development is similar to the evolutions in the province of organic creation."[58] While Semper's examples came from the ancient world, the stage was set for a similar ethnographic understanding of western architecture in the present day.

In order to argue for the superiority of western architecture, contributors to the *Inland Architect* combined European theories of architectural evolution made popular by Viollet-le-Duc and Semper with the contemporary craze for "Anglo-Saxonism" or "Aryanism." When the WAA was established in 1884, the architect Sidney Smith raised a toast to the new institution on behalf of the Royal Institute of British Architects. "Greece is the foundation of all architecture," he said. "It gradually extended west until it reached Europe and Great Britain. In this country it commenced in the east again . . . It is gradually extending west, and in the west we expect to see its greatest development in the United States."[59] Smith's comments echo the popular nineteenth-century belief that white Americans were descended, via the medieval Anglo-Saxons, from the original Indo-European peoples, the Aryans, who lived in central Asia.[60] The English, the Germans, and the Americans all believed they were descended from this hearty race, characterized by their strength, independence, and innate love of freedom.[61] When Jenney spoke admiringly of the Aryan race, with their practical common sense and sturdy buildings, he sited western architecture firmly within this racial ideology.

The politician and future president Theodore Roosevelt promoted the superiority of the westerner in his series of books *The Winning of the West* (1889–96), where he compared early American frontier society to the Germanic fortified villages of the Middle Ages.[62] Roosevelt's books popularized the ideology of manifest destiny. The frontiersmen's "inheritance of sturdy and self-reliant manhood helps them greatly," he wrote. "Their blood told in their favor as blood generally does tell when other things are equal."[63] In his famous essay "The Significance of the Frontier in American History," delivered at the 1893 World's Columbian Exposition, the historian Frederick Jackson Turner supported Roosevelt's argument, and enshrined the frontier mythology in American history. Like Roosevelt, Turner proposed that the frontier experience had formed the character of the American people: that the land had shaped the settlers rather than vice versa.[64] He described the westward migration of the white race as a "natural" process of civilization: an ever westward-moving frontier, occupied first by small farms, then towns, then cities. Overturning earlier nineteenth-century ideas of innate racial difference, Turner believed that the frontier was largely responsible for perfecting the Anglo-Saxon character. His theory of the frontier allowed for, even depended on, the incorporation of recent white immigrants into a single race of Americans with a common social goal.

Ideas of evolution and assimilation formed the basis of a story of origins for Chicago's architecture and people. In the *Inland Architect*, architecture shared the same characteristics as the new "American" being formed in the West. It and he were independent, practical, and strong. The natural model of evolution and adaptation, to which both architectural and human form was thought subject, provided an explanation not only for a healthy new style but also for failed models of inadequately assimilated forms, described as alien, weak, and diseased. In 1888 the Chicago architect Allen Pond applied the Darwinian doctrine of the survival of the fittest to architecture when he wrote, "Time unerring destroys the freak and the abnormal thing; and only the normal creation, that which is in harmony with itself and its environment and which fulfills the law of the type, prevails against the destructive forces of nature and persists."[65] Pond and his brother Irving drew clear parallels between architectural and bodily pathologies (fig. 1.10). In 1891 Irving, who had been a pupil of Jenney's at the University of Michigan, published "Architectural Kinships," an essay that explicitly linked architectural and human (in his view, racial) physiognomy.[66]

In terms of late nineteenth-century racialist theories of human development through strong bloodlines, the Boston architect H. H. Richardson represented the rootstock of an original American architecture in the pages of the *Inland Architect*. Richardson was extremely influential on western architects in the early to mid-1880s, when his Romanesque revival buildings were portrayed as the authentic architectural expression of the Aryan ideal. In the years following his death in 1886, he was described as a kind of architectural frontiersman whose hearty strain must not be allowed to die out.[67] The desire for the bold, the vigorous, and the vital, and above all the truthful, in the persona of Richardson was a response to the fragility and falseness of the cobbled-together styles of Victorian eclecticism. Root credited Richardson with curing America of the delicate and weak Queen Anne style. In its place, he claimed, Richardson had forged a vibrant new national style out of an imperfect and impure medieval form, the Romanesque, using the "great vigor and masculinity of his genius."[68]

In this way of thinking, the bold and vital Richardsonian Romanesque hastened the natural process of architectural evolution, correcting and healing the

1.10 Illustration from Irving Pond, "Architectural Kinships," *Inland Architect and News Record* 17, no. 2 (March 1891): 22. Pond compared the distinctive architectural style of various races to their clothing and physiognomy. Used by permission from Ryerson and Burnham Libraries, Art Institute of Chicago.

horrifying mutations of the past while nurturing a hardy new native species. Richardson reached the height of his fame in Chicago with the construction of his Marshall Field Wholesale Store on Adams Street, two blocks west of LaSalle (1885–87; fig. 1.11). This immense building, designed as a heavy U-shaped volume, ornamented only by its rough stone surface and by a series of large arched windows, was widely praised for its massiveness and simplicity. Referring to this building, Sullivan famously exclaimed, "Here is a man for you to look at . . . a man that lives and breathes, that has red blood; a real man, a manly man; a virile force . . . I mean that stone and mortar, here, spring into life."[69] In these terms the heavy, plain, and unornamented walls of Chicago buildings designed in emulation of the Richardsonian Romanesque represented not only the direct expression of their unfussy commercial programs but also the strength and tremendous energy of a native westerner perfectly adapted to his rugged climate.

ARCHITECTURE AND ANARCHY

The metaphors of the native and the foreign that dominated discussions of Chicago architecture in the 1880s were drawn not only from books but also from very real struggles taking place on the streets of the city. If H. H. Richardson represented the ideal westerner, his antithesis was the foreign-born radical labor activist, heir of the failed German revolution of 1848 and the Paris commune of 1871, who railed against Americans' wealth and property, and aimed to destroy the very buildings they were most proud of. As tall buildings rose along LaSalle Street, an increasingly powerful labor movement challenged the vision of a prosperous western metropolis. Richardson's death coincided exactly with an era of unprecedented organized labor activity in Chicago. He died at his home in Brookline, Massachusetts, on April 27, 1886. The devastating Haymarket bombing occurred in Chicago a week later, on May 4. These were years of great anxiety for the architecture profession as building workers' unions increased in membership and activity, and a growing anarchist movement threatened to overthrow the city's ruling institutions. From 1881 to 1886, just as the tall office building was being invented, the new type was already under threat. Anarchists, largely recent immigrants, attacked not only the city's defining edifices but also the organic ideal upon which they rested. In the years following the Haymarket affair, architects feared that Richardson's legacy of organic architecture would be lost in an unstable city torn apart by political conflict.[70]

While immigrants were needed to fuel the city's economy, their arrival in large numbers also represented a threat to the supposed natural processes of evolution and assimilation through which the city was to prosper. German immigrants formed a huge minority in late nineteenth-century Chicago, comprising nearly a third of the population in 1880. Along with Slavs and Bohemians, they settled in ethnic enclaves to the north, south, and west of the city.[71] Their culture and language were preserved through the agency of churches, newspapers, and social clubs. Because of their strong sense of ethnic identity and perceived sympathy for radical politics, Germans and eastern Europeans were seen as a threat to "Americanization," that is, the harmonious mixing of immigrant groups to create a healthy and strong new race. These groups were widely viewed by English speakers as racially distinct from "white" Americans.[72] (The Irish, who had arrived slightly earlier, had already become more or less assimilated into the category of "Americans" or "whites."[73])

While the large German minority in Chicago contained representatives of all classes and professions, including many architects, these immigrants were particularly active in workers' associations, including craft unions.[74] The labor movement in Chicago gained power in the 1860s, when union leaders nationwide promoted the regulation of the workday to ten and then eight hours. Even though most business owners fiercely opposed unionization, Chicago's labor leaders achieved some success in this regard the early 1880s, due in part to the tacit support of the city government. At that time the police force, under the control of the Democratic mayor Carter Harrison, identifying with working-class tradesmen and laborers,

1.11 H. H. Richardson, Marshall Field Wholesale Store (1885–87), Adams Street between Franklin and Fifth avenues. This building, erected two blocks west of LaSalle Street, inspired many Chicago architects. Louis Sullivan believed it was built according to organic principles and represented the strength of character of the American West. Used by permission from the Chicago History Museum; ICHi-19131.

cooperated with orderly strikes by refusing to help employers protect nonunion labor. Because of this cooperation between organized labor and city government, workers came to believe that Chicago might become home to a new working-class democracy. The city could become an urban utopia, a success where the agrarian socialist utopias of the previous generation had failed. However, these working-class political goals were to go unrealized. The labor movement in Chicago was affiliated with a number of radical factions whose extreme rhetoric and actions eventually forced a split between the city government and the unions.[75]

The years 1883 to 1887 were turbulent ones for the Chicago building industry. H. H. Richardson's Marshall Field Wholesale Store (1885–87), Burnham and Root's Rookery (1885–88), and Adler and Sullivan's Auditorium (1886–89) all suffered delays when masons, bricklayers, and carpenters struck again and again in support of shorter hours and higher wages (fig. 1.11).[76] In general, architects opposed the demands of the building trades unions, since labor disputes disrupted their own work and prevented their clients (business owners and real estate developers) from doing theirs. Throughout the strikes architects pushed for building to continue, and supported the use of nonunion, even convict labor in place of striking workers.[77]

While strikes continued on building sites and demonstrations filled the streets, a powerful war of words was carried out in the press, including journals aimed at architects (the *Inland Architect*), real estate interests (the *Economist*, the *Building Budget*), and radical workers associated with the building trades unions (the German-language *Arbeiter-Zeitung* and the English-language *Alarm*). The *Arbeiter-Zeitung*, edited by a German upholsterer turned activist and journalist, August Spies, and the *Alarm*, edited by the American typographer Albert Parsons and his seamstress wife, Lucy Parsons, were printed in the same offices, located on Fifth Avenue (now Wells Street) very close to the heart of capitalist business on LaSalle Street. These papers maintained that the propertied class had assumed total and unlawful control over the so-called unpropertied, denying them the true value of their labor and forcing them into starvation and crime. Turning away from the mainstream trade union movement, the *Arbeiter-Zeitung* and the *Alarm* were dedicated to the destruction of class rule by means of armed revolutionary struggle.[78]

Parsons and Spies were members of the Social Revolutionary Congress, formed in Chicago in 1881. Calling for the armed organization of workingmen, the congress formed the International Working People's Association in 1883. The IWPA was the basis for a robust anarchist movement in Chicago, a group that could claim three thousand members by 1886. It promoted a strong working-class counterculture, complete with highly visible parades, marches, and demonstrations. The demonstrations sometimes turned violent as anarchists clashed with the police and with private militia. As the Communards in Paris had recently shown, the nature of warfare was changing—it now took place on the streets, with little differentiation between soldiers and civilians (fig. 1.12).

The IWPA's manifesto, drafted in part by Spies and Albert Parsons, was modeled on the Declaration of Independence. It declared the group's dedication to the "destruction of the existing class rule, by all means i.e. the energetic, relentless, revolutionary and international action" and the "establishment of a free society based upon co-operative organization of production."[79] The manifesto advocated arbitration instead of courts of justice, asylums instead of prisons, cooperative production instead of the wage system, and the exchange of goods based on value rather than a capitalist economy. With its strident rhetoric disseminated through the pages of the *Alarm* and the *Arbeiter-Zeitung* and in the fiery speeches declaimed at demonstrations, the IWPA had a strong effect on the attitudes of the middle class toward the labor movement in general.

Along with the IWPA, radical labor organizers within the building trades characterized their movement in explicitly nonnativist terms. In doing so they offered a direct challenge to the organicist and regional doctrine espoused by Chicago architects. Labor leaders saw themselves not as natives of any particular place but as part of an international brotherhood of workers. "In the cause of labor there is no nationality, sex, creed or color," Parsons wrote in 1886. "Economic subjection is international, so also must be the protest."[80] The movement refused to recognize the flag of the United States, flying instead the black flag of the international anarchist movement (fig. 1.13).[81] The desire for a worldwide uprising of workers was antithetical to the local architects' belief in the development of a harmonious western society out of the acclimatization of different races. For the anarchists, a new society would arrive not through evolution but through revolution.

Yet both capital and labor enlisted the same language of organicism to argue their respective causes. The *Alarm* argued that "anarchy is the practical application of natural law to all the affairs of life."[82] It declared, "Under natural law, or in the absence of government and authority, men could not help but act right, since none would be or could be protected in doing wrong, in other words, crime, or the violation of natural rights would then bring its own punishment on the perpetrator."[83] This, the paper believed, was the true realization of American independence from Europe. The social critic Henry George, the so-called Prophet of California, popularized the concept of natural law in his book *Progress and Poverty* (1881). According to George, the national economic depres-

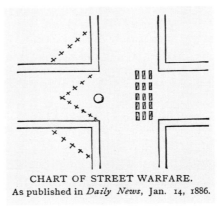

CHART OF STREET WARFARE.
As published in *Daily News*, Jan. 14, 1886.

1.12 *(top)* "Chart of Street Warfare. As Published in *Daily News*, Jan. 14, 1886." This diagram was entered into evidence at the Haymarket bombing trial. Based on an 1885 drawing published in the socialist weekly *Alarm*, it illustrates a strategy for armed urban warfare. It shows how armed anarchists (*crosses*) might overcome a column of policemen (*hatched rectangles*) at the intersection of two streets. The illustration is from a book published by Chicago Police Department Captain Michael J. Schaack, *Anarchy and Anarchists* (Chicago: F. J. Schulte, 1889), 438.

1.13 *(bottom) An Anarchist Procession.* The anarchist black flag is flown in Chicago on a Thanksgiving Day march in 1884. As this illustration shows, the flag-bearing anarchist leaders were often women. From Michael J. Schaack, *Anarchy and Anarchists* (Chicago: F. J. Schulte, 1889), 78.

sion of 1873 had been caused by fundamental inequities of the capitalist system, especially land and property ownership, which reduced renters to the status of serfs. Since land was not the product of labor, he claimed, it should not be owned and the rental system should be abolished. He also believed that workers were entitled to the products of their labor, not an unfair monetary approximation of its value.[84] George's book provided fodder for the revolutionaries of the IWPA who declared, "This system is unjust, insane and murderous. It is therefore necessary to totally destroy it with and by all means."[85]

In their fight against the propertied class, radicals saw the tall office building as a direct target. It was the symbol of speculation and property ownership, the twin evils of anarchist thought. Lucy Parsons, a former slave who had come to Chicago from Texas with her husband in 1873, vividly argued this point in the pages of the *Alarm*.[86] Though she had no professed interest in the aesthetic form of the tall office building, Lucy used powerful architectural imagery in her criticism of the city's treatment of the poor. Drawing a direct relationship between the buildings in the Loop and the conditions of the destitute living in their shadows, she described them not as architects did, as exemplars of a bold new style that had evolved from the needs of the people, but as symbols of capital's oppression of the workers. In 1885 she wrote, "We build magnificent piles of architecture whose dizzy heights dazzle us, as we attempt to follow with our eye along the towering walls of solid brick, granite and iron, where tier after tier is broken only by wondrous panes of plate glass. And as we gradually bring the eye down story after story, until it reaches the ground, we discover within the very shadow of these magnificent abodes the homeless man, the homeless child, the young girl offering her virtue for a few paltry dollars to hire a little room way up in the garret of one of them . . . Yet it was their labor that erected these evidences of civilization."[87]

Lucy and Albert Parsons promoted anarchy as the answer to an unjust society, and advocated the use of dynamite to destroy capitalist institutions. Under their editorship, the *Alarm* tried to coopt the sympathies of the "mechanic," or skilled building worker, by persuading him that effort expended in building "jails, courthouses . . . law and insurance offices" was an ultimately useless form of production benefiting only the wealthy.[88] They called workingmen to arms, advocating the bombing of banks and other public buildings. Architecture was property, and for the anarchists well versed in the philosophy of Pierre-Joseph Proudhon, property was theft.[89] With his hands, each individual laborer was capable of making only a small part of any building. With explosives, or "infernal machines," as they were called, he had the ability to destroy at a scale usually controlled only by the architect.

The Parsonses depicted dynamite as the gift of modern science to the workingman, and printed detailed recipes for its manufacture and use in such articles as "Explosives: A Practical Lesson in Popular Chemistry. The Manufacture of Dynamite Made Easy."[90] While it is difficult to say how real these anarchists' threats were, they were taken in deadly earnest by the police and by the military. In an 1884 report, General Philip Sheridan, commander of the United States Army and leader of the Chicago militia, warned that anarchists could easily manufacture explosives, and that banks, public buildings, and "mercantile houses" represented prime targets.[91] In January of 1885 an anonymous messenger left a crude explosive device at the main office of Burnham and Root's recently completed Chicago, Burlington and Quincy Railway offices on the corner of Franklin and Adams streets, directly across from the Marshall Field Wholesale Store. Though police disarmed the bomb before it could explode, its existence was widely reported as evidence that the anarchists were about to abandon words for action.[92]

Richardson's transmutation of stone into art found its opposite in the anarchist's ability to shatter it, to turn that stone back into dust. In a widely distributed manifesto called "Word to Tramps" (1884), Lucy Parsons, whose dramatic language and powerful imagery enlivened the otherwise repetitive and didactic tone of the *Alarm*, advised homeless workers considering suicide to blow themselves up in front of the new mansions lining Prairie Avenue.

Stroll you down the avenues of the rich and look through the magnificent plate glass windows into their voluptuous homes who have despoiled you and yours. Then let your tragedy be enacted here. Awaken them from their wanton sports at your expense. Then send forth your petition and let them read it by the red glare of destruction. Thus when you cast one lingering look behind, you can be assured that you have spoken to these robbers in the only language which they have ever been able to understand, for they have never yet deigned to notice any petition from their slaves that they were not compelled to read by the red glare bursting from the mouths of the cannon, or that was not handed to them on the point of a sword . . . Each of you hungry tramps who read these lines, avail yourselves of those little methods of warfare which Science has placed in the hands of the poor man, and you will become a power in this or any other land. Learn the use of explosives![93]

But Marshall Field's architect had perhaps anticipated the threat to his wealthy patrons, and acted against it in advance. A suicide bomb would have been ineffective against Richardson's Glessner House, built on South Prairie Avenue between 1885 and 1887 (fig. 1.14). The monolithic stone house turned its heavily fortified back on the street, and opened up only to the refuge of a private internal courtyard.[94] This monument to domestic security simulated the solidity and strength of a fortified castle, standing fast against alien invaders of all kinds.

The Glessner House is symptomatic of a larger fear. As a result of militant anarchist rhetoric, the middle classes in Chicago fully expected to see their city come under attack, with results as potentially devastating as the great fire of 1871.[95] Ironically, when a dynamite bomb was exploded, it was employed not in the Loop but in the working-class area of the Haymarket, on the west side of the Chicago River (fig. 1.15).[96] On the evening of May 4, 1886, a relatively small group gathered to listen to speeches by Albert Parsons and other anarchist leaders. As the meeting began to disperse, an unknown assailant threw a bomb, killing several police officers and wounding others (fig. 1.16). On June 5, 1886, thirty-one anarchists were indicted for the crime and eventually eight were charged with conspiracy to commit murder. After a lengthy and highly publicized trial, four men, including Albert Parsons and August Spies, were sentenced to death and hanged.[97] The Haymarket affair solidified middle-class opinion that those responsible for strikes in the building trades as well as in other industries, were nothing but foreign fanatics intent on destroying the American way of life. A cartoon published in *Harper's Weekly* soon after the Haymarket bombing sums up this view of German radicals in America (fig. 1.17). The caption reads: "LIBERTY (to go if you do not like the institutions of our Republic) OR (commit murder and you will be punished with)

1.14 *(top)* H. H. Richardson, Glessner House (1885–87), 1800 South Prairie Avenue. The heavily fortified design for this house may have been influenced by the perceived threat to Chicago's wealthy property owners posed by bomb-throwing anarchists. From J. J. Glessner, *The Story of a House* (1923).

1.15 *(bottom)* Haymarket Square; S. L. Stein Publishing Co., ca. 1893. The Haymarket, a commercial marketplace to the west of downtown across the Chicago River from the financial district, was a popular meeting place for labor demonstrations in the early 1880s. The monument memorializing the policemen killed during the Haymarket bombing can be seen at the bottom right. Courtesy of the Library of Congress; LC-USZ62-134212.

1.16 *(opposite)* *The Anarchist-Labor Troubles in Chicago. The Police Charging the Murderous Rioters in Old Haymarket Square on the Night of May 4th*; from sketches by C. Bunnell and Chas Upham in *Frank Leslie's Illustrated Newspaper*, May 15, 1886, pp. 200–201. The climax of a decade of escalating urban violence, the Haymarket bombing made the threat of class warfare seem real. Courtesy of the Library of Congress; LC-USZ62-75192.

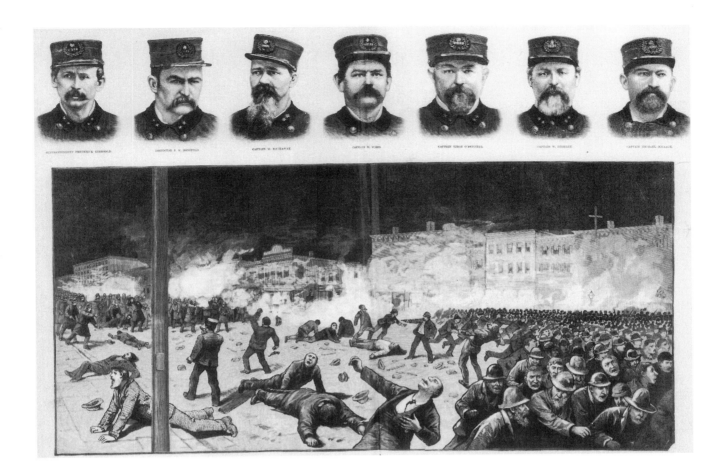

DEATH." The anarchist with his bomb, standing on the American flag, is given the choice of the hangman's noose (operated by Uncle Sam) or a steamer back to "Hamburg or Bremen" (with Lady Liberty showing the way).

In 1889 the Chicago police captain Michael Schaack wrote, "The anarchists of Chicago are exotics. Discontent here is a German plant transferred from Berlin and Leipsic [sic] and thriving to flourish in the west. In our garden it is a weed to be plucked out by the roots and destroyed."[98] As part of this rhetoric about the native and the foreign, the battle line between architecture and anarchy was clearly drawn (fig. 1.18). Building owners, contractors, and architects joined ranks behind the mainstream press in opposing the unions, seeing them as incubators for anarchist activity.[99] *Inland Architect* articles describing the evolution of a new American style in the West represented by the tall office building appeared side by side with editorials condemning strikes by the building trades unions. When the bricklayers went on strike in 1883, the editors announced, "The bricklayers union is deserving of no sympathy whatever."[100] In June of 1886, immediately after the Haymarket bombing, they claimed, "It is a healthful sign for the future prosperity of the laboring classes" that they are not now so easily led by "professional agitators" demanding an eight-hour day, because ultimately "labor blames capital for that which it is itself most to blame."[101] An editorial published in the Chicago real-estate journal the *Building Budget* summarized this opinion. Arguing that the profession of architecture and the system of anarchy promoted by the Parsonses

1.17 *(above)* Thomas Nast, *Liberty or Death*; engraving, from *Harper's Weekly*, June 5, 1886. This cartoon critical of immigrant radicals in America was published in the wake of the Haymarket bombing. The full caption reads, "LIBERTY (to go if you do not like the institutions of our republic) OR (commit murder and you will be punished with) DEATH." Used by permission from the Chicago History Museum; ICHi-03666.

1.18 *(left)* Police monument—Haymarket Square, erected 1888. Photograph by A. Witteman. Erected to honor the police dead, the sculpture is by Johannes Gelert and the base is by John Wellborn Root. A separate statue honoring the executed anarchists was erected in Waldheim Cemetery in Forest Park outside Chicago. Used by permission from the Chicago History Museum; ICHi-14452.

and their colleagues were purely antithetical, the writer had nothing but praise for the prosecution of the anarchists convicted for inciting the bombing: "Architecture and massive masonry are symbols of law and order, and the iconoclast longs to pull them down. When society becomes unsettled, and property is rendered insecure, men are not disposed to launch out in beautiful and substantial structures . . . The anarchist is the plain and practical foe of the architect and builder. Art, indeed, and anarchy cannot exist together. They are as antagonistic as light and darkness, cosmos and chaos, order and confusion."[102]

Talk of social revolution was effectively put to an end by the Haymarket bombing. Though the labor unions continued their action into the 1890s, calls for radical change were repressed. The goal of the unions changed from abolishing the wage system altogether to working within it to raise the standard of living by increasing wages. "After 19 years of agitation, the eight hour movement is pronounced a failure," the *Inland Architect* triumphantly announced in May of 1886.[103] Socialist and anarchist activity was brutally put down by the police, who rounded up and arrested hundreds of suspects. The events of that year—mass demonstrations by the working class, violent strikes followed by a dynamite attack and effective martial law—had an enormous impact on Chicagoans' view of their city. They struck a blow to dreams of an organically ordered frontier society where immigrants of many races came together to form an independent race of Americans. The possibility of an urban utopia, whether capitalist or socialist, seemed to be dead. But as we will see in the following chapters, during the late 1880s and early 1890s Chicago architects attempted to keep this dream of a harmonious and organic city alive through their projects for tall office buildings, which they saw not only as commercial structures erected for financial profit but also as civic structures designed to reunify the populace; not urban problems but urban solutions.

2 LOUIS SULLIVAN'S DEMOCRATIC ARCHITECTURE AND THE LABOR MOVEMENT

CHAPTER

Louis Sullivan's description of his architecture as the aesthetic manifestation of American, specifically Midwestern, democracy is a cornerstone of architectural history in the United States. In his 1896 essay, "The Tall Office Building Artistically Considered," he set down his vision of democratic architecture as a celebration of the "potential energy" of the raw, unfinished city around him, and of the steel-framed and terra-cotta-clad building as its ideal medium.[1] Historians have identified the Wainwright Building in St. Louis as the one in which he achieved a "revolutionary architectural mode," the symbol of America's technical and social progress.[2] With its delicately ornamented lower stories, entrance, and cornice, Adler and Sullivan's design for the Chicago Stock Exchange on the southwest corner of LaSalle and Washington streets, completed in 1894, is recognized as the finest example of this new type in Chicago (fig. 2.01). Sullivan used ornament as a metaphor for democratic society. In his writing he repeatedly emphasized the link between innovative design and democracy, between building and what he called the "social organism," arguing that architecture would only become a living art when it was "of the people, for the people and by the people."[3] His desire for an architecture that truly expressed the will of people is particularly poignant when we remember that he was writing at a time of deep division in Chicago society. In the years immediately following the Haymarket bombing of 1886, the organization of industrial society was in dispute. In Sullivan's field, building owners, real estate men, architects, engineers, contractors, and building tradesmen were engaged in a fierce battle over how buildings should be constructed and by whom, and in the service of which larger urban and social ideals.

When the editor of the *Building Budget* wrote in 1886, "The anarchist is the plain and practical foe of the architect and builder," he summarized the general opinion of the architecture profession in the aftermath of Chicago's failed social revolutionary movement of the early to mid-1880s.[4] Sullivan's work must be seen in this context. His principal task was to create an architecture that expressed the triumph of business and technology over forces that threatened to destabilize the city. His design for the tall office building was a political manifesto about the fractious relationship between art and labor, and ultimately about the future of industrial society and its governance. In its rhetorical intent, his delicate ornament, so often described as an architectural textile covering the skeleton frame of the building beneath, might be compared to the embroidered banners calling for social revolution that were paraded through the streets of Chicago at this time (figs. 2.02 and 2.03). Much as these banners did, his ornament proclaimed a new industrial world.

Debate about the so-called Chicago construction—where an internal iron or steel frame supported the weight of the building, allowing it to be both taller and lighter—had both aesthetic and political elements. For architects and their

2.01 Adler and Sullivan, Chicago Stock Exchange (1893–94), 30 North LaSalle Street. This building was the finest example in Chicago of Sullivan's self-described "revolutionary architectural mode," an architecture expressive of both American democracy and the new "Chicago construction." Historic American Building Survey, ILL, 16-CHIG, 36-1. Courtesy of the Library of Congress.

clients this new form of construction was valuable because it bypassed the powerful bricklayers union and the delays caused by that organization. The Chicago construction involved the assembly of mass-produced, prefabricated cast-iron and terra-cotta pieces connected to a metal frame with anchors and brackets, a cheaper, lighter, and faster method of construction than the masonry wall. Sullivan recognized that terra-cotta had an advantage in the battle for control over the building site. Its use transferred the performance of aesthetic expression from the hands of the craftsman to the hands of the architect. Sullivan's success in creating an industrial ornament for the tall office building secured his position in history. He overcame the perception that Chicago building was the work of engineers and laborers, built in the service of capital. He reclaimed architecture for Chicago, and the tall office building for art.

THE BUILDING TRADES DISPUTES IN CHICAGO

Beginning in the early 1880s, businessmen bankrolled the construction of increasingly higher office buildings in downtown Chicago, especially in the financial district along LaSalle Street. Yet despite the volume of new construction, the building industry was extremely volatile. Changes in the local and national economy created a cycle of booms and busts in rapid succession. Land prices rose and fell sharply, as did rents. The cost of building materials changed dramatically from season to season, and so did the availability of labor. As a result of economic and technological uncertainty, labor and capital came into conflict, with acute consequences for the architecture profession. In examining this time and place, architectural historians have paid special attention to the tectonic transition from masonry to steel-framed structures, and the new aesthetic that resulted from this transition. By comparison, relatively little attention has been paid to the transformation of the process as well as the product of building, a transformation that resulted in profound changes to what Howard Davis has called the "culture of building."[5] The commissioning, design, and construction of tall office buildings demanded not only new materials, new structures, and new ways of building, but also new relationships between building owners, architects, engineers, contractors, and tradesmen.

Between 1883 and 1900, disputes in Chicago's building trades grew exponentially as the process of building became industrialized.[6] The use of fireproof materials, terra-cotta cladding, and structural cast iron as well as modern heating, lighting, and plumbing rapidly transformed the practice of building. As the production of building materials and the construction of buildings became partially mechanized, building tradesmen saw the value of their labor reduced. Not only could machines replicate some of the tasks performed by humans, they also worked more quickly and for no pay. For example, the invention of the Chambers machine in the early 1880s led to a threefold increase in brick production that flooded the market for bricks, resulting in lower wages and unemployment. The nail industry faced the same problem after the introduction of the nail-making machine, and carpenters were under threat from woodworking machinery.[7] At the same time, new trades appeared. Ironworkers struggled to find their place in the building industry amid conflicts with masons and carpenters over matters of jurisdiction.[8] As a result, building workers began to organize, condemning the use of labor-saving machinery and demanding more control over the building process as well as better pay and working conditions.[9]

Starting in 1883 and lasting well into the 1890s, a series of strikes crippled the building industry in Chicago, causing huge work disruptions on building sites throughout the city, and on the tall buildings being erected along LaSalle Street in particular (fig. 2.04).[10] In 1887 a strike by both the bricklayers' and carpenters' unions in Chicago resulted in thirty thousand building trades workers being locked out by contractors determined to break the power of the unions. These strikes were prompted by support for the national eight-hour movement. Formed in Chicago in 1885, the Eight Hour Association began lobbying for an official eight-hour workday that would start on May 1, 1886.[11] From the beginning, the eight-hour-day issue gained a larger social significance than mere working hours. It signified the ability of workers in an industrial economy to determine the conditions of their own labor and compensation, and to participate as active citizens in a just society.

As Joseph Siry has explained, the first and most significant building whose construction was disrupted by strikes was W. W. Boyington's eclectic Chicago Board of Trade, built between 1883 and 1885 at the southern end of LaSalle Street (fig. 2.05). The building was designed as a celebration of the wealth that the railroads, along with the grain, lumber, and meatpacking industries, brought to the city. But labor leaders saw it differently. For them it represented capitalism's tyrannical rule over the working class, and for this reason it became a particular target for attack. In 1883 its construction was halted by a strike called by the powerful United Order

2.04 (top) A Strike. The Walking
Delegate Sowing the Seed of Discontent. Building unions employed
powerful "walking delegates" as
their representative on the building site. Architects and contractors
feared these delegates, because
they had the power to call a strike
on a moment's notice. From Michael
J. Schaack, Anarchy and Anarchists
(Chicago: F. J. Schulte, 1889), 114.

2.05 (bottom) W. W. Boyington,
Chicago Board of Trade (1883–85),
LaSalle and Jackson streets; S. L.
Stein Publishing Co. This building,
symbolic of Chicago's newfound
wealth, was the site of vigorous disputes between labor and capital. Its
construction was halted by strikes on
the part of stonemasons and bricklayers, and a large crowd of angry
anarchists and socialists picketed its
1885 opening. Used by permission
from the Chicago History Museum;
ICHi-00255.

of American Bricklayers and Stonemasons. In 1885 the banquet celebrating the building's inauguration was disrupted by a loud demonstration held on the streets outside, led by the anarchist leaders Lucy and Albert Parsons.

At the same time it came under attack politically, the Board of Trade was also attacked aesthetically because of Boyington's extravagant use of several different historical styles and colors in its design. Referring to the political protests surrounding it, the New York critic Montgomery Schuyler said of this much-maligned monument: "It is difficult to contemplate its bustling and uneasy façade without feeling a certain sympathy with the mob of anarchists that 'demonstrated' under its windows on the night of its opening. If they were really anarchists, it was very ungrateful of them, for one would go far to find a more perfect expression of anarchy in architecture."[12] Though satirical, these comments reveal a connection between discussions about the way the tall office building should look and the prevailing social turmoil in Chicago. Schuyler's criticism was all too clear: a heavily ornamented building, exhibiting many different styles at once, was no better than the uncivilized mob, ignorant or defiant of the proper modes of behavior.

Architects and contractors actively worked against the labor movement. As we saw in chapter 1, during the worst period of labor unrest the *Inland Architect* continually voiced its criticism of the striking workers and their leaders. Its editors refused to see any validity in the eight-hour cause, arguing that work hours and wages ought to be regulated only by the law of supply and demand, not by artificial control mechanisms.[13] They laid the blame for industrial unrest at the feet of "professional labor agitators," who they believed did not represent the majority of building workers.[14] Writing of the 1887 dispute between the Master Masons of Chicago and the bricklayers' union, the editors claimed that the unions were led by "socialist cranks."[15] These instigators were not even real workers, since "it is the incapable man, the botch whom no employer wants on any terms who is always descanting on the 'rights of labor.'"[16] Architects aimed to strengthen their control over building by lobbying the Illinois legislature for a state licensing law. Passed in 1897, this law sharply defined the professional rights and responsibilities of both architects and contractors. In response to years of strikes, building contractors banded together in 1899 to form the Building Contractors' Council, with the explicit aim of breaking up the powerful union organization, the Building Trades Council. This aim was achieved by mid-1900. Throughout the twentieth century, the building trades unions were never as powerful as they had been in the 1880s.[17]

Through his own practice and membership in professional organizations like the Western Association of Architects (later combined with the American Institute of Architects), Louis Sullivan was intimately familiar with the fractious relations between architects, contractors, and building workers' unions.[18] As Joseph Siry and Robert Twombly have shown, the Auditorium Building, his first attempt to find a new aesthetic expression for the large-scale commercial building, was dogged by a long, drawn-out labor dispute, an experience that left Sullivan suffering from nervous exhaustion when the building was completed in 1889.[19] These events prompted him, along with other Chicago architects, to explore alternative construction methods that were less dependent on the skills of traditional building workers. They also prompted him to establish a new idea of organic architecture, one that depended less on the collaborative creation of large groups of building craftsmen, and more on the individual interpretive power of the architect.

THE "CHICAGO CONSTRUCTION"

The tall office buildings built in Chicago around 1890 represent the transition from one process of construction to another, a process that would define discussions of modern architecture for the next fifty years. The introduction of the steel-framed building was not only due to a desire on the part of building owners for larger, taller buildings that could be erected quickly—it was also the result of industrial action on the part of the bricklayers. Strikes by masons and other building trades unions precipitated the widespread use of the newly invented "Chicago construction," steel-framed buildings encased in a lightweight cladding of brick and terra-cotta.[20] As Henry Ericsson, a Chicago builder and early member of the bricklayers' union, later claimed, the use of the iron and steel frame "soon released building from dependence upon the prior erection of massive walls of brick and stone, and thus set in motion a revolution in the technology of modern building and altered fundamentally the brick and stone mason's relation to the building industry."[21] The Chicago construction caused a fundamental rift with an older ideal of architecture as organic expression. The new technology allowed the architect to fundamentally redefine himself in relation to the building craftsman, as traditional skills were no longer necessary. Late nineteenth-century American architects repositioned themselves as managers of the specialized, technical knowledge of others. Louis Sullivan saw himself as the one person able to synthesize this knowledge and give it artistic expression.

Adler and Sullivan were quick to take advantage of the Chicago construction. While their Auditorium was built of heavy granite requiring the cooperation of hundreds of masons, in his structural plan for the Chicago Stock Exchange made in 1893, Dankmar Adler utilized a steel frame. The thirteen-story building, which contained the trading floor and business offices of the exchange on its lower floors and rental office space above, was designed as an E-shaped plan with a long façade facing LaSalle Street and three short wings projecting to the west. Clad in white enameled brick, the rear light wells ensured that adequate natural light would reach each of the interior offices. On the street side a series of six bay windows achieved the same effect. Sullivan's role was to articulate the interior functions on the outside of the building with an elaborate terra-cotta façade (fig. 2.06). He framed six yellow, terra-cotta-clad vertical tiers of bay windows with two darker, horizontal terra-cotta bands, and used the same material for the cornice and the entry level, above and below. These bands were embossed with an organic motif representing the fecundity of the natural resources of the Midwest. First implemented on the Wainwright Building, this juxtaposition of vertically stratified but relatively plain wall surface with a carpet of densely ornamented terra-cotta around the lower stories and cornice became Sullivan's much emulated signature style. Formally revolutionary, these buildings represent not only the aestheticization of the steel-framed building but also the aestheticization of industrialized building production.

The Chicago construction inaugurated a fundamental break with the aesthetic ideals of a previous generation of American architects, who, as we saw in chapter 1, took the English art critic John Ruskin as their guide. Though he may be described as a follower of Ruskin in many respects, Sullivan's theory of the role of ornament in architecture represents a challenge to that of Ruskin in one essential area. Like Ruskin, Sullivan believed that the true art of architecture was to be found in the adaptation of material and structure to need, not in the external application of fashionable styles. However, the link Ruskin made between ornament and the just disposition of a moral society suffers a significant turn in Sullivan's imagination. For Ruskin, Gothic ornament was beautiful because it registered the mark of craftsman's hand. He saw it as an authentic form of labor requiring the harmony of mental and physical effort. At a larger scale, he held up the collaborative participation of the medieval craftsman in the process of building as an allegory of the participation of the workingman in the governance of society.

The association Ruskin made between craft and a moral society held sway in mid-nineteenth-century American architecture. In 1859 the New York architect Leopold Eidlitz repeated this idea when he wrote in the *Crayon*, "When men labor no more because they are interested in the work they perform, but simply to sustain life, the very foundations of society are breaking up, and the strongholds of morality, honesty, and happiness are crumbling into dust."[22] Like Ruskin, Eidlitz claimed a relationship between the Gothic style and democracy through the figures of the carpenter and the stonemason, equal collaborators in the building process. New York and Chicago architects continued to follow the model of the Ruskinian Gothic in the design of important public buildings up until the late 1880s. However, even as they employed the Ruskinian Gothic style, industrialization was encouraging them to question the link between neo-Gothicism

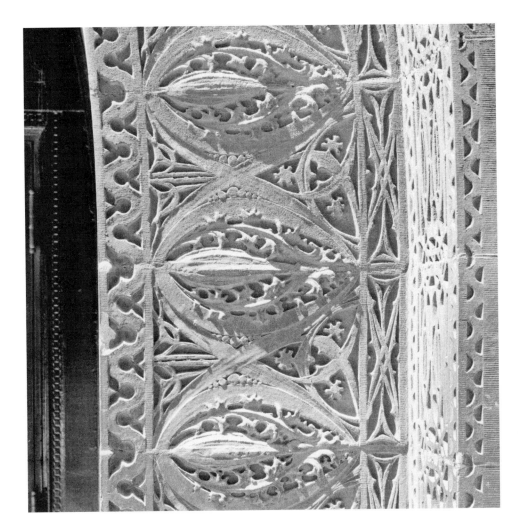

2.06 Adler and Sullivan, Chicago Stock Exchange, entranceway detail. Sullivan created a new industrial ornament, replacing the personal expression of the stonemason that the previous generation of architects had valued so highly. Historic American Buildings Survey, ILL, 16-CHIG, 36-5. Courtesy of the Library of Congress.

and social harmony. For example, in 1865, at the same time that Peter B. Wight completed his Venetian Gothic–style National Academy of Design in New York City (fig. 2.07), James Bogardus and his peers were erecting cast-iron stores and warehouse buildings throughout Lower Manhattan. While these commercial buildings were initially dismissed as engineering, not architecture, some critics could see that the old argument about building as a metaphor for cooperation was about to change.

In 1859 the architect and critic Henry Van Brunt argued that the basis of architectural production had become inextricably severed from the idealized medieval world celebrated by Ruskin.[23] In "Cast Iron in Decorative Architecture," an essay that serves as a direct precursor to Frank Lloyd Wright's famous 1901 lecture, "The Art and Craft of the Machine," Van Brunt questioned the Ruskinian ideal of the nobility of individual labor. Medieval work methods are impossible to employ in modern-day New York, he argued, because buildings are no longer made by individuals but by large organizations like the newly formed general contracting companies. He wrote that modern architecture, "to express our spirit best, is not one of personal thought and aspiration in the workman; it is not one where the individual irregularities of genius or enthusiasm may find scope in tender or grotesque idiosyncrasies of detail; but rather one of system, and, as regards the workman one of organized subordination; it is essentially an architecture of strict mechanical obedience."[24] In other words, the freedom of the craftsman has given way to the precise synchronization of the industrial process (fig. 2.08).

From an early period, Chicago architects were acutely aware of their changing role in the face of new building materials and new methods of construction.[25] In an 1878 letter to the Regents of the University of Michigan arguing for the reestablishment of its lapsed Department of Architecture and Design, William Le Baron Jenney described the need for architects as replacements for "mechanics" or skilled workers, who were being trained less and less as general craftsmen and more and more as specialists qualified for a particular trade.[26] The growing use of cast iron and terra-cotta in construction helped architects like Jenney to reimagine the process of design. It gave them the opportunity to redefine their role as the true "artists" who would shape the new architecture, since building workers were increasingly not generalists but highly skilled craftsmen or unskilled laborers, each of whom worked on specific and separate tasks.

This redefinition of the architect's role was especially important in Chicago, where the tall office building was barely recognized *as* architecture by contemporary critics. The employment of materials and techniques entirely outside the architectural tradition led critics from Europe and the cultural elite in the Northeast to argue that this new type was not "art" in the accepted sense. Instead, they saw it as a product of engineering and construction, built in the service of capital. For example, in 1894 the French architect Jacques Hermant famously criticized Burnham and Root's Monadnock as "no longer the work of an artist responding to particular needs with intelligence and drawing from them all of the possible consequences. It is the work of a laborer who, without the slightest study, superimposes 15 strictly identical stories to make a block then stops when he finds the block high enough."[27] In this way the tallest and most imposing of Chicago's commercial buildings was dismissed as the work of a laborer, not a designer. (Quite perversely, as I outline in the postscript, when the tall office building was later recognized and given value by European critics, it was valued precisely for its ap-

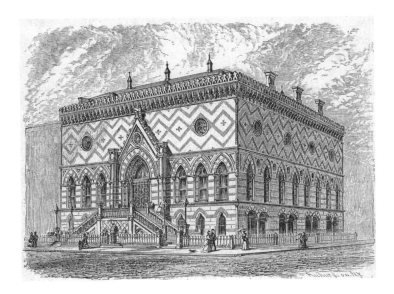

parent lack of design. When modernist architects praised the Chicago skyscraper, they argued that the walls had been left in their "natural" state, that here the partnership of business and construction was allowed to "speak for itself."[28])

The tectonic transition from masonry to curtain walls was not quickly or easily accepted. In the Ruskinian paradigm, the value of architecture, both aesthetic and moral, was tied to its weight, and the correctness of building was judged by the labor that went into creating it. Arguing that iron could never be the basis of true architecture, Eidlitz declaimed, "Iron never can, and never will be, a suitable material for forming the main walls of architectural monuments. The only material for that purpose always has been, and now is, stone . . . Nature herself has made all her strongholds of stone; and we, of necessity, have always done, and will always do the same with our structures. We need the effect of its weight, and bulk, and impenetrableness, which qualities are not to be replaced by any other material now known."[29] Since nature built her structures out of stone, it would be unnatural to build in any other way. The task of the Chicago architect, then, was to convince the public that the design of the steel-framed office building involved aesthetic labor, even though this labor took a different form from that required to erect a stone building.

Chicago architects struggled to reconcile new construction methods with the traditional language of architecture. They actively experimented with all kinds of new materials, both practical and fantastic. Before terra-cotta emerged as the dominant cladding material, first metal was considered, and then glass. Early discussions centered on cast iron, since that material had been in widespread use structurally and ornamentally since the 1860s. In the early years of its use, most critics in Europe and the northeastern United States viewed cast iron as a cheap and tasteless simulation of stone. Up until the 1870s it was widely described as an industrial material not suited to the art of architecture. Nevertheless, the appearance of two- and three-story cast-iron storefronts in Chicago, including those by George Johnson on Lake Street dating to the 1850s, led architects to speculate about the possibility of a whole new style based on iron construction.[30] The influential French architect Eugène-Emmanuel Viollet-le-Duc employed delicately curved metal arches that followed the biomorphic lines of earlier Gothic structures. But this quirky and idiosyncratic style was largely incompatible with the

2.07 (left) Peter Bonnett Wight, National Academy of Design (1865), Fourth Avenue and Twenty-third Street, New York City. Engraving by James H. Richardson, from William Leete Stone, *History of New York City* (1872). The leading architects of New York City utilized the Ruskinian Gothic for their most culturally significant buildings. Picture Collection, The Branch Libraries, The New York Public Library, Astor, Lenox and Tilden Foundations. Used by permission from the New York Public Library.

2.08 (right) "Building the great steel-framed skyscrapers—working high above the street—New York City." Stereo card by Underwood and Underwood, ca. 1906. By the turn of the twentieth century, steel-framed construction had become the norm for large-scale commercial buildings in both New York and Chicago, and the practice of building construction had become industrialized. Courtesy of the Library of Congress; LC-USZ62-69629.

rational and strictly orthogonal steel-framed grid employed in commercial buildings in America, except perhaps on surface ornament.

As buildings grew higher and ornamental ironwork became a legitimate building art, architects wondered if metal could be used to clad tall office buildings. In 1885 Nathan Clifford Ricker, professor of architecture at the University of Illinois, discussed the possibility that iron construction might lead to the development of a new style of American architecture made entirely of metal, especially if techniques like electroplating could be developed to color its surface. In 1899 the Boston-based critic Clarence Blackall, who was sympathetic to the aims of Chicago architects, suggested that tall office buildings might be clad entirely in metal.[31] Reporting on Burnham and Root's early plans for the Masonic Temple in June of 1890, the *Chicago Tribune* reported that the final cladding material of the temple had not yet been decided, and "if it were not for the danger of fire from surrounding buildings the whole exterior would be of steel."[32]

Along with cast iron and steel, aluminum attracted particular attention.[33] In 1885 Ricker suggested the newly discovered metal alloy as a possible replacement for cast-iron façades, due to its "fine color" and the fact that it is "not easily affected by atmospheric influences."[34] In an 1892 speech to the Chicago Architectural Sketch Club, the terra-cotta manufacturer Fritz Wagner predicted the next building craze would be "in the line of aluminum and glass."[35] Spurred on by glass manufacturers and by the example of greenhouse architecture, the idea of an all-glass building received some speculative attention.[36] But while these new materials excited the imagination, the metal-and-glass building remained unrealized in nineteenth-century America. When it came to cladding the Chicago construction, terra-cotta tile had unassailable advantages over metal and glass: it was fireproof, and it was readily available.[37]

One might argue that terra-cotta tile is as important a material as steel in the creation of an aesthetic for modern architecture. Both materials were necessary to create the kind of tall yet lightweight structure that would offset the high land costs and poor soil quality in Chicago. Though terra-cotta is an ancient material that has been used since classical times, terra-cotta tile is a product of industrialization. It became available in the Chicago region starting in 1868, when the Chicago Terra-Cotta Company was formed under the directorship of Sanford Loring, Jenney's sometime business partner. It was most successfully promoted by that company's successor, the Northwestern Terra Cotta Co., founded in 1877.[38] At this time the material was used for fireproofing and as a replacement for heavy and costly decorative stone ornament. By 1883 Chicago had two terra-cotta works in operation.[39] The bricklayers' strike of that year encouraged architects to think about other applications for the material, and by the end of the decade terra-cotta had become the preferred material with which to clad the tall office building.

Cheaper than stone and lighter than brick, terra-cotta could be produced and fabricated relatively quickly, and installed without the use of skilled labor.[40] While skilled modelers were required to sculpt the initial form from which the mold was constructed, this mold could be used again and again. The unfired surface of terra-cotta could be machine pressed into a variety of ornamental patterns, and it could be covered with almost any color and glaze.[41] But this flexibility raised further problems. What should the terra-cotta-clad tall office building look like?

The rapidly increasing use of terra-cotta generated a series of critical essays attempting to place it within the architectural tradition. In an 1894 article, "Steel and Terracotta Buildings in Chicago," the engineer George M. R. Twose criticized the majority of Chicago architects for using the aesthetic traditions of one system of construction (masonry) to mask another (steel).[42] The hybrid result, he believed, was disturbing to look at, because it reduced the bulk of what was apparently masonry to the point where it did not seem capable of performing its structural function. Twose argued that terra-cotta ought to be thought of as a material in its own right.[43] He called for new guidelines for the use of terra-cotta as cladding, since those that Ruskin had set down for natural materials in relation to truth and authenticity no longer applied. Twose was one of the first writers to realize that this material represented not only the mechanization of cladding's practical aspect, since the material could be quickly and cheaply manufactured and erected, but also the mechanization of its aesthetic, since new colors, shapes, and patterns could be created and almost infinitely reproduced. In fact he worried that terra-cotta was becoming too precisely manufactured, and this perfection, attainable only through a mechanized production process, was aesthetically undesirable. Near-absolute seriality was the visible evidence that the built world had ceased to be handcrafted, that mechanization had taken command.[44]

Terra-cotta cladding made its dramatic debut in the form of the twelve-story Tacoma Building, built in 1889 on the corner of LaSalle and Madison streets, a few blocks north of the Home Insurance Building, the Rookery, and the Chicago Board of Trade. The Tacoma was designed by Holabird and Roche and built by the George A. Fuller Company, a construction firm operated by the Boston architect and engineer George A. Fuller (fig. 2.09).[45] While its rear party walls were clad in common brick, the two street façades were made up of a gently undulating, terra-cotta and glass curtain wall. In the early twentieth century some commentators with firsthand knowledge of the building claimed that representatives of a local terra-cotta company had suggested the use of a steel frame to the architects so that their product might be employed on the exterior, reversing the usual hierarchy where the structure is thought to dictate the external form.[46] While this material was praised for its utilitarian benefits, the Tacoma also received a great deal of criticism. The *Chicago Tribune* commented that the building appeared fragile, as if a blizzard could knock it down. The newspaper concluded that the Tacoma was the product of "the owner's desire to get control of as much space as his ground would warrant," and that the end result had no aesthetic value whatsoever.[47] Architects and critics were at an impasse. The new system of construction was faster to erect than masonry. It enabled taller buildings with more rentable area, and it bypassed the control the radical bricklayers' union held over the building process. Yet the aesthetic effect was not yet accepted as a true expression of American art.

SULLIVAN'S INDUSTRIAL ORNAMENT

Louis Sullivan's success lay in his aesthetic response to the transition from masonry to steel-framed structures. This response synthesized the seemingly irreconcilable: the Ruskinian ideal of organic expression and the incontrovertible fact of the Chicago construction. Where Daniel Burnham laid claim to the architect's superior powers of organization, these kinds of managerial skills held little interest for Sullivan. Instead, he concentrated on aesthetics as the proper mode of endeavor for the architect. Though he professed to be concerned with architecture

as the natural outgrowth of its social and political world, he seldom addressed contemporary problems directly. Yet while his writing suggests a disengagement from everyday concerns, existing as it does in the lofty and often impenetrable realms of poetry and philosophy, at the same time he was actively involved in the problems of the architecture profession in the early part of his career. His essays may be seen as a commentary on the larger debate about the relations between art and labor, albeit disguised in naturalistic metaphor. While "The Tall Office Building Artistically Considered" (1896) is Sullivan's best-known essay, another work, "Ornament and Architecture" (1892), is perhaps more revealing, because it divulges his sophisticated understanding of the consequences of separating the art of building from the craft of it.[48] This essay succinctly summarizes the aesthetic problem of the new technology of the Chicago construction, and hints at the underlying issue of labor conflict. Because of the unique technical makeup of the Chicago construction, Sullivan wrote, it was now possible to imagine building form and exterior cladding as two distinct parts, where the form was derived from practical considerations and the cladding gave it artistic expression.

Like other American architects of the time, Sullivan sought to separate his work from that of the builder or "mechanic" by establishing an opposition between originality and tradition.[49] While the craftsman was limited by traditional practice, the architect was freer to invent a new style, using his creative imagination to employ new materials in new ways. Though he had a close relationship with the men who modeled his terra-cotta ornament, especially Kristian Schneider, Sullivan did not consider them creative collaborators.[50] Instead, he believed the design of ornament, and by extension the expression of the needs of society, was the purview of the architect alone. As Frank Lloyd Wright later wrote of terra-cotta, the material is "as sensitive to a creative brain as a dry plate is to the lens of the camera."[51] That is, the method of production, casting, enabled direct communication between the mind of the architect and the finished product, with minimal translation on the part of the building worker.

Sullivan reinforced the divide between the architect and the mechanic, creating a hierarchy where the aesthetic skills of the architect were placed above those of the craftsman. While he believed it was possible to separate form and ornament, he also believed that no building could truly be described as architecture without an organic and harmonious ornament emphasizing and expressing its inner form. He was opposed to the idea that plain construction was more honest and aesthetically pleasing than consciously conceived design. Though the tall office building was a natural and spontaneous product of culture, he believed it was not yet art until the architect had given it artistic expression.[52]

Sullivan's ideas about the architect's role in the building process and the proper artistic expression of the tall office building were in line with the defenders of industrial capitalism, who saw the American city as the natural product of a democratic society. Like theirs, his concept of democracy was not a formal system of government but a feeling of personal freedom existing equally in all men, a feeling that only art could make manifest. Sullivan's idea of democracy was heavily influenced by that of Walt Whitman, who believed that the democratic spirit must take root in men's hearts and emotions rather than in law.[53] Echoing Whitman, Sullivan wrote, "democracy will begin to unfold itself to us as the expression of the individual."[54] "Democratic freedom implies and demands self-respect, self-control, individual responsibility, and individual accountability," he claimed.[55]

2.09 Holabird and Roche, Tacoma Building (1887–89), LaSalle and Madison streets. Chicago Architectural Photographic Co. The terra-cotta-clad Tacoma was one of the first buildings in Chicago to explicitly express its internal steel frame on the exterior façade. Holabird and Roche chose to use dark-colored terra-cotta, chromatically mimicking traditional stone and brick construction. Photography Collection, Miriam and Ira D. Wallach Division of Arts, Prints and Photographs, The New York Public Library, Astor, Lenox and Tilden Foundations. Used by permission from the New York Public Library.

While he subscribed to the rhetoric of "western architecture" promoted by the *Inland Architect*, Sullivan's own ideas of aesthetic form had more to do with personal ethics than with finding a regional or national style. He did not want other architects to copy him, but rather to find their own modes of expression. "Genius is the simple unsophisticated power to see, hear and feel Life!" he wrote. "Therefore Genius in man is nothing other than the historic aspiration of Democracy."[56] In his eyes, the political role of architecture lay not in the collaborative labor of the craftsmen who made it but in the artistic expression of the lone architect-genius who designed it. In 1888 Sullivan was chairman of a committee of forty-eight members of the Western Association of Architects charged with drafting a code of ethics. In his report on behalf of the committee, he provided a brief statement of his own views on the issue, in which he reiterated his belief that the architect was most properly engaged in matters of aesthetics. While he believed that the architect owed a responsibility to his clients, and to the greater public, he owed the greatest responsibility to "the artistic side of practice."[57]

Early in his career, Sullivan attempted to situate these democratic ideals in relation to building practice. He was deeply engaged in the labor issue—indeed, no Chicago architect could avoid it. In 1890 he argued in favor of the "individual contract system" as opposed to the "general contract system," fearing the exploitation of the individual craftsman under the latter approach. His report on this issue contains a telling quote from Ruskin: "In all buying consider first, what conditions of existence you cause in the producers of what you buy."[58] But despite this early engagement with the sticky issue of labor relations, by the late 1890s Sullivan had become disillusioned with professional organizations and their ability to effect the social change he sought. His 1908 manuscript, *Democracy, A Man Search*, never published in his lifetime, presents a damning indictment of the industrial city under capitalism, including both the bosses and the unions, whom he saw as equally hypocritical and corrupt.[59] As Sullivan's personal vision of democratic architecture began to fade, his disdain for collective action grew stronger.[60]

With his terra-cotta and cast-iron ornament, Sullivan believed he had succeeded in giving aesthetic expression to the industrially produced tall building. Between 1889 and 1894, the skyscraper became the symbol of a democratic society. His buildings—the Stock Exchange, the Schiller Building, and the Schlesinger Mayer Store in Chicago, the Wainwright Building in St. Louis, and the Guaranty Building in Buffalo—succeeded as icons on the city skyline. He designed them as towers to be seen from all sides, piercing the datum of the surrounding buildings, symbolizing the triumph of American business. However, while he designed them in relation to the street with great sophistication, he did not design them in relation to each other. He seldom ventured to imagine what part the tall office building could play in the urban form of the industrial city, beyond a purely symbolic role. Only one of his essays, written in 1891, touches on this larger urban question. In it Sullivan proposed an early version of the setback solution that would dominate the New York City skyline after 1916. (That same year, he experimented with the consequences of these restrictions in his never built design for an extremely tall and siteless "Odd Fellows Hall" [fig. 2.10].[61]) He attempted to balance the building owners' desire to build as high as possible so as to maximize their investment through rental income, with "public welfare," the need to keep the streets filled with light and air. But this proposal stopped at the scale of the building. It was in keeping with his basic democratic philosophy that the rights

of the individual to build as he wished
could be compatible with the rights
of the wider population, if each acted
thoughtfully with regard to the other.
"It seems to me a subject not at all
debatable that here in Chicago the
freedom of thought and action of the
individual should not only be maintained, but held sacred," he wrote.[62]

Sullivan's success lay in designing
the tall office building as a three-
dimensional object to be seen in the
round rather than a two-dimensional
façade designed to be seen only from
the public street.[63] After 1889, however,
he never again undertook a project
with the programmatic complexity
of the Auditorium Building, nor did
he attempt to make the tall building

2.10 Illustration from "Chicago—
Proposed Odd Fellows Temple,"
Graphic 5 (December 19, 1891):
404. Louis Sullivan's design for a
thirty-six-story building for the Illinois Branch of the Fraternal Association of the Independent Order of
Odd Fellows is made up of several
smaller towers joined together. This
unrealized project shows how Sullivan imagined that a very tall building could be monumental, but at the
same time responsive to its urban
environment.

a truly public structure. The public dimension of his tall office buildings was limited to that of symbolic images on the skyline, images whose aesthetic value came
from simple massing and complex ornament. Though Sullivan sat on the board
of directors of the Municipal Art League, a society devoted to "stimulating civic
beauty," he was generally uninterested in city planning, seeing urban design as yet
another form of false authority.[64]

By 1900 the heroic skyscraper, the ideal Sullivan had helped realize in the 1880s,
was no longer fashionable, victim to the City Beautiful movement and its desire
for urban reform. Sullivan famously criticized the neoclassical architecture inspired by the World's Columbian Exposition as being the result of "feudal" forces.
He opposed Burnham's grand civic visions as a conformist illusion designed to
swindle the masses.[65] As he described it, truly democratic architecture exceeded
the ability of any one person to imagine it. It could not be organized or predicted.
It would occur spontaneously or not at all. As David Van Zanten has written, in
Sullivan's later work ornament takes on the significance held by planning in the
work of Burnham and other Progressive-era architects.[66] He invested in it all his
desires for the future of a democratic society.

While they are works of art, just as he intended them to be, Sullivan's ornamented curtain-wall façades were banners advertising an optimistic view of the
future of American society under capitalism. Paid for by business interests, these
banners were designed and built to counter those being vigorously waved on
the streets below. What sympathy Sullivan may have had with the striking workers of Chicago and the anarchist leaders lay in their common rejection of what
they saw as arbitrary and corrupt forms of social control (including planning and
professional organizations) in favor of a politics of personal responsibility. Both
Sullivan and the anarchists rejected bureaucracy in favor of an eternally truthful
"natural law."

However, while labor leaders clung to the writing of Ruskin and later William
Morris, Sullivan abandoned the English prophets of organicism.[67] The difference between the Ruskinian and Sullivanian ideas of organic architecture is one

of national self-identity and aspiration. While Ruskin idealized the worker, Sullivan's hero was the businessman, the embodiment of American individualism. His anthropomorphic praise for H. H. Richardson's Marshall Field Wholesale Store—"Here is a man for you to look at . . . a man that lives and breathes, that has red blood; a real man, a manly man"—is praise for the strength and independence of the capitalist entrepreneur and not that of the stonemason.[68]

In the mythology of the American frontier, a mythology that Sullivan never abandoned, individualism ruled over collective action. Any man could become a successful entrepreneur and use his power to effect change on society. Along with the rest of the American middle class, Sullivan believed the divide between capital and labor was an artificial one that could be broken down altogether by individual will. The millionaire industrialist Andrew Carnegie expressed this optimistic view of American society best in his 1889 essay "Wealth," when he claimed that any common man could aspire to membership of the middle class, and further, that the middle classes had the burden of distributing wealth so that all might be provided for.[69] Carnegie and Sullivan both believed in the transformative potential of capitalism and industrial society.[70]

Sullivan's familiar theories concerning the appropriate design of the tall office building, illustrated by his design for the terra-cotta-clad, steel-framed Chicago Stock Exchange, developed in the context of a struggle between labor and capital that played out in the streets of the city, especially on LaSalle Street, the site of Chicago's financial power. His view of democratic architecture reflected contemporary debates over the future of industrial society, the struggle on the part of American architects to define themselves as a profession, and the violent building trades disputes that disrupted the practice of architecture in Chicago from 1883 until 1900, precisely the years in which he achieved his greatest fame. Unlike Burnham and Root, who rejected ornament altogether in the design of their Monadnock, seeing it as a distraction to the citizens of a busy industrial metropolis, Sullivan attempted to recuperate ornament for the industrial age, embracing the design freedom that new methods of production afforded him. The use of cast iron and terra-cotta allowed ornament to be mass produced and industrially assembled. Here the building worker's control over the building process was loosened, and the architect's vision transferred directly to the face of a building through the medium of drawing and the process of casting. In this context Sullivan took the authentic experience the building worker achieved through handicraft, as Ruskin and his followers had described it, and relocated it in the mind of the architect. In short, he accepted the industrialization of the building process and granted the power of democratic expression to the architect alone. The architect, not the craftsman, was the new symbol of democracy.

3 THE MONADNOCK

JOHN WELLBORN ROOT AND THE ART OF PURE COLOR

CHAPTER

Burnham and Root's severe building design for the Monadnock at Jackson and Dearborn streets, completed in 1889, is in many ways antithetical to the elaborate industrial ornamental Adler and Sullivan created for the Chicago Stock Exchange. The heavy brick building is almost devoid of ornament, relying only on its rich purple-brown color and abstracted curves at the corners, base, and attic for aesthetic effect. But despite their differences, these architects had the same goal: to find the appropriate aesthetic expression for a tall office building in a highly unstable urban environment. While the Monadnock was first interpreted as an abstracted version of the Egyptian style, within a few short years of its completion it was heralded as a frank expression of its program and construction, without any style at all. Late nineteenth-century American critics repeatedly described the Monadnock as a revelation of the commercial building in its "natural" state, that is, without artificial embellishment. In the early twentieth century the building was canonized as one of the first American buildings to embody the modern spirit. Modernist architects and critics described it as the genesis of a new movement. However, despite these claims the Monadnock does not fit easily into the narrative that has been constructed for it. Its apparent artlessness was far from an abdication of authorial responsibility. On the contrary, the unusual design was a deliberate strategy on the part of its architects to produce an aesthetic expression for a new building form.

In their design philosophy, both Daniel Burnham and John Wellborn Root followed the principles of organicism promoted by the Western Association of Architects and the *Inland Architect*. In a series of essays published in the magazine between 1885 and 1890, Root claimed that the business block should be designed not only in response to new interior functions, but also in response to the "distracted perception" engendered by the modern metropolis. He described the dulling of perception in modern city dwellers and imagined how architecture might ameliorate this effect through simple massing, uncomplicated skylines, and plain monochromatic surfaces. Root's writing reveals the influence of emerging theories of empathy, and provides us with a different view of the Monadnock—not as the unconscious product of a new industrial age, but as a carefully considered aesthetic response to the environment of Chicago, a response in which color and form would work hand in hand, and without recourse to ornament in the accepted sense. With their design for the Monadnock Burnham and Root attempted to counter the chaos and disorderliness of the streets with an architecture of calm and repose.

EXPERIMENTS IN THE FORM OF THE SKYSCRAPER

Burnham and Root had been in practice together since 1873, but the early years of their partnership were plagued by the national economic recession. Consequently, they built little until the early 1880s. Burnham's enterprising spirit and Root's design talent served them well when the building boom began in earnest. During the early years of this decade, the partners completed a group of tall office buildings at the southern end of LaSalle Street near the new Chicago Board of Trade building that secured their reputation as talented and original young architects. These included the Counselman Building (1884), the Insurance Exchange (1885), and the Rookery (1886). Together these buildings presented an alternative to the rampant eclecticism of the Board of Trade—the adaptation of historical styles toward a new simplicity. "The random application of ornament of all sorts, without thought or purpose, is the crying evil of modern architecture," Root wrote in an 1885 essay entitled "Architectural Ornamentation."[1] Decoration, he believed, must always be subordinate to form in the design of a commercial building. It might be employed so as to accentuate special features, such as the entrance, or the rhythm of the structural bays, but it should always be balanced by large stretches of undecorated surface. The model for such decoration is always found in nature, Root claimed. He believed that ornament was alive and expressive when it was modified by what he called the "constructive," or structurally rational, aspect of building, and irrelevant when separated from it.

This essay and another, "Style," published in 1887, articulated an organic rationalism that clearly influenced Louis Sullivan, who expressed similar thoughts about the relationship between ornament and form in the same journal a few years later. In their own work Burnham and Root used the early tall office buildings they built near the southern end of LaSalle Street as design exercises, exercises that received much praise from contemporary critics. The plain, rose-colored brick, granite, and terra-cotta Counselman Building was praised for eschewing ornamentation in favor of "massiveness and durability."[2] The Insurance Exchange and the Rookery established a new form for the tall office building in the financial district that was much admired and copied. Like H. H. Richardson, who was designing the Marshall Field Wholesale Store a few blocks away at the same time the Rookery was being built, Burnham and Root concentrated on emphasizing the commercial building as a singular volumetric mass (at least from the street front), detached from its surroundings on three sides, solid and heavy, with ornament subordinate to the overall form (fig. 3.01).[3] While the Rookery was more ornamented than the Marshall Field Wholesale Store, the two buildings were widely seen as setting a new standard for commercial architecture. By 1887 Burnham and Root were the acknowledged experts in the new "commercial style."[4]

Burnham and Root began to design the Monadnock in the early 1880s. Although its appearance is extreme, it may be seen as an extension of the same design philosophy that produced the Rookery. The eight-year process of design and construction afforded plenty of time for reflection, and the demands of its clients provided an opportunity to refine the aesthetic the young firm had established in its earlier buildings. The site was 70 feet by 200 feet, on the corner of Jackson and Dearborn streets, three blocks east of the Rookery (fig. 3.02). Though this part of Dearborn Street was relatively remote then, the site was economically desirable for several reasons. Encouraged by the construction of the Board of Trade building

3.01 *(top)* Burnham and Root, the Rookery (1885–86), southeast corner of LaSalle and Adams streets. Photograph by J. W. Taylor. Critics both inside and outside Chicago praised the Rookery as setting the standard for a new generation of tall office buildings. Historic American Buildings Survey, HABS ILL, 16-CHIG, 31-10. Courtesy of the Library of Congress.

3.02 *(bottom)* "From Adams Street, Looking South"; from *Rand McNally's Bird's-Eye Views and Guide to Chicago* (Chicago, 1898). Situated to the south of the existing business district, the Monadnock (marked "7" in this illustration) occupied an unusually small site facing a group of federal buildings to the north, including the central post office ("5"). Burnham and Root's Great Northern Hotel (1889–91) lay diagonally across Dearborn Street to the north ("8").

on Jackson Street, the entire business district had slowly moved south from its original location near the Main Branch of the Chicago River. At the same time, railroad companies were buying up land even further south of the city for new terminal buildings, so the area around south Dearborn Street was ripe for speculative development (the Monon Building by John Van Osdel and the Manhattan Building by William Le Baron Jenney were completed nearby at about the same time as the Monadnock). Finally, the fact that the site had only one short shared boundary made it desirable, since building owners were anxious to avoid legal disputes over party walls.[5] In this location the Monadnock could be built almost "in the round," with three exterior walls facing streets, and only one short wall shared with another site to the south. (The owners of the Monadnock later purchased the adjacent site for an addition designed by Holabird and Roche.)

The Monadnock was commissioned by the Boston real estate developers Peter C. and Shepherd Brooks, regular clients of Burnham and Root since 1881.[6] The Brooks brothers had been investing in Chicago real estate since the 1860s, and they considered the business blocks they built in that city as purely speculative investments. Famed for his stinginess, Peter Brooks was quick to encourage technological innovation in the cause of economy. Wanting his buildings to be as plain as possible, he emphasized the architectural characteristics of firmness and commodity over delight. In commissioning the Monadnock, he made his usual request that the architects refrain from superfluous ornament, and restrict themselves to "the effect of solidity and strength, or a design that will produce that effect, rather than ornament for a notable appearance."[7] As a result of these instructions, as well as the dimensions dictated by the narrow site and the real estate formula that decreed sixteen stories as offering the best rate of return on investment, the Monadnock was to become the most influential of all the buildings designed by Burnham and Root.

The Monadnock took five years to design and another three to build.[8] Though the Brookses purchased the site as early as 1881, they did not announce the project to the press until October of 1885, when a short notice appeared in the *Building Budget*, Chicago's real estate journal, noting that the project would cost $850,000.[9] An initial sketch for the building made at this time shows a narrow, thirteen-story building (fig. 3.03). The short Jackson Street façade has a lotus-blossom motif adorning the eleventh-floor spandrels, a plain and massive stone entrance, and a curved cornice in imitation of an Egyptian pylon. Predominantly vertical, the façade is broken by stringcourses at the third, fourth, and eleventh floors. Between the first and the third floors the exterior walls are canted inward, generating a gentle curve. However, this design was not to be realized. The Brookses delayed construction, waiting for the real estate market to improve at the southeastern end of the Loop, a district still dominated by warehouses at the time.

In 1889, as the real estate boom was reaching its peak, the *Inland Architect* published another scheme for the site.[10] Although designed as a singular monolith, the new building was actually legally two structures, the Monadnock and the Kearsage, reflecting the complex family ownership of the building.[11] Both structures were named for mountains in New Hampshire, and perhaps influenced by Ralph Waldo Emerson's poem "Monadnoc," which celebrated New England's "airy citadel." Between the initial scheme of 1885 and the new drawing of 1889, the Monadnock had undergone a surprising simplification (fig. 3.04). The lotus-blossom ornament, the stringcourses, and the classical base had gone. The batter was more

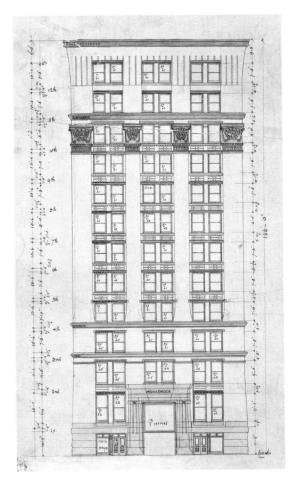

pronounced, and the previously flat walls were broken by a series of projecting bays starting at the third-floor level, cantilevering over the street. Instead of a clear horizontal separation of floors with a hierarchy of importance derived from the classical orders, including an ornamented base and attic, the walls of the Monadnock swept upward, in a series of regular bays to a gently outward-curving cornice, with no ornament to interrupt the verticality of the walls' sixteen-story height. Instead of heavy, double-height doorways, its entranceways were small openings topped by a simple stone lintel. Instead of grouped series of windows separated by pilasters and decorative spandrels, there was a homogenous grid of identical small rectangles puncturing the heavy walls. While the narrow southern wall, soon to be hidden by Holabird and Roche's southern extension, was made of rough "common" bricks, the three street façades were made of narrow "finished" bricks of a curious purple-brown color.[12] In a highly unusual design decision, this material took the place of ornament. Burnham and Root gave all their attention to the way these special bricks curved to form the batter of the wall, and chamfered the corners and base of the oriels at the bottom of the bay windows. The windows themselves were regularly repeated identical openings, with no ornament beyond a thin sill. The cornice at the top reflected the gentle curve of the base.

The Monadnock was radical in its aesthetic, but not in its use of structure. In keeping with the latest real estate trends, the building was now sixteen stories (215 feet) high. By 1889 the equation balancing rental return and the cost of building

3.03 (left) Burnham and Root, the Monadnock, original sketch of Jackson Street elevation, 1885. This preliminary design by John Wellborn Root is in an abstracted Egyptian style. The thirteen-story building is divided into five horizontal sections; the top two are disguised as a high cornice. Used by permission from Collection Centre Canadien d' Architecture / Canadian Centre for Architecture, Montréal.

3.04 (right) The Monadnock Office Building, Chicago. Burnham and Root, Architects; from Inland Architect and News Record 14, no. 5 (November 1889). This sketch shows a radically simplified design. All ornament has been abolished in favor of a delicately contoured, dark purple-brown brick. The building is now sixteen stories, and there is no horizontal division between floors. Used by permission from the Avery Architectural and Fine Arts Library, Columbia University.

dictated that this size would be the most profitable, and most buildings of this height incorporated some element of steel framing.[13] However, the conservative Brooks brothers and their architects decided to stick with masonry walls that had to be over 4 feet thick at the base. With startlingly plain walls of dark-colored brick presenting a smooth and unrelenting face to the street, the designers made no attempt to break up the mass of the building; indeed, they seemed to use every formal device possible to emphasize it.

In plan the building was simple, as the narrow site could support only a single double-loaded corridor, opening onto an inner and outer office on both sides. The interior walls had a 3-foot-high marble wainscot with oak trim and feather-chipped glass window panels above, so as to get light into the central corridor.[14] Today the long corridor continues to resemble the corridor on an early train, with the offices on either side like private railway carriages. Ornamental open staircases are cast-aluminum from street level to the first floor and cast iron above.

In 1893 Holabird and Roche was commissioned to design a southern addition, legally two new buildings called the Katahdin and Wachusett, also named for mountains in New England.[15] The Katahdin, planned first, has skeleton framing inside and masonry exterior walls like the original. The Wachusett is the only part of the building to be entirely steel framed. Although the addition follows the basic color and massing of the original, its façade has a stringcourse of orna-ment above the second story, creating a more pronounced base; the entrances are of a grander scale; and an ornamented cornice was added in a neoclassical style.[16] Though this addition is markedly more traditional than its predecessor, the Monadnock remains an extremely unusual building.

Few contemporary critics recognized any value to Burnham and Root's austere design. The Monadnock seemed a radical departure from the firm's earlier work. The Rookery and the contemporaneous design for the ornamental Woman's Tem-ple (1890–92), both on LaSalle Street, were praised for their graciousness and ac-knowledged as the joint triumphs of Root's career. "There is a distinction between the Woman's Temple and the Monadnock Building," wrote an anonymous author in the anthology *Industrial Chicago* (1891). "The first is an architectural house, the second an engineers."[17] Another writer in the same collection was kinder to the Monadnock, calling it a "thoroughly puritanical" example of the commercial style, which he compared favorably to the "riotous" Rookery, but still unfavorably to the "perfectly dressed" Woman's Temple.[18]

Some critics attempted to redeem the Monadnock by seeing it as a variation on the Egyptian style made fashionable by Owen Jones's *Grammar of Ornament* (1856). This interpretation was easier to see in the original design than in the finished building. An article in *Industrial Chicago* called the Monadnock "a gigantic structure without ornament, save the Egyptian cornice," concluding hopefully, "the design of the architect was to be lavish in interior equipment, merely showing strength in the exterior, and in this he has succeeded." The same author also saw Egyptian influence in Burnham and Root's "Chicago" building, built for the Northern Hotel Company in 1890 in anticipation of visitors to the World's Columbian Exposition. This building was described as having an entablature that was "an ornamental min-iature of the Egyptian cornice of the Monadnock-Kearsage."[19] The architectural historian Donald Hoffman has reinforced this stylistic interpretation, arguing that the profile of the building is based on the bell-shaped columns the Egyptians had derived from the papyrus stem, a motif that Jones had illustrated in abstracted form. Hoffman notes that the name *Chicago* derives from an Ojibwa word for the wild onion plant, whose bulb might be compared to the papyrus.[20]

The Egyptian style seemed particularly suited to Chicago because of topographic similarities between the midwestern city and Cairo, at the mouth of the river Nile.[21] More particularly, the German architect and theorist Gottfried Semper's interest in Egyptian forms may have had an influence on the design of the Monadnock. During the time the building was being designed, Root was translating a section of Semper's *Der Stil in den technischen und tektonischen Künsten* (1860–63) that contained a passage describing the simple masses of Egyptian buildings sitting on the sandstone banks of the Nile.[22] The built representation of an early civilized culture, Egyptian forms were believed to be especially applicable to a young country like the United States. Given such an analogy it was possible to imagine a general Egyptian influence in the architecture of the city as a whole, and to liken the squat, square, boxlike office buildings with their interior light courts to the palace-temples of Egypt. Some Chicago critics believed they might have found the germ of a new architectural language in these imagined similarities of topography and civilization. However, this interpretation had little lasting impact beyond Chicago. For East Coast and European visitors to the city, the Monadnock represented something entirely new: the frank expression of business without attempt at ornament at all.

THE BUILDING THAT SPEAKS FOR ITSELF

The Monadnock gained national and international attention in 1893, when Chicago was host to the World's Columbian Exposition. Visitors came to see both the fair and also the tall office buildings in the downtown Loop. In the copious articles and books written about Chicago architecture dating from this time, the tall office building was described as something thoroughly new. European and East Coast critics did not recognize Egyptian or any other stylistic references in the design of the Monadnock. Nor did they credit the Chicago architects Burnham and Root with creating a unique aesthetic. Rather, they were convinced that the tall office building did not have any relationship to "style" in the accepted architectural sense; instead, they saw it as the pure expression of commerce, unmediated by design.

Contemporary critics described Chicago's tall office buildings as evidence of an anonymous, industrial architecture that threatened the development of American art. The first mention of the Monadnock outside Chicago is in a review of the city's building projects published in *Harper's Weekly* in October 1891, several months before it was completed. The author described the building rather doubtfully, noting how different it was from other Chicago high buildings, and ending his review with the comment that "there can be no question as to its loftiness."[23] While the article is accompanied by an illustration of the Monadnock as well as several other buildings mentioned, including Jenney's Manhattan Building, Adler and Sullivan's "New German Opera House" (the Schiller Building), and the Masonic Temple, strangely it is the only building not identified by name in the caption (fig. 3.05).

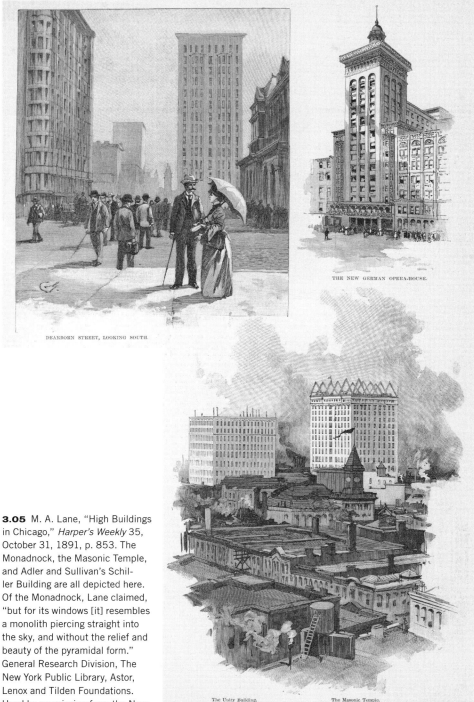

DEARBORN STREET, LOOKING SOUTH.

THE NEW GERMAN OPERA-HOUSE.

The Unity Building.   The Masonic Temple.
HIGH BUILDINGS IN COURSE OF CONSTRUCTION IN CHICAGO AS VIEWED FROM THE "ROOKERY."

3.05 M. A. Lane, "High Buildings in Chicago," *Harper's Weekly* 35, October 31, 1891, p. 853. The Monadnock, the Masonic Temple, and Adler and Sullivan's Schiller Building are all depicted here. Of the Monadnock, Lane claimed, "but for its windows [it] resembles a monolith piercing straight into the sky, and without the relief and beauty of the pyramidal form." General Research Division, The New York Public Library, Astor, Lenox and Tilden Foundations. Used by permission from the New York Public Library.

As Arnold Lewis has shown, European critics often used the Monadnock as an example of what may result when individual architectural creativity is removed from construction.[24] As we saw in chapter 2, in an 1894 review of Chicago building, the French architect Jacques Hermant derided the Monadnock as "the work of a laborer." Some American critics, however, turned this apparent lack of concern with style in the accepted sense into an advantage.[25] The New York critic Barr Ferree, a strong supporter of Chicago architects, was the first writer to describe the

Monadnock as truly modern because it was *without* style. Reviewing it in early 1892 for *Architecture and Building*, he wrote, "there are no attempts at façades, as they are generally understood in architecture, no grouping of windows, no ornamental appendages, nothing but a succession of windows, frankly stating that the structure is an office building, devoted to business, needing and using all available surface."[26] Though the design was simple, "and perhaps in New York would be condemned as bald and wanting in some architectural features," the result, he thought, was satisfactory. The architecture was good because the ends of business were answered. Writing six months later in the English *Builder*, an anonymous critic called the Monadnock a fine example of Chicago's artistic resolution of the problem of the high-rise commercial building. With its massive flat walls, the critic wrote, the building is left in its "natural state," without any attempt at façade-making.[27]

Critics continually praised the Monadnock's "naturalness." Writing in the *Architectural Review* in 1893, Robert D. Andrews claimed that the building had "the proud distinction of being perhaps the only important modern building in the country that has not been 'painted on after it was finished.'"[28] Andrews championed the Monadnock as a piece of architecture entirely without precedent, and again as "natural." It is a work of art, he said, because like all works of art it "corresponds to an ideal . . . the truthful external expression of internal nature, life or purpose." Although the ideals of business (clarity, precision, logic, and exactness) are not necessarily the highest we might aspire to in art, he noted, they are the only ideals the business building ought to express. In this way he admired the Monadnock for its truthfulness to its utilitarian program. Here at last was a building that spoke for itself.

Montgomery Schuyler, another New York critic, was perhaps the staunchest champion of the Monadnock. While he criticized D. H. Burnham and Co.'s Reliance Building of 1894 for being too flimsy, he believed the Monadnock radiated the gravity of modern business life. Its lack of ornament, he felt, was not the omission of art. "On the contrary," he said, "the success of it comes from a series of subtle refinements and nuances that bring out the latent expressiveness of what without them would in truth be as bald as a factory."[29]

Conveniently for critics who saw the Monadnock as the expression of business, an example of the architect restraining his personal creative instincts in favor of pragmatic functionalism, the provenance of the building is unclear. Unlike Sullivan's oeuvre, there is no story of artistic genius told about the Monadnock, only hints that the building's owners may have had a large hand in its final design. The dramatic change between the first and final schemes has led many critics and scholars to speculate about the degree of Root's involvement in the finished building, a story lent credence by an otherwise adulatory biography of Root by his sister-in-law Harriet Monroe published in 1896. Monroe wrote that, exasperated by Root's lack of compliance with the client Brookses' demands for simplicity, the brothers' agent, the real estate developer Owen Aldis, usurped him as designer of the Monadnock in favor of Burnham.[30] Whether Monroe was speaking from personal knowledge or repeating a popular story will probably never be known.

As Burnham's fame increased around the turn of the century, the story of Root's reluctant involvement in the Monadnock grew to the point where it was widely believed that he had nothing at all to do with the design. From 1896 to 1921, several critics, including Schuyler, Andrew N. Rebori, and Burnham's biographer Charles Moore, all stated that Burnham was the sole designer of the Monadnock. Rebori, in particular, saw the building as a heroic example of structural expressionism on Burnham's part.[31] However, this was not the universal opinion at the time. A 1905 article in the *American Architect* praised the building and credited Root with its creation.[32] There is also evidence to oppose Monroe's version of events. According to Miles Berger, who has researched the real estate interests behind the tall office buildings in Chicago, Aldis was a great friend of Root's. This makes the story that Aldis went to Burnham behind Root's back seem unlikely.[33] Only one constant remains in all these stories: those who wish to criticize the building's design see the client's interests outweighing those of the architects, and those who wish to praise it believe the architects managed to retain aesthetic control. The idea that a unique aesthetic expression may have arisen from the conjunction of economic and aesthetic desires is seldom considered.

In architectural histories the fine balance between art and commerce in the design of the tall office building is often paralleled with the personalities of the architects involved. The great success of Burnham and Root and Adler and Sullivan in skyscraper design has been attributed to the perfect balance of business sense and artistry between the partners—Burnham and Adler representing pragmatism; Root and Sullivan, imaginative design sensibility. Similarly, the failings of Jenney, and of Sullivan after Dankmar Adler left their partnership, are usually attributed to a deficiency in one of the necessary components. Jenney's work is characterized as technologically innovative but artistically mediocre, since he relied on a series of draftsmen for the design of his façades.[34] Swinging too far in the other direction, Sullivan's later work, highly colorful and ornamented, is sometimes seen as irrational and unchecked by logic. Given this precisely calibrated balancing act, it seemed hard for critics to believe that Burnham and Root, whose most famous buildings up to that time were the Rookery and the Woman's Temple, were capable of creating the severe and restrained Monadnock. It was easier to imagine business concerns taking over as the client, supported by Burnham, enforced his demands for a purely functional business building, uncompromised by design.

Because of Burnham's reputation for understanding architecture as a business first and an art second, the version of the story in which Burnham alone was the designer supports the belief that the Monadnock was an unmediated response to the demands and conditions of commerce. In these terms, the Monadnock could be presented by American critics of the late 1890s and early 1910s as a case of a building where business speaks for itself. But in this interpretation a strange thing happens to the building's finely molded brick walls. Despite their incredible solidity and refinement, they became conceptually invisible, neutral representations of the interior structure and program. As we will see, a careful reading of Root's own writing reveals that the simplicity and massiveness of the Monadnock were a deliberate aesthetic strategy on the part of its architects; that the building was designed not as an expression of structure or material or business alone, but in response to the effects of business on the city.

THE TALL OFFICE BUILDING IN REPOSE

The Monadnock was an experiment in the design of the tall office building. While he never discussed the design of his own buildings directly, the essays that John Wellborn Root published in the *Inland Architect* between 1883 and his death in 1891 help us understand the designer's intentions. Root shared the organic philosophy of his colleagues in Chicago, but he was equally interested in questions of reception and perception as they were being discussed in contemporary art, aesthetics, and psychology. After reading his essays carefully, it is possible to conclude that the simple, massive, and monochromatic Monadnock was the result of a deliberate aesthetic strategy designed to respond to the particular sensibility of the metropolitan dweller.

The conclusion that the Monadnock is a paradigmatic example of form following function depends on the belief that business is rational and ordered. In fact, the building was intended to lend the multiple interior functions an exterior appearance of stability and permanence they did not necessarily have. As we have seen, the Monadnock was not home to a single company but a speculative office building. Its proximity to the Federal Courthouse meant that it had myriad tenants, including lawyers, architects, engineers, and patent draftsmen, a now-obscure trade. The common metaphor for such a building was the beehive, a place where hectic, furious activity takes place on a huge scale, dependent on a minute division of labor, organized by an almost infinite series of intricate and invisible patterns. The number of people and the scale of activities taking place within the Monadnock were fascinating yet incomprehensible to outside observers. In 1896 the *Chicago Tribune* reported that the population of the building was larger than that of many small towns in Illinois. In 1900 the same paper reported that the Postmaster of Chicago had divided the Monadnock into four postal zones and dedicated four mail carriers to it. These mail carriers made deliveries six times a day to 6,000 inhabitants occupying 1,200 rooms, handling 25,000 pieces of mail each day (fig. 3.06).[35]

Because of its complex internal program, the tall office building presented a challenge to accepted methods of planning and design. In 1887 the *Building Budget* reprinted an article by the English architect Lawrence Harvey explaining the Beaux-Arts method of planning.[36] Using Charles Garnier's Paris Opera House as an example, Harvey explained that the internal functions of a building must be expressed on the exterior of a building in a hierarchical manner. In the case of the Opera House, the stage was given most prominence. In turn, the lesser functions were given external expression in relation to their place in the hierarchy. In cases where the individual parts of a building do not have a clear hierarchy of parts, "such as most administrative buildings, blocks of residential flats and offices," Harvey suggested an alternative method

3.06 "Most Remarkable Postal District in the World: Four Carriers Who Never Get Out of One Chicago Building," *Chicago Daily Tribune*, July 8, 1900, p. 49. This article explained that the Monadnock (including the southern addition by Holabird and Roche) was so large that it was considered a separate postal district. The 6,000 people who occupied 1,200 offices inside received six mail deliveries a day except on Sunday, when there were three.

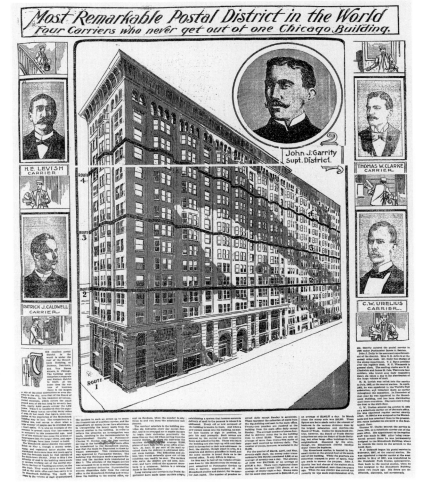

of design, the "architectural packing-case," where disparate functions are given coherence by their enclosure in a simple volume.[37] While Chicago architects generally followed Beaux-Arts planning maxims, in the case of the business building the interior functions were simply too numerous and irregular to be coherently represented. Although they believed tall office buildings like the Monadnock were prime examples of organic architecture, in their design they subscribed to the "packing-case" method.

In his writing, Root emphasized that it was the architect's job to correct rather than reflect the disorganized and haphazard forms assumed by business organizations. In other words, he did not want to represent the interior reality of business life (chaotic, hurried, fragmented, and impossible to comprehend). Instead, he and Burnham used architecture to give stability, rationality, order, and coherence to functions that appeared to have none. Further, they argued that the form should be monolithic and plain, since metropolitan dwellers were too busy to appreciate fine detail. Unlike Sullivan, Root did not attempt to ornament the tall office building with fields of delicate flowers and leaves, however abstracted. For the sake of both aesthetics and hygiene, he wrote, the exterior form should be kept simple.

The theme of blindness, of the near-invisibility of the tall office building among the hustle and blur of the downtown world and the smoke of its polluted environment, pervades contemporary writing about Chicago. When Barr Ferree visited the city in 1892, he noted a "genuine metropolitan atmosphere . . . The streets are crowded . . . with hurrying, bustling people, intent on business and with scarce time to gaze at the attractions in the shop windows."[38] If the busy inhabitants of Chicago's streets had no time to window-shop, argued Root, they certainly had no time to appreciate delicate ornament placed high up on downtown buildings. He believed that delicate details were unnecessary on tall office buildings, simply because they would not be seen (figs. 3.07 and 3.08).

It is as absurd to decorate with intricate ornament commercial structures on busy streets as to approach a man at the corner of Madison and State Streets and begin to talk of the last poem by Austin Dobson. And the absurdity does not end with the failure to attract attention: the ornament so neglected becomes dead by virtue of such neglect and we become like street vendors, who, by constantly crying in unheeding ears, stifle their own voices . . . Not only does the repose of a design demand that ornament be applied with accent and a sense of rhythm, but stretches of undecorated surface are essential to the value of such ornament as may be used . . . Each detail in a building goes for little with the general public, and . . . they are more impressed by the use of certain materials, by the general arrangement of masses, by the effect of lightness or solidity, and by the mere quantity rather than quality of ornament.[39]

Echoing a larger discussion about municipal sanitation, he supported his aesthetic argument with a hygienic one, claiming that such decoration was undesirable because it would collect dirt and dust. In the design of the tall office building, Root believed the architect should employ simple massing, uncomplicated skylines, and plain surfaces of a single, monochromatic material to create a sense of "repose" in the viewer.

The word *repose* appears over and over again in American architectural writing of this period as an important attribute for civilized buildings. In 1884 William Le Baron Jenney had suggested an aesthetic opposition between repose and the

picturesque when describing the difference between public and private build-ings.[40] The quality of variety, so attractive in the domestic designs promoted by Andrew Jackson Downing and Alexander Jackson Davis in the mid-nineteenth century, was not suitable for public buildings, he believed. In an address to the Chicago Architectural Sketch Club in 1889, Jenney claimed: "The buildings [of today] are like people, full of a nervous, restless energy; quaint, picturesque, strik-ing perhaps, but rarely restful . . . Business building should have a quiet dignity, a simple, massive grandeur that will not grow tiresome, that will, by the very sight of them, tend to rest men from the worry and turmoil of the struggle for bread."[41] Critics came to agree that the sheer mass of Chicago's tall buildings rendered or-nament irrelevant, and the idea of architectural repose, or simplicity, was central

3.07 "Dearborn St., North from Van Buren, Chicago." Stereo card by H. C. White Co., 1906. The base of the Monadnock can be seen on the left, with the Federal Building and Holabird and Roche's Marquette be-yond, and the Great Northern Hotel opposite. John Wellborn Root be-lieved it was pointless to ornament tall office buildings, because that ornament would go unnoticed by busy city dwellers walking on the streets below. Courtesy of the Library of Congress; LC-USZ62-51776.

3.08 Cityscape view northeast from the roof of the County Building toward the Schiller Building (on the left, with a tower on its roof) and the Masonic Temple (on the right, in the background); glass negative, from the *Chicago Daily News*, 1907. The design of the Monadnock must be seen in the context of the heavily polluted atmospheric environment surrounding it. The haze of smoke and fog enveloping the city made it particularly difficult to appreciate detailed ornament on the façade of tall office buildings. Used by permission from the Chicago History Museum; DN-0004955.

to their positive reception. In 1892 a British reviewer wrote of them that "their finest quality is that of immensity, and the less the fronts are broken up, the less the walls are interrupted by piers and by strings, the more imposing the structure and the more tremendous the effect."[42] In an 1891 review of Root's work, the architect Henry Van Brunt suggested that just such a superfluity of ornament had marred the design of the Rookery. Comparing the interior court to a Piranesi etching, he criticized it for its "feverish energy" and "absence of subordination and repose."[43]

This response to the problem of the tall office building, the turn toward simple massing rather than ornamental refinement, was allied with new theories of perception being explored at the same time by some American architects. The idea particularly attracted the Czech émigré Leopold Eidlitz, a New York–based architect, and a friend and mentor to Richardson, Wight, Schuyler, and a whole generation of American architects and critics in the 1860s and '70s.[44] His peculiar version of architectural organicism, which he described in *The Nature and Function of Art, More Especially of Architecture* (1881), was closely related to German theories of Einfühlung, or empathy, although it predates widespread understanding of the idea in the United States.[45] In this book Eidlitz described physical energy as the basis of all architectural creation and perception. He believed it is the corporeal action of doing mechanical work, or carrying loads, that we recognize when we look at architectural form. Eidlitz's definition of beauty as the expression of an idea through matter was especially influential for Root.[46]

In his writing, Root used the same metaphors of distraction and attention, motion and rest that German aestheticians employed to formulate a new
understanding of the way we perceive art. In his 1886 "Prolegomena zu einer
Psychologie der Architektur" and *Renaissance und Barock* (1888), the Swiss art
critic Heinrich Wölfflin proposed a psychological basis for our perception of
the built environment, claiming that we understand architectural form through
identification with the movement implied in it.[47] This empathetic approach is
in some ways an extension of the concept of organicism, because architecture
is considered analogous to a living body, subject to the same physical stresses
and strains.

By the 1890s theories of empathy were entering the American discourse on
aesthetics. For example, the Chicago-based journals the *Open Court* and the
Monist published regular excerpts from, and reviews of, books by European aestheticians such as Theodor Lipps, Ernst Mach, Georges Hirth, Alfred Binet, and
Henri Bergson for consumption by an American audience.[48] Lipps's theory of
empathetic perception was summarized succinctly in an 1898 review of *Raumästhetik und geometrisch-optische täuschungen* (1897), in which Lipps is quoted: "The
column acts as I act when I pull myself together and rise from my seat . . . I
cannot perceive the column without picturing it as invested with the activities
which I have experience of in myself."[49] Chicago architects also knew of these
ideas through the work of the New York architect Henry Rutgers Marshall, one
of the most prominent American contributors to the discourse on empathy
in the United States. Marshall forms the most solid link between these new
aesthetic theories and Chicago architecture, since his introductory essay, "The
Science of Aesthetics," was published in both of Chicago's professional journals,
The Inland Architect and *The Building Budget*, in 1890.[50]

When Burnham and Root designed the Monadnock, they took this empathetic approach into account, imagining how busy Chicagoans would view the
building as they rushed down Dearborn and Jackson streets, pushing past other
pedestrians and dodging horse-drawn carts and omnibuses on the way to their
jobs in other office buildings, to the railway station, to the department stores, to
the Board of Trade and the Stock Exchange. In their design they responded to
a commonly expressed idea, that the senses of contemporary city dwellers had
become dulled by the continuous demands made on them by this hectic urban
landscape. In his 1903 essay, "The Metropolis and Mental Life," the German sociologist Georg Simmel provided a definitive description of what he saw as the
physical adaptation of modern man to the modern city. He called this physi-
ological change, in which the city dweller muted his own nervous response and
deadened himself to the many demands of the urban world, a "blasé attitude."[51]
In colloquial terms, Simmel's modern man develops a "thick skin" in order to
resist the demands made on his nerves by the multiple sensory stimuli of the city
street. In these terms the Monadnock might be characterized as a blasé building; psychologically its thick skin presented a restful surface to the eyes of those
viewing it (fig. 3.09).[52] Where the art nouveau style of the same period was the
overt expression of a restless and nervous society undergoing extreme change,
Burnham and Root intended the Monadnock as an antidote to it.[53] They believed
this large, plain building ought not to further upset already rattled nerves, but
instead to anchor and stabilize them.

THE ART OF PURE COLOR

Theodore Starrett, an architect who worked for Burnham and Root during the long process of the Monadnock's design, claimed that the building was an experiment in the aesthetic potential of brick.[54] This potential included not only its form but also its color. In an 1889 article showing the radically revised design for the building, the Chicago real estate paper the *Economist* reported that while "uniform material is everywhere employed (brick) . . . no two parts of the building will have the same color value."[55] Though the perspective rendering accompanying the article shows the entire building to be a single dark color, reflecting the monochromatic effect of the purple-brown brick eventually used, this passage suggests that the architects may have originally intended the three street façades to be polychromatic. In her biography of Root, Harriet Monroe wrote, "many persons remember his desire to grade the color of the building from brown bricks at the bottom to yellow at the top."[56] Indeed, Root had proposed such a scheme

3.09 The Monadnock, detail of base. The massive base of the Monadnock presents a plain and reassuringly solid surface to the street. Photograph by the author.

for an earlier building, the Rialto. In 1885 the *Building Budget* reported that "it is understood that the architects propose making a bold departure from the usual manner of erecting the outer walls, by using pressed brick of varied colors instead of as uniform shade as is generally done."[57] The fact that this color scheme was not carried out in the Rialto or the Monadnock has been ascribed to its expense, but perhaps this no-doubt startling effect was simply too extreme for the architect's clients. What remains is Root's expressed desire that architects experiment with color as a primary aesthetic effect.

Root had a long-standing fascination with the power of color to speak directly to the emotions. In an 1883 essay, "Art of Pure Color," he discussed the possibility of an architecture whose effect depended on color rather than ornament.[58] His writing shows a thorough understanding of the debates about form and color, figuration and abstraction, in contemporary painting. As the first president of the Chicago Art Guild, in 1883 he presided over a "White and Gold" evening, an event perhaps influenced by the American painter James McNeill Whistler's recent London art show, also designed in white and gold.[59] In his essay on color dating from the same year, Root referred to the famous libel case between Ruskin and Whistler, prompted by Ruskin's criticism that Whistler's atmospheric and almost abstract paintings were nothing but a pot of paint flung in the face of the public. In his own defense Whistler used the analogy of music to suggest the possibility of a visual art of pure feeling, without any attempt at formal representation. Root sided with Whistler, arguing that painting was evolving into an "art of pure color." Applying Whistler's philosophy of painting to building, Root claimed that architecture too might gain its effect from color rather than ornament. He believed that, rather than being subordinate as decorative elements, terra-cotta tile, stained glass, and mosaics, with their deep, pure, and brilliant pigments, could take on a central role in the aesthetic of the built environment. As in contemporary painting, architecture might cease to be defined by hard edges, he thought, and instead suffuse its inhabitant with an ever-changing glow of colored light. Root's essay was contemporaneous with the French symbolist Gustave Kahn's "The Aesthetic of Polychrome Glass" (1886), which explicitly linked colored glass architecture to the evolution of modern perception.[60] Like Kahn, Root talked about the increasing sophistication of color perception and speculated about the effect of polychromy on modern nerves.

Root's belief in the immediacy of color perception was central to most avant-garde art movements of the late nineteenth century. In contemporary art theory, color, like music, was thought to represent a direct appeal to the senses, without mediation by the brain. Unlike conventionalized figural representation, it was thought to be a kind of natural language, perceived physiologically rather than intellectually. Root described the experience of color as direct, while that of form was indirect. He likened form to a newspaper that must be read, while color creates a direct emotional response.[61] Without the mediation of iconographic symbolism or historical allusion, it seemed to provide a way back to a natural connection between man and his environment that had been lost in the chaos of the industrial city.

The idea that man's color perception was continuously evolving was frequently repeated in nineteenth-century writing on architecture and design, where color appreciation was often used as an indicator of cultural development. In his *Grammar of Ornament*, Jones had proposed an evolution of color perception, from an original recognition of only primary colors in ancient times to a more developed understanding of secondary and tertiary tones.[62] The English color theorist George Field believed that the cultivated mind could appreciate a rational relationship between colors, while the "vulgar uncultivated sense" regarded colors as "individually distinct, without order or dependence, the arbitrary inventions of fancy."[63] He used the argument that children desire bright and gaudy things while adults have a more sophisticated appreciation of color to support this contention.

Turning this idea on its head, the Hungarian social critic Max Nordau held up the swirling, restless lines of the art nouveau and Jugendstil styles, with their ripe and florid colors, as signs of a general cultural degeneration.[64] Nordau implied that the fashionable taste for such styles was a general symptom of societal instability resulting from "unnatural" urbanization. Root, however, took the more positive view that a refinement of color appreciation might induce a cultural *regeneration*. While primary colors were associated with an undeveloped aesthetic sense, appreciation of them could be seen as "natural" rather than savage. Acting directly on the mind and body, without the mediation of historical allusion, color seemed to provide a way back, to noble savagery, and also a way forward, to an era beyond present-day materialism, toward a modern spirituality.

Like many fin-de-siècle painters and designers, including Piet Mondrian, Wassily Kandinsky, and Bruno Taut, Root drew not only on scientific and psychological theories for his belief in the power of color but also on contemporary mysticism.[65] In the early 1870s both Burnham and Root were members of the Union Park Temple on the West Side of Chicago, a Swedenborgian church.[66] Members of the "New Church," as the sect was known in America, followed the teachings of the eighteenth-century Swedish scientist and mystic Emmanuel Swedenborg.[67] According to Swedenborg's "doctrine of correspondences," the physical world is an imperfect copy of a spiritual world whose invisible order may be seen only by the enlightened. Swedenborgians believed that the sun's light is the visible manifestation of God on earth, and that color mediates between everyday life and the higher realm. The three primary colors correspond to the three essential aspects of the Holy Spirit: red is love, blue is faith, and yellow is life. As a young man, Root repeated that triumvirate in "Faith and Science," an essay written for a Swedenborgian tract around 1876. Critical of contemporary materialism, he believed that truth exists in a "higher sphere" in which spirits commune, unburdened by matter.[68] Root was aware of the aesthetic expression of this idea in the work of the American painter George Inness, another follower of Swedenborg.[69] In Inness's later work, color became the means to show the spiritual value inherent in the physical landscape. Root praised Inness, along with Camille Corot and J. M. W. Turner, as "Impressionists" who used color to reveal the metaphysical.[70]

Despite his innovative use of materials, Root remained convinced that the truth of architecture dwelt in ideas.[71] It should not mimic the visible world of structure and program, he believed, but express the invisible metaphysical truths lying behind the material world. When he claimed that architecture was becoming overly concerned with its own technical makeup, it is clear that, as for Sullivan, Root's definition of the function of the tall office building was not pragmatic or utilitarian but social and spiritual. He believed a new architectural aesthetic might train human perception, extending its capabilities, and in doing so help the modern city dweller evolve to a higher state of consciousness. Through colored architecture the dystopia of modern life might be overcome, and an authentic experience returned to. Burnham and Root's design for the Monadnock is a unique aesthetic expression. Although the precise question of authorship remains unclear, there is little doubt that the unusual building is the combined result of the desire for simplicity on the part of the client, Burnham's business acumen, and Root's aesthetic philosophy.

Near the end of his essay "Art of Pure Color," Root described a vibrantly colored city made of terra-cotta tile, stained glass, and mosaics. "Think for a moment what our streets might become," he wrote, "if to the somber grays of stone or reds of brick were added the full, unfading bloom of glass, marble and tiles. These combined by artists of sensibility . . . would fill our cities with the eternal joy of color."[72] This image prefigures the delicately colored illustrations made by the artist Jules Guerin for Burnham's 1909 *Plan of Chicago*, paintings that depict a harmonious vision of a beautiful city, bathed in the light of the rising and setting sun. The Monadnock may have been Burnham and Root's imperfect first attempt to realize this ideal. Here the two men arrived at a new aesthetic for the tall office building, one based in form and color rather than ornament. They also pointed toward a new urbanism; one in which the visual confusion of the city, with its cacophony of historical references and different voices, could be reconciled.

4 THE MASONIC TEMPLE
THE DOUBLE LIFE OF A CIVIC SKYSCRAPER

In their respective designs for the Stock Exchange and the Monadnock, Adler and Sullivan and Burnham and Root used very different aesthetic strategies to account for the form of the tall office building. Where Sullivan sought an ornament suitable to its increasingly industrial method of construction, Burnham and Root concentrated on color and pure form, arguing that the city itself provided the stimulus formerly offered by ornament. Both these strategies fall squarely within the rhetoric of organicism espoused by the *Inland Architect*, where the exterior form of a building responds, apparently spontaneously, to the social and physical climate in which it is built, and the materials from which it is made. This chapter will focus less on the exterior form of the tall office building than on attempts to reimagine its program as a truly public enterprise instead of one restricted solely to business interests.

Daniel Bluestone has described the appropriation of civic forms such as cupolas, turrets, statuary, and monumental entrances in commercial buildings like W. W. Boyington's Columbus Memorial Building (1891) on State Street.[1] In their pretensions to public significance, such buildings may be described as "civic skyscrapers." In the early 1890s Burnham and Root designed two of the most prominent civic skyscrapers in Chicago, the Woman's Temple (1890–92), built for the Woman's Christian Temperance Union (WCTU) at LaSalle and Monroe streets, and the Masonic Temple (1890–92), built for the Chicago Order of Freemasons at State and Randolph streets.

As their names suggest, these curious buildings were imagined as both secular and sacred, commercial buildings and "temples." Through groups like the WCTU and the Freemasons, the tall building, often maligned as the product of greed, speculation, and usury, was brought into the service of civic reform. The two temple buildings symbolized the moral goals of the organizations that built them, the redemption of the industrial city through religion, service, and art. In the case of the Masonic Temple, Romanesque gables and dormers distinguished it from its more businesslike neighbors. A mansard roof in the manner of a French chateau did the same for the Woman's Temple (fig. 4.01). But at the same time, these buildings were also intended to generate capital, containing space not only for civic functions but also for rental offices and stores.

Contemporary critics celebrated the two temple buildings as the future of the American city, the evolution of the office block from pragmatic business box to beautiful civic icon. The twenty-two-story Masonic Temple in particular attracted international attention for its height and unusual hybrid program. The uppermost floors contained Masonic Lodge rooms as well as a theater and a rooftop observatory, while the bottom half of the building contained stores and a restaurant. Inside the typologies of street, lobby, and shopping arcade were gathered together vertically by an internal atrium stretching the full height of

4.01 Burnham and Root, Woman's Temple (1890–92), LaSalle and Monroe streets. Photograph by Barnes-Crosby. The magnificent design and large scale of the temple reflected the ambitious social goals of the Woman's Christian Temperance Union. Used by permission from the Chicago History Museum; ICHi-19133.

the building. The culmination of other magnificent light courts designed by Burnham and Root, this one served as a prototype for a new kind of public space, one that was bright, clean, and peaceful in comparison to the dirty, dark, and noisy streets outside. However, it was not always easy to unify commercial interests with social ideals. In the Masonic Temple the dream of a democratic society met the reality of an emerging mass culture. While it was one of the most architecturally successful versions of the tall office building as civic skyscraper, it was also one in which the contradictions inherent in the modern American city were exposed.

GENDERED SPACES FOR CIVIC REFORM

Though the Freemasons were an established fraternal order, and the Women's Christian Temperance Union a relatively new one, the two organizations had the same basic social and urban agenda in commissioning new buildings. In 1891 the *Chicago Tribune* described the two temples as "great buildings in the erection of which sentiment is mingled with cold business policy."[2] "Cold business policy" referred to the planned construction of rental office space in order to financially sustain the operation of each organization. But the "sentiment" involved was no less serious. In both cases the architecture was to represent a social ideal: the feminine virtues of temperance and Christian morality in the case of the WCTU, and the masculine virtues of loyalty, wisdom, and self-reliance in the case of the Freemasons.

The WCTU and the Freemasons were two of the larger members of a group of voluntary social organizations that played an important role in nineteenth-century American society. Starting in the early 1800s, so-called fraternal organizations such as these attracted thousands of members throughout the United States.[3] While apolitical, these groups had a significant influence on social and urban policy in the last two decades of the century. Made up largely of white middle-class men and women, they were the vehicles through which a new vision of social and urban unity was projected in the Gilded Age. Fraternal societies were a way to systematize and enforce moral order at a time when the disintegration of traditional social ties seemed imminent. Through the rituals associated with each group, individuals were symbolically reborn as members of a single organization with common goals.

Freemasonry provided a model for other groups. Following English and Scottish tradition, the colonists imported Freemasonry to America in the eighteenth century, founding the first Lodge in Philadelphia in 1730. The society proved particularly popular in the revolutionary era as a secret male order dedicated to bringing about social perfection. In fact Benjamin Franklin and George Washington were both Freemasons, as late nineteenth-century Masons recalled proudly when they linked their contemporary efforts back to the early days of nation building. After a period of anti-Masonic activity in the 1820s, when fears of the order's secret influence on business, politics, and the church reached a crescendo, it became more popular than ever. From the 1860s to the 1880s, countless secret male lodges were formed in the Masonic mode, often appropriating Masonic ritual and lore wholesale.[4] These groups included the Odd Fellows, the Knights of Pythias, the Benevolent and Protective Order of Elks, the Ancient Order of United Workmen, and the Modern Woodmen of America. They all adhered to the same goals of self-improvement, fellowship, and community service as the Free-masons. These organizations were particularly attractive to Civil War veterans who sought to extend the military virtues of duty, honor and comradeship into civilian life. Through groups such as these, newly arrived immigrants formed new social bonds outside their own ethnic group.

Women were attracted to fraternal organizations, though they were not allowed to join. Separate women's groups modeled on the Freemasons first appeared in the 1850s and reached their peak in the 1890s as women sought to extend their influence beyond the home.[5] They became active in shaping the city and civic life through voluntary organizations such as the Young Women's Christian Association, the Salvation Army, the College Settlement Association, and the Women's Christian Temperance Union. These organizations aimed to rescue the inhabitants of the industrial city, especially new immigrants, from poverty, disease, and crime. They created what Daphne Spain has called "redemptive places" in the larger American cities: settlement houses, kindergartens, libraries, public bathhouses, and playgrounds.[6] By providing basic services for the poor, these women's groups helped new arrivals assimilate, teaching them how to wash, dress, eat, read, and play like Americans. In most cases these redemptive places were located away from downtown, often in buildings designed for other purposes.

The most prominent of these female-run institutions in Chicago, Jane Addams's Hull House, was one of the few to occupy a purpose-built complex. Built between 1889 and 1908, Hull House was designed by the Chicago architects Irving and Allen Pond in the style of a sixteenth-century English manor house.[7] Here Addams and her fellow social workers provided inexpensive and nutritious food for the poor, along with amenities such as a kindergarten, nursery, and music school. If Hull House was unusual in the programmatic specificity of its design, it was typical in its siting. Built at the intersection of Halsted and Polk streets in the Near West Side of Chicago, it was purposely located close to its immigrant constituents.

While Addams and other women's groups restricted their efforts to poor residential areas, in 1887 Matilda Carse, president of the Chicago Central Woman's Christian Temperance Union, announced she would build the headquarters of the WCTU right in the middle of the Loop on LaSalle Street, among the banks, insurance offices, and stock exchanges that marshaled the financial reserves of the Midwest (fig. 4.02).[8] The WCTU shared similar aims with the settlement movement: social reform through the education of the poor, and the preservation of the moral and physical health of the family. Carse had numerous objectives in commissioning the Woman's Temple. She wanted to build a lasting monument to the WCTU and its founder, Frances Willard, and a place where the organization could perform its mission: educating the working class about the evils of alcohol. She also wanted to create a source of revenue for the WCTU. Financed by a stock company in a manner similar to other large office buildings, the Woman's Temple shifted the issue of temperance from the feminine realm of the private home to the heart of Chicago's masculine world, the city's economic and political center. In 1895 Willard said of the building, "It is the only attempt yet made by women to concentrate in architectural forms the thought and purpose of home protection."[9]

Signaling the breadth of her ambition, Carse hired Burnham and Root, the most famous Chicago architects of the day, to design her building. John Wellborn Root made an initial sketch for a different, smaller site in 1888. When it was published in the *Inland Architect*, this design was criticized as too plain for a client with such lofty aspirations.[10] Root was soon persuaded by Daniel Burnham and his architect friends to add a chateaulike roof and more terra-cotta ornament to the façades. The second version of the Woman's Temple had an H-shaped plan with a recessed front instead of a light well. The ground floor was given over to public activities, including rooms for daily gospel temperance meetings, places where "the rum-cursed victims of the legalized liquor traffic could find a refuge."[11]

The centerpiece of the whole design was Willard Hall, a large ground-floor auditorium designed to accommodate seven hundred people. It was decorated with allegorical paintings and stained glass representing Mercy, Justice, Purity, and Temperance, all depicted as female figures and executed in the Pre-Raphaelite manner by the English artist Walter Crane. Lavishly decorated in marble and bronze, Willard Hall was to be the new center of an international cause: women's rights. The *Chicago Tribune* reported, "It will be the Faneuil Hall of a worldwide woman's movement and the Mecca of women in every country who sigh for enlargement of their sphere."[12] It should be noted, however, that Willard Hall had an entrance off Monroe Street entirely separate from the main building entrance on LaSalle Street. Though the WCTU wanted to unite its quasi-sacred temperance mission with that of commerce, the two spheres were not allowed to mix at the level of the individual building user.

At the same time that the Woman's Temple was being completed, Burnham and Root were at work on another civic skyscraper, the Masonic Temple at State and Randolph streets. For contemporary critics the two buildings represented the aesthetic flowering of the tall office building, the moment in which the type shook off its distasteful association with commerce and became a truly beautiful piece of public art. Architects generally viewed the Woman's Temple as the more successful of the two projects, though the Masonic Temple was the more popular tourist attraction. In 1891 the *Chicago Tribune* praised the Woman's Temple as approaching "the ideal of office buildings. It appeals to the eye in a manner wholly

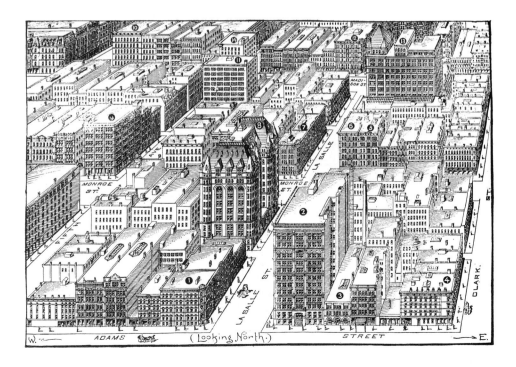

4.02 "From Adams Street, Looking North on La Salle"; from *Rand McNally's Bird's-Eye Views and Guide to Chicago* (Chicago, 1898). The Woman's Temple (marked "8" in this illustration) was prominently located on LaSalle Street, adjacent to the city's most prominent business buildings, including the Home Insurance Building ("2").

unlike any of the 'dry-goods box' giants which are becoming so common."[13] When it was about to be demolished in 1922, Robert Craik McLean, editor of the *Inland Architect*, remembered the Woman's Temple as the apotheosis of the "romantic period in American architecture."[14]

THE CIVIC SKYSCRAPER AND THE CHICAGO CONSTRUCTION

Just like the Woman's Temple, the Masonic Temple was situated in the heart of the Loop, and it too was a deliberate attempt at a civic skyscraper, a tall office building designed for the greater good of the city (fig. 4.03). Paradoxically, the building, with its attention-getting design, was financed by a nominally secret society, the Order of Freemasons, which desired a site for a Scottish Rite Consistory and its Illinois headquarters.[15] The building was to be an urban advertisement for the Masonic ideal of voluntary brotherly fraternity. Since 1884 the Masonic order responsible for commissioning the new building, the "Oriental Consistory," had been housed in rooms designed for them by Peter B. Wight on the fifth and sixth floors of H. H. Richardson's neo-Gothic American Express Building at Monroe and State streets, completed in 1874.[16] The order soon outgrew these rented rooms, and in early 1890 the *Chicago Tribune* announced plans for a monumental new building, as high as any in the city. This building would "honor Masonry, much as the Auditorium has honored its promoters."[17] In this way the Freemasons wanted to equal or surpass Adler and Sullivan's celebrated Auditorium Building, which had been completed only a year earlier.

The Oriental Consistory had been pondering the construction of a grand Masonic Lodge in Chicago for twenty years, and the upcoming World's Columbian Exposition offered the perfect opportunity to realize this dream. Norman T. Gassette, a lawyer and Grand Master of the Chicago Order of Freemasons, wanted to construct a building so magnificent that it would attract the attention of the

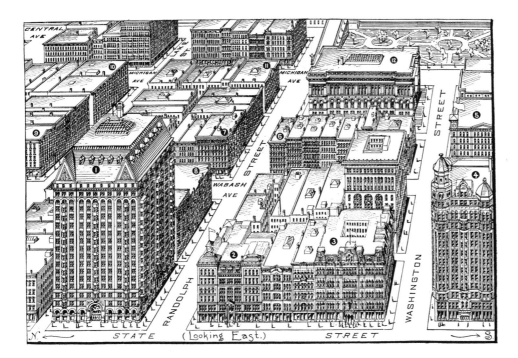

4.03 "From State Street, Looking East"; from *Rand McNally's Bird's-Eye Views and Guide to Chicago* (Chicago, 1898). The Masonic Temple (marked "1" in this illustration) was located two blocks north of the Columbus Memorial Building ("4") on State Street, the main commercial thoroughfare of Chicago.

world. He promoted it as being more than a regional headquarters for all Masonic bodies in Illinois, believing that the temple would be a public testament to the order's strength and progressiveness, "commensurate with the future of Chicago as the pivotal center of the continent and the metropolis of the world."[18] The Masons would benefit from rampant real estate speculation fueled by the fair, and the large number of visitors it attracted would provide an audience for the new building. In January of 1890 the organization purchased a valuable site on the northeast corner of State and Randolph streets, the terminus of several streetcar lines, planning to raze the existing five-story building and replace it with a tall office building of least twelve stories. It raised finances by setting up a stock company with $2 million in capital. "Every Mason is expected to subscribe to the stock, to show his pride, and because it will pay," the *Chicago Tribune* reported.[19] From the beginning the fraternal and commercial goals for the Masonic Temple were inextricably intertwined.

The design and construction of the Masonic Temple was closely followed in the architectural and popular press. Early newspaper reports stated that the building would be twelve to fourteen stories, the third-highest structure in Chicago, and would contain a "European Hotel" with about 850 rooms as well as Lodge quarters. The height of the building increased with every new report. A small sketch elevation showing the principal features of the proposed building— a large arched entranceway on State Street, a tall shaft made of vertical bands of bay windows, and two gables on top—was published in several local newspapers in June of 1890, when the building permit was issued. The accompanying stories reported that the building would be the highest in the world at eighteen stories, or 240 feet.[20] By November, when Burnham and Root had completed the plans, the Masonic Temple was to be twenty-two stories high, 275 feet above the street grade (fig. 4.04). The hotel idea was now forgotten. Instead, the building was to house retail shops on several floors with office spaces above, and an interior "rotunda" finished with plate glass and marble open to the sky.[21] Below the rooftop level, four floors were given over to Masonic rooms, armories, a drill hall, and a banquet hall in the Egyptian and Gothic styles. There was also an "Oriental Consistory," a meeting hall where Masonic degrees were conferred, equipped with a dramatic stage and pipe organ, and a Scottish Rite preceptory.[22]

Following a solemn ground-breaking ceremony involving a parade of four thousand Masons, including the Sublime Princes of the Oriental Consistory and members of the Scottish Rite in full regalia of black clothes and white aprons, construction was begun in November 1890.[23] The temple was formally dedicated in May of 1892. At twenty-two stories the completed building was visible from far around, dwarfing its closest neighbors, none of which exceeded seven stories (fig. 4.05).[24]

In their design for the Masonic Temple, Burnham and Root had a number of precedents in mind. In 1873 Philadelphia Masons had erected a grand Masonic Temple on Penn Square (fig. 4.06).[25] This building, the result of a design competition, was typical of the Masonic buildings erected in the mid-nineteenth century, although larger in scale. Designed by James H. Windrim in an eclectic style resembling a Gothic cathedral with oriental ornament, it was dedicated to Lodge activities only. Three years later Napoleon Le Brun created a different Lodge type, an elaborate Second Empire–style Masonic Temple on Twenty-third Street and Sixth Avenue in New York City (fig. 4.07).[26] This five-story building was unusual in that it contained rental space on its lower floors, setting a precedent for

4.04 *(left)* "The Masonic Temple, Chicago's Great Sky Scraper (265 ft), Randolph and State Streets." Stereo card by E. W. Kelley, ca. 1909. The Masonic Temple loomed high above the surrounding streets. Courtesy of the Library of Congress; LC-USZ62-51773.

4.05 *(below)* "Panorama of Chicago." Photograph by J. W. Taylor, ca. 1902. The Masonic Temple may be seen in the far middle distance of this panorama. By 1890 the typical height of a new office building in downtown Chicago was sixteen stories. However, most buildings of that height were erected in the financial district along LaSalle Street, near the Chicago Board of Trade. The twenty-two-story Masonic Temple was built in the older commercial district along State Street, where few of the surrounding buildings exceeded seven stories. As this view shows, the Masonic Temple dominated the skyline, challenged only by the railway depots and grain elevators near the lakeshore. Courtesy of the Library of Congress; LC-USZ62-113500.

combining sacred and secular activities in large urban Masonic halls. Burnham and Root's building may be compared to Le Brun's in its civic aspiration. Like his, it mimicked the commercial buildings around it in size and scale, adding the ornamental trappings that signified cultural importance.

Following Le Brun's example, the new Masonic Temple in Chicago hybridized sacred and secular functions within an office building. It conformed to the same historicizing logic of tall office building design that Burnham and Root had employed in the Rookery, in which neo-Gothic motifs were borrowed to frame the iron structure underneath. The building followed the same basic exterior form as the Rookery: a tripartite division into base, shaft, and attic, although a steep double-gabled roof exaggerated the height. The exterior façade of the first three stories was granite, punctured on the State Street side by a 42-foot-high arched entrance portal. A fourteen-story shaft of gray brick and terra-cotta-clad pilasters pierced by shallow bay windows rose above this base to meet the double-gabled attic roof. Although it was structurally unnecessary, Burnham and Root complied with the tectonic symbolism of masonry construction. The lower floors appeared heavier, with smaller window openings, while the higher floors had larger ones.

The design of the temple was particularly important, because Freemasonry is based on a set of architectural metaphors. Each Lodge is the symbolic reconstruction of the ancient Temple of Solomon, and each Mason the symbolic inheritor of a set of values associated with the craft of masonry—strength, self-reliance, and loyalty—which he learns through the reenactment of various sacred rituals.[27] By the late nineteenth century, Masonic practice included advanced levels, or "Lodges," including the York Rite and Scottish Rite, whose rituals took the form of plays performed before large audiences.[28] These plays were extravagant theatrical productions with casts of hundreds, intricate costumes, and elaborate stage sets. They required specialized spaces and props akin to a theater, and were enacted only rarely. The Oriental Consistory was a Scottish Rite Lodge, so a large theater was included at the top of the temple for the plays.

Because these rituals give initiates access to the world of Masonic knowledge, and are fiercely guarded as a consequence, Lodge rooms were traditionally raised up above street level to keep out prying eyes. In raising its Lodge twenty stories in the air, the Masonic Temple in Chicago exaggerated this secrecy to an extreme level. Yet at the same time, the highly visible building advertised the power of the Masons to shape the city.

As we have seen, John Ruskin and his followers saw the collaborative effort of masons on the great medieval cathedrals as a metaphor for the role of individuals in a democratic society. Though the Chicago Freemasons saw themselves as symbolic descendants of the medieval masons, as a group they were quite separate from the building craftsmen of their own time. While the popularity of Freemasonry reflected a desire to maintain an earlier and simpler way of life, the rise of the bourgeoisie as a separate class created a rift with craft workers that only grew wider as industrialization changed the nature of building work.[29] The Knights of Labor and early trade unions had grown out of trade-based fraternities that were very similar to the Freemasons in their rituals, membership, and goals. However, the middle-class Freemasons had no interest in joining with contemporary building workers as the latter struggled to find a place for themselves within industrialized processes of construction.

While they prided themselves on providing a masculine alternative to the dominant business interests in the city and on being open to all, Freemasonry was largely restricted to the middle class. The high initiation fees (from $15 to $75) dissuaded working-class applicants, as did the cost of acquiring elaborate costumes.[30] Besides the cost of membership, the long-standing animosity between the Freemasons and the Roman Catholic Church was a powerful deterrent to Catholic immigrants from eastern and southern Europe. In 1884 Pope Leo XIII issued an encyclical condemning the Masons, an act that incited a great deal of anti-Catholic feeling among American Freemasons, reinforcing their belief in the superiority of the assimilated American over the immigrant workingman.[31] During the labor conflicts of the 1870s and '80s, the Chicago Freemasons became overtly militaristic, taking up arms and marching en masse in support of the local militia against striking workers. Nonetheless, they were able to preserve the mythology of the premodern artisan as ideal citizen in the face of violent conflicts between workers and their bosses on Chicago building sites.

The design of the Masonic Temple reflected the alienation of the building worker in its use of new construction practices. Like other high buildings being erected in Chicago at the time, it was steel framed. As the *Chicago Tribune* noted, "In this structure, a type of the American school of architecture, the masonry is only to protect the real supports of the building, steel beams."[32] The ancient craft of masonry was relegated to ornament and fire protection. (At one point there was even a radical proposal to clad the entire building in steel, not brick or stone.)[33] Like other business organizations, the Chicago Order of Freemasons elected to side with progress, which in Chicago meant industrialization and mechanization rather than the preservation of traditional crafts. The Masonic Temple, symbol of an ancient order, was the newest and tallest example of a building technology putting contemporary masons out of work. In their promotional handbook, the Masons noted that "there has been some criticism upon the appearance of simplicity of the exterior walls of this building. But in this very particular they will stand as a perpetual monument to the Master mind of the architect who designed them."[34] With these words, the Masons transferred the creativity and skill behind the act of building from the mason to the architect.

In the search for the appropriate formal expression of steel construction, some critics felt the Masonic Temple came close to providing an answer. In 1892 the *Chicago Tribune* praised the architects of the Monadnock and the Masonic Temple for leaving the central shafts of these buildings in a "natural state," thereby expressing "power and mightiness."[35] However, the Masonic Temple was not canonized in twentieth-century architectural histories in the same way that the Monadnock and the Reliance were. In the end the building was remembered not for its architecture but for its spectacle. For a select few citizens, the Masonic Lodge rooms offered spaces of civic enlightenment and community. The Freemasons continued to hold meetings in the building until 1924, when the temple was sold to new owners.[36] Beyond that, these rooms were hired out for art exhibitions, musical concerts, religious meetings, and educational lectures, promoting the unity of all Chicago's citizens and their shared cultural growth.[37] But the building had a double life. While the civic goals of the Masonic Temple were communicated by its enormous size and height, and by the Lodge rooms within, designed to accommodate secret ceremonies of brotherhood, visitors to Chicago were captivated by its commercial aspect: the rooftop theater and observatory, and the fashionable stores inside.

THE "CITY IN ITSELF"

While its owners saw the Masonic Temple as a place to promote the fraternal ideal of active civic participation, the building also contributed to the creation of passive civic spectatorship—what Vanessa Schwartz has called the "spectacularization of city life."[38] Between 1890, when the city was awarded the World's Columbian Exposition, and 1893, when the fair opened, Chicago desperately aspired to compete with the urban pleasures and entertainments of European cities. American tourists flocked to Paris for its theaters, grand department stores, and boulevards designed for strolling. With their design for the Masonic Temple, Burnham and Root took those multiple activities and incorporated them into a single building type, the skyscraper. The rooftop observatory presented the city as an object for viewing. The magnificent atrium produced a new kind of urban crowd: consumers captivated by the mass-produced goods on display behind the store windows. If the outside walls of the Monadnock were designed to focus attention through plain and simple massing and monochromatic color, the atrium inside the Masonic Temple was a place of deliberate diversion. It subdued its inhabitants, distracting them with a phantasmagoria of commercial abundance. The Masonic Temple was a visual fantasy, a fantasy that exposed both the excitement and the shock of modern urban life.

The Masonic Temple became Chicago's answer to the recently completed Eiffel Tower in Paris. Its image was reproduced over and over in postcards and magazine articles. In 1894 *Scientific American* compared the Masonic Temple to the Statue of Liberty and Trinity Church in New York, the Capitol in Washington, and the Ferris wheel at the fair (fig. 4.08).[39] In 1897 Mayor Carter Harrison described the temple as one of the "Seven Wonders of the City," along with the Union Stock Yard, the drainage canal, the great grain elevators, the system of water supply, the elevated railroad, and the parks and boulevards.[40] In the same year, the temple featured in one of the Edison Company's earliest films, which depicted the junction of State and Madison streets as the "busiest corner in Chicago" (fig. 4.09).[41] The building achieved such fame that it became subject to a popular swindle in which con men offered to sell it to tourists for a bargain rate.[42] The Freemasons had more than achieved their goal of producing a high building equal to the wonders of the world: they had produced an icon.

The tall office building was not only a place of business, it was also a tourist destination, and the Masonic Temple was one of the first structures of the type in Chicago designed with tourism as one of its primary functions.[43] Beginning in the early 1880s, visitors were encouraged to go to the top of such buildings, both to see the view and to tour the marvel that was the building itself. In an 1892 article on Chicago in *Harper's Weekly*, Julian Ralph noted that visitors to the World's Columbian Exposition would no doubt want to tour the city as well as the fair. Though the recently completed parks and lakeshore improvements were pleasing attractions, Chicago's tall buildings provided the greatest novelty. "Frames of steel, enclosed with mere envelopes of masonry," Ralph wrote, "invite strangers to flit up and down in their light and often elegant interior courts, in the swift express elevators with which they are all provided."[44]

The Masonic Temple was a hybrid typology. Combining the office building, the arcade, and the department store, it was the realm of both men and women, of shopping and tourism as well as business.[45] In 1892 *Moran's Dictionary of Chicago*, one of the many guidebooks published for visitors to the fair, dubbed the Masonic Temple a "city in itself," claiming with enthusiastic hyperbole, "everything that can be found in the modern city may be found and obtained in the Masonic

4.08 *(left)* "A City Under One Roof—The Masonic Temple," *Scientific American* 70, no. 6 (February 10, 1894): 1. The Masonic Temple is compared in size and grandeur to the Statue of Liberty, Trinity Church in New York City, the Capitol in Washington, DC, and the Ferris Wheel at the World's Columbian Exposition of 1893. Science, Industry & Business Library, The New York Public Library, Astor, Lenox and Tilden Foundations. Used by permission from the New York Public Library.

4.09 *(right)* "Bargain Day on State St., Chicago," ca. 1899. Apart from its unprecedented height, the Masonic Temple was notable for its innovative program. The building was a major attraction for shoppers and tourists alike, containing a vertical shopping arcade up to the ninth floor, with offices above, and a theater and observatory on the roof. Courtesy of the Library of Congress; LC-USZ62-93763.

Temple. The business interests are so varied that a man or woman might live within its walls for an entire year without ever going or sending outside for any necessities and very few luxuries of life."[46] The entrance portal led visitors into an atrium lined with interior balconies and clad in Italian marble, with elaborate bronze columns extending the full height of the building (fig. 4.10). This 300-foot-high central light shaft was capped by a glass dome and serviced by a semicircular array of fourteen elevators running up the east side of the building. In an unusual and financially daring move, the lower half of the Masonic Temple housed a ten-story shopping arcade. Grand Master Norman Gassette had decided that the floors of this arcade would not be numbered, but named in honor of distinguished members of the Masonic order. This was principally "to do away with the idea of altitude," since rental space on the ninth or tenth floor was daunting to potential retail tenants.[47] Shoppers could wander around galleries on each shopping level, looking through huge sheets of plate glass into stores selling "Chic Paris Hats" and other fashionable commodities, "exactly as in a street."[48] The largest restaurant in the city occupied the basement.

Four elevators ran express to the top. For 25 cents they would carry visitors up to the rooftop observatory, palm garden, and theater (fig. 4.11). These elevators were a spectacle unto themselves, as passengers could both see and be seen as they made their ascent. Along with the "El," the elevated train system that defined Chicago's Loop, the elevators mechanized travel through the city in an entirely new way, presenting a futuristic urban experience for visitors.[49] An 1891 rumor had it that the Masonic Temple would incorporate a stop on the Lake Street "El" line so that passengers could alight directly into the second level of the building.[50] While this rumor was unfounded, it hinted at a possible future connection between high-rise buildings and high-speed commuter travel, a science fiction fantasy come to life.

The rooftop observatory, rising 330 feet in the air, presented another new attraction, an aerial view of Chicago, tamed and presented for visual consumption. To the east lay the endless expanse of Lake Michigan dotted with white ship's sails; to the west, the smoke of industries and factories with the prairie beyond; to the north, the fashionable green residential area of Lincoln Park; and to the south, for one short year, a distant view of the white domes of the World's Columbian Exposition. Filled with flowers and plants, the rooftop could accommodate two thousand visitors at once. It was entirely enclosed by a heavy glass roof and walls that could be opened during the summer months. In winter it was heated by steam pipes. If the scenic views and the sensation of being so astonishingly high were not of sufficient interest, the management provided musical concerts and refreshments.

Even if visitors came at night, the city was still visible, reproduced in electric form. The rooftop theater advertised an electric lantern show, "a most wonderful and realistic reproduction in miniature of the world-famed court of honor in the World's Fair; the artistic masterpiece of the nineteenth century, showing with absolute fidelity the noble architecture that made the White City famous throughout the civilized world. The Prismatic and MacMonnies Fountains with real water effects and the thousand other ever changing beauties of the never-to-be-forgotten scene."[51] In this way the rooftop observatory and theater were an improved version of the panoramas and dioramas that captivated American audiences in the mid-nineteenth century. Like them they were precinematic spaces where the new urban landscape was presented for visual consumption.[52]

The lavishly decorated interior atrium of the Masonic Temple was also an image designed to be consumed, an image of an idealized urban space dedicated to shopping and leisure. The atrium, or light court, evolved from the pragmatic need to bring light into the building interior in an era before affordable and reliable electric lighting was available. In commercial buildings these courts were at first utilitarian spaces and not meant to be seen. In the 1880s they began to be imagined as public

4.10 *Stairway and Galleries from Elevators and Rotunda. Interior Views of the Masonic Temple, Chicago. Burnham and Root, Architects*; from *Inland Architect and News Record* 20, no. 5 (December 1892). The interior atrium was imagined as a grand public space, an extension of the street outside. Clad in bronze and marble, it extended up all twenty-two stories of the building and was lit by a glass dome above. Used by permission from the Avery Architectural and Fine Arts Library, Columbia University.

spaces providing the kind of public amenities found in hotels, arcades, and department stores. Sumptuous glass-covered atria were first employed in hotels, like the Rotunda lunchroom of the Astor House Hotel in New York by James Bogardus (1852) and the seven-story entrance court of the Palace Hotel in San Francisco (1875), which was lined with white iron galleries.[53] Borrowing from these models, the interior court of the office building was transformed from a simple enclosed backyard

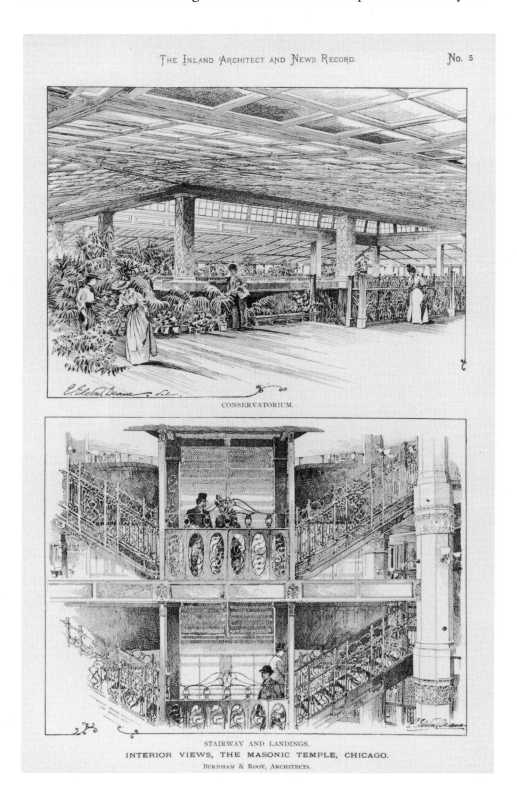

THE INLAND ARCHITECT AND NEWS RECORD. No. 5

CONSERVATORIUM.

STAIRWAY AND LANDINGS.
INTERIOR VIEWS, THE MASONIC TEMPLE, CHICAGO.
BURNHAM & ROOT, ARCHITECTS.

4.11 *Conservatorium and Stairway and Landings. Interior Views, The Masonic Temple, Chicago. Burnham and Root, Architects*; from *Inland Architect and News Record* 20, no. 5 (December 1892). The rooftop level of the Masonic Temple, containing an observatory, palm garden, and theater, was a major tourist attraction for the city. Used by permission from the Avery Architectural and Fine Arts Library, Columbia University.

to a place of public gathering, whose decoration could act as a substantial draw, allowing the building owners to charge higher rents for the offices surrounding it.

The morphology of the Chicago grid contributed to the invention of the extravagantly decorated interior light court. Since daylight can usefully penetrate only about 30 feet into a building, light courts were employed in lots wider than about 80 feet, where the interior spaces would otherwise be dark and difficult to lease. As Carol Willis has shown, the city's large, almost square blocks, measuring over 300 feet wide, made the interior light court a necessity for buildings occupying an entire lot.[54] From about 1880 until 1910, the typical Chicago office building was a large hollow box, penetrated by a central light court. Burnham and Root pioneered this type with their design for the Chicago, Burlington and Quincy Railway Building (1882–83) at Franklin and Adams Streets. This building contained a six story glass-roofed light court. Lined with white marble and surrounded by iron galleries, this court was made into an artistic feature. The company perfected the light court in the Rookery on LaSalle Street (1886) and the Society for Savings Bank in Cleveland (1887–90). The Rookery's light court depended on the sumptuousness of its ornament rather than height for its artistic effect (fig. 4.12). A horizontal space, not a vertical one, its glass roof caps it at the second-floor level. The Society for Savings Bank extended its atrium higher, to ten stories.

In Chicago Edward Baumann and Harris W. Huel's Chamber of Commerce Building (1888–89) at LaSalle and Washington Streets is the immediate precedent for the light court of the Masonic Temple. It ascended twelve stories of the building, reaching a height of 200 feet. The light court in the Masonic Temple set a new standard for height, extending through all twenty-two stories of the building, over 300 feet. Visitors were encouraged to think of this court as a public space, a more perfect extension of the street outside. Paradoxically, as a number of newspapers reported, the erection of the temple actually made the exterior street a more inhospitable place. The corner on which it stood was notorious for the wind-tunnel effect created by the adjacency of tall buildings: icy gusts of wind lifted women's skirts, blew men's hats off, and generally turned everyone around (fig. 4.13).[55]

In its earliest incarnation, the tall office building was a masculine domain inside and out: its public spaces were home to the cigar stand, the barbershop, the shoeshine chair, and the lunch counter. Female visitors, including suburban ladies

4.12 (left) Interior light court of Burnham and Root's Rookery, LaSalle Street; S. L. Stein Publishing Co., ca. 1893. The sumptuous interior atrium of the Rookery is a precedent for that at the Masonic Temple. Historic American Buildings Survey, HABS ILL, 16-CHIG, 31-12. Used by permission from the Chicago History Museum.

4.13 (right) "Wind and Sleet Make the Masonic Temple Corner Difficult of Navigation," *Chicago Daily Tribune*, February 5 1898, p. 3. While the interior atrium of the Masonic Temple was designed as a new form of public space, outside it created a wind tunnel effect that made the surrounding streets inhospitable.

on the way to appointments with their stockbrokers, lawyers, and doctors, passed quickly through. Female workers such as clerks, stenographers, and switchboard operators were rare until the 1890s. Because the Masonic Temple combined the program of the office building with that of the arcade and the department store, it combined the multiple and gendered functions of the city in a new interior public realm. It has been suggested that Root may have been influenced in his design for the Rookery by the Parisian department stores he saw on an 1886 trip to Europe, such as Louis-Charles Boileau's Bon Marché (1869–76) and Paul Sédille's Printemps (1881).[56] If the atrium of the Rookery was an attempt at something similar, the Masonic Temple took the precedent even further. Like a department store, it catered to a retail market with much decoration and large advertising signs. Like the arcade, it was designed as the extension of the street.

The vertical atrium connecting shopping, offices, restaurants, and theaters was deliberately theatrical. While the exterior of the Masonic Temple referred to masonry construction even though it was a steel-framed building, the interior walls of the atrium provided the opportunity to express this new construction method without reference to architectural precedent. Here Root's fondness for dark colors, for the subtle bloom of variegated brick, was checked in the interests of maximizing daylight. Instead, he clad the columns, wainscots, and soffits of the shopping levels with white marble and alabaster. The floors and walls were decorated with colorful mosaics and mural painting.[57] Only above the tenth floor stores, where offices looked out onto other offices, did he revert to glazed, white terra-cotta tile, a utilitarian material used to reflect daylight down into deep light courts. (An example of what this may have looked like may be seen in the upper levels of the light well in the Rookery [fig. 4.14].)

The building materials of the industrial age—iron, glass, and glazed terra-cotta tile—were made palatable in the interior light court before they appeared on the exterior of public buildings. This was an opportunity to show that these materials could offer more than just the practical benefits: they could also be beautiful. Iron, an integral part of the building's structure, was cast and wrought into highly intricate ornamental forms. The Winslow Brothers, the Chicago firm responsible for much of the decorative ironwork in Chicago's tall buildings, including the Masonic Temple, the Monadnock, and the Reliance, proudly displayed photographs of the work it had done in its magazine, *Ornamental Iron*.[58] Unlike the white-painted iron storefronts of the 1850s and '60s, this ironwork was painted a darker color, contrasting with its white background so there was no confusion between structure and surface. Newly available plate glass lined the Masonic Temple's atrium, making the goods displayed behind the store windows part of the internal decorative scheme. At night the glass dome was illuminated by electricity, creating a kaleidoscopic display of colored lights.

The Masonic Temple was a spectacular building. Though it was commissioned and designed as a place of high culture, it attracted events aimed at a growing mass audience. In 1895 a couple were married on the temple's roof, an early example of a novelty wedding. The building's height tempted daredevils to perform amazing feats of athleticism both inside and out. In 1898 Fred Schinner, a professional bicyclist, attracted publicity by running up all twenty-two stories of the Masonic Temple as part of his race training. At the turn of the century, Jehan Bedini, a juggler, caught a turnip dropped from the top of the atrium onto the tines of a fork held between his teeth. (A traveling entertainer, he repeated this trick at the City Hall in Los Angeles and the San Francisco *Chronicle* building.) In 1905 visitors rushed to the rooftop observatory to witness an airship piloted by Roy Knabenshue of Toledo, Ohio, pass by on a flyover of the city. (Knabenshue had originally intended to circle the rooftop of the temple, but was prevented from doing so by the chief of police.) This feat was repeated by not one but dozens of airships during a 1907 air show.[59] Around the same time, the rooftop theater entertained crowds with a rotating bill of vaudeville acts, including "Papinta—The World Famed Mirror Dancer," "The Wonderful Faust Family—Australian Acrobatic Marvels," "Mamie Remington and her Ragtime Pickaninnies," "Master Duffy, the Napoleon of Miniature Comedians," and "Dixon, Bowers and Dixon—The Three Rubes."[60]

Despite the Masonic Temple's attractions, tenants and visitors struggled to reconcile the thrill and the horror of life lived high in the air. The building's height presented not only delightful views but also an ever-present fear of falling. While the elevators were a novel entertainment, they were also tests of the trustworthiness of new technology. A series of elevator accidents in the Masonic Temple around the turn of the century killed three people and injured several more. In 1892, shortly after the building opened, Charles Chanter, a botanist from Wisconsin, was crushed between an elevator car and a beam on the fifteenth story. In 1901 John L. Collins was caught between an open door and the bottom of an elevator car on the fourteenth floor. Crushed, he fell to his death in the basement 200 feet below. His fall was illustrated in a lurid diagram in the *Chicago Tribune* (fig. 4.15).

4.14 *(left)* The upper stories of the light well of the Rookery, ca. 1967. The glazed white terra-cotta used here was originally employed as a utilitarian material designed to bring light down into the heart of large office buildings. It was not used on street-facing façades until the mid-1890s. Historic American Buildings Survey, ILL, 16-CHIG, 31-2. Courtesy of the Library of Congress.

4.15 *(right)* "Death from Long Fall in the Masonic Temple," *Chicago Daily Tribune*, July 26, 1901, p. 12. The Masonic Temple was the site of a series of tragic accidents. The open elevator cages contributed to a number of deaths by falling.

In 1907 Edward C. Tombit, an elevator operator, was killed and two other men seriously hurt when their car dropped from the fifteenth floor to the basement because of a snapped cable. In 1911 four men were injured when a passenger elevator fell eighteen stories. In 1912 William C. Tracy Clow, a railroad clerk, accidentally fell down an elevator shaft from the eighteenth floor to the basement.[61]

Fire was another danger. In 1904 a fire broke out in the fifth-floor offices of Robert Friedlander and Co., manufacturers of X-ray apparatus, when a lit match was carelessly discarded, causing some of the company's X-ray vacuum tubes to explode. In the panic the building's elevators were almost overwhelmed, although four thousand people were eventually evacuated without serious injury. In 1907 three hundred people attending an assembly hall dance were evacuated because of a fire caused by overheated hydraulic rods in the elevators.[62]

Given these terrible accidents, it is hardly surprising that some visitors were afraid to venture into an elevator or up to the roof. The Masonic Temple provided for these customers too. Numerous nerve doctors and other health specialists had their offices in the temple, including the Nerve Seed Company (useful if a trip to the observatory in the elevator made one "nervous, dizzy and faint"), H. Boardman Rising's Training School for Physical Culture ("send for my pamphlet on Muscles and Corpulency"), and Professor Wilson's Magneto-Conservative Garments (for "nervous prostration, paralysis, varicose veins, and locomotor ataxia").[63]

The temple also attracted those for whom such treatments and devices had failed. Its fascination as a public spectacle extended to those who used the building to publicize their own deaths. Between 1898 and 1914, eight people committed suicide by jumping from the atrium or the roof. In 1898 Alfred C. Greenleaf, an unemployed bookkeeper, committed suicide there after first attempting to take his life in the Chamber of Commerce, where he was caught in the act of climbing over the railing on the twelfth floor of the rotunda and ejected from the building. He then went to the Masonic Temple atrium, ascended to the sixteenth floor, and jumped, witnessed by scores in the rotunda below. In 1907 Anna Normoyle, a twenty-year-old girl visiting her stenographer friend at the offices of the Sterling Electric Manufacturing Company, threw herself into the open court from a fifteenth-floor window. In July 1911 G. A. Wright, disturbed by three days of heat stroke, jumped over the gallery railing, also at the fifteenth floor. The *Chicago Daily News* published a photograph taken from the spot he jumped, looking over the balcony into the atrium below (fig. 4.16). Later that year a machinist, J. F. Greek, crawled out on a beam from the nineteenth floor and jumped. His body first struck a cigar stand on the atrium floor and then a man standing nearby, breaking both of his arms. Following Greek's death, heavy nets were stretched across the rotunda at the fourth and twelfth floors. However, this did not deter Casper Rasmussen, a twenty-two-year-old insurance solicitor, who in 1912 climbed onto the roof and jumped, landing on the roof of the Ryerson Building fourteen stories below. Rasmussen's death was described as a possible case of a recently discovered mania called "leap lust" by the *Chicago Tribune*. Less than a year later Henry Korthagen paid 25 cents admission to the building's observatory and jumped from the roof onto State Street. His was the third suicide at the Masonic Temple within twelve months.[64]

Perhaps the most poignant of the suicides in the Masonic Temple was that of John Konwinski in December of 1913. A career criminal, self-professed socialist, and "martyr to the cause of criminology," Konwinski launched himself from the

eighteenth floor into the interior light court, landing on a steel safety screen recently installed on the ninth floor.[65] Before he died he composed a will instructing that his body be donated to science. Writing of himself in the third person, Konwinski claimed he had been "born almost a stranger into the world. He could not adapt himself to the environment that was given him by society. His condition has caused many a mental strain and intellectual misery by brooding over problems of existence in general." He hoped "that dissection might indicate why his life had been directed toward crime."[66] Konwinski's death was a highly self-conscious expression of the social estrangement felt by many inhabitants of the industrial city. Despite the civic groups who aimed to convert the new building type to a locus for new kinds of community, the skyscraper could not conquer the alienation of a tragic few.[67]

4.16 Main lobby of the Masonic Temple, as viewed from a gallery several floors above it; glass negative, from the *Chicago Daily News*, July 3, 1911. Some deaths in the Masonic Temple were not accidental. This photograph accompanied a newspaper story about the suicide of George A. Wright, who leaped to his death from the fifteenth floor. Used by permission from the Chicago History Museum; DN-0057206.

THE FAILURE OF THE FUTURE VERTICAL CITY

The Masonic Temple gradually fell into decline in the early years of the twentieth century. The experiment in vertical shopping failed within four years, probably because such a distribution of stores did not facilitate easy access from the street. The once prosperous jewelry firm of Giles Brothers, who leased space in the fourth floor of the Masonic Temple when it first opened, failed by 1893. Critics speculated that the company had not survived its move from a busy ground-floor store on the corner of State and Washington.[68] Though the observation deck remained open, the Roof Garden Theater was forced to close in 1905 when a new city ordinance prevented crowds larger than five hundred people from gathering more than 45 feet above street level.[69] The Temple Theater was closed in the 1920s when it had lost its reputation for high-quality entertainment—in 1921 police censors caused a near riot there when they tried to prevent the performance of a risqué stag show advertised as "Girls! Girls! Girls!"—and live theater was losing its audience to the movies.[70]

By the late 1920s the era of Chicago's tall buildings seemed to be over. The Masonic Temple was one of many such buildings from the 1880s and '90s to be demolished in these years. In the Depression-era economy, one- or two-story "taxpayer" buildings, or even parking lots, replaced skyscrapers on many downtown lots where low rents could not support high property taxes.[71] In 1922 the Masonic Temple Trust sold its building to a group of Chicago businessmen for $3.1 million, only $100,000 more than the building had cost to build thirty years earlier. The new owners renamed the Masonic Temple the Capitol and announced comprehensive renovation plans, which were never carried out.[72] In June 1939 the Arthur Rubloff Real Estate Company demolished the building, claiming it was forced to do so in order to avoid the expense of shoring up the foundations against the new subway line being constructed under State Street.[73] When it was built in 1892, the twenty-two-story Temple had replaced a five-story building. In December 1939 it was replaced by a two-story art-deco movie theater, the Telenews, designed by architects Shaw, Naess and Murphy.[74] The tall office building was no longer profitable or desirable in downtown Chicago.

Some local critics, like Al Chase, real estate editor of the *Chicago Tribune*, hoped the renovation of the Monadnock building in 1938 would signal a new attitude toward the first generation of Chicago skyscrapers, buildings that were not yet universally accepted as historically significant.[75] By the mid-twentieth century Graham Aldis, the Monadnock's manager, could claim, "Its simplicity and fine proportions have won it international renown among architectural critics, some of whom find it a forerunner of the present modern or 'functional' style."[76] But the Masonic Temple's significance was not similarly recognized. Aesthetically it seemed old fashioned, even an embarrassment. Its stylized façade could not compete with the sleek art-deco buildings being erected around it. Its highly ornamented interior seemed anachronistic once the vertical shopping arcade had failed.

Through the design of civic skyscrapers like the Woman's Temple and the Masonic Temple, the tall office building was transformed from a private enterprise designed for real estate profit into a public edifice representing the goals of a reformed civic life. These buildings offered community halls alongside business offices and stores, as well as a new kind of public space in downtown Chicago. But this linking of civic goals to commercial ones also represented their undoing. As programmatically progressive and technologically advanced as the Masonic Temple was in 1892, it could not keep up with the realities of the real estate economy in the early twentieth century. Although it was aimed at creating a society of civic participants, ultimately it remained answerable to the individual demands of profit and loss and to a fickle public of mass consumers.

5 THE RELIANCE BUILDING
URBAN SANITATION AND SKYSCRAPER REFORM

The splendid architecture of the Masonic Temple's interior atrium, a lightweight screen of marble, iron, and glass, was a rehearsal of sorts for the new architecture bounding the streets of the American metropolis. With the completion of D. H. Burnham and Co.'s Reliance Building nearby on State Street in 1895, the shiny, pale terra-cotta surface first used to reflect light deep into the interior of tall buildings became an exterior aesthetic (fig. 5.01). According to early twentieth-century historians of modern architecture, the Reliance was a short-lived step in the evolution of the wall from load-bearing masonry to completely transparent curtain. However, this transition was more complicated and less direct than it seems. If the solidity of masonry had become unsuitable because of structural and programmatic constraints, in 1890 the tall office building had symbolic and functional requirements that made phenomenal transparency undesirable.

Chicago architects established an aesthetic for the terra-cotta and glass curtain wall, situating it not merely as a simulacrum of brick and stone, or as the precursor to glass, but as a tectonic entity in its own right. This new surface was designed not only to let light in but also to protect the interior from the dangerously polluted environment outside. Greeted with ambivalence by critics, the Reliance received unreserved praise only in relation to discussions of urban sanitation. This was entirely fitting, since the building was designed to accommodate the downtown offices of fashionable doctors and dentists. Clad in the same pale enameled tiles used for hygienic purposes in hospitals, kitchens, and bathrooms, it was designed to convince the world that the skyscraper was not a threat to the city after all but a solution to the problems of dirt, disease, and pollution. The Reliance was an idealized vision of the tall office building in a reformed industrial city.

"A GLAZED TERRACOTTA TOWER"

The Reliance Building was built on a very important site in Chicago, the southwest corner of State and Washington streets, the center of the city's main shopping thoroughfare.[1] Although the site is small, measuring only 85 feet by 56 feet, it garnered high rents, because it faced two major commercial streets. In 1890 the site's owner, William Ellery Hale, a well-established real estate speculator, commissioned architects Daniel Burnham and John Wellborn Root to draw up plans for a new building that would house the original Carson Pirie Scott and Co. department store on the ground floor with offices above.[2] Hale was impatient to begin building and would not wait for the leases on the existing building to run out before demolition. He instructed his architects to begin constructing a new building literally underneath the old one. The first stage of construction, the opulent ground-floor and basement-level store designed by Root, was completed in 1891 (fig. 5.02).

5.01 *(opposite)* Burnham and Root / D. H. Burnham and Co., Reliance Building, southwest corner of State and Washington streets (1889–95); photograph by Barnes-Crosby, ca. 1904. Used by permission from the Chicago History Museum; ICHi-19252.

5.02 *(left)* Entrance of the Reliance Building. John Wellborn Root designed the ground floor with large plate-glass windows surrounded by dark, red-brown granite spandrels and bronze window frames. This story was constructed underneath the existing building, and originally occupied by the Carson Pirie Scott Department Store. Photograph by the author.

This new façade consisted of large plate-glass windows supported by dark red-brown granite spandrels and bronze window frames. Inside, Carson Pirie Scott's two story quarters were richly decorated with mahogany woodwork, alabaster walls inlaid with gold and glass, marble mosaic floors, and ceiling paintings by Burnham and Root's decorator, William Pretyman. In an era before electricity could provide sufficient interior lighting, the department store was designed to receive as much daylight as possible. Shallow light wells tiled with white enameled brick and paved with glass brick on the sidewalk allowed natural light down into the basement.

Two major events separate the completion of the lower levels of the Reliance in 1891 and the resumption of construction in 1893: the World's Columbian Exposition and the death of Root. Between 1890 and 1893 Burnham and Root were occupied with the design of the fair, with little time left over for private commercial work. When Root died suddenly in January of 1891, Burnham assumed responsibility for the fair, spending the next three years on it almost exclusively. In 1893, when the exposition was over and he was ready to resume his regular practice, Burnham had to rebuild his office for commercial work. He named three men as his new partners: Ernest Graham (his longtime assistant), Edward Shankland (his engineer), and Charles Atwood, a promising young architect whom Burnham had brought out from New York to work on the fair. Graham was the office manager and Burnham's right-hand man, Shankland was in charge of construction management, and Atwood replaced Root as the firm's chief designer.[3] "Burnham and Root" became "D. H. Burnham and Co." In July of 1893 Atwood was given the task of designing the upper floors of the Reliance.[4]

The design and construction of the Reliance reflected the new makeup of Burnham's firm, and the new realities of the construction industry. Just as Burnham modeled his professional office on the corporate organization of his big-business clients, dividing it into separate departments, each with its own responsibility, his contractor of choice, George A. Fuller, streamlined building construction. Trained as an architect at MIT, Fuller started his construction company in Chicago in 1882, just as the revolution in building practice was beginning. He was a new kind of contractor, a coordinator of all the aspects of building rather than a specialist in one particular trade, and he built the majority of tall office buildings erected in Chicago in the 1880s and '90s.[5] As the contractor for Holabird and Roche's recently completed Tacoma Building, he had experience with the latest advances in the Chicago construction. Working alongside Atwood and Shankland, he took full advantage of the new technique in the design of the Reliance. To the amazement of Chicagoans, the George A. Fuller Company demolished the existing upper stories at the site and erected a slender sixteen-story steel frame in their place, all in the last two weeks of July, 1894 (fig. 5.03).[6] Soon afterward the rear two party walls were clad in common brick, with the expectation that adjacent buildings would soon be hiding them (these party walls are still visible looking north on State Street [fig. 5.04]). The Northwestern Terra Cotta Co. manufactured the cream-colored, enameled terra-cotta tile used on the two street façades, while the Diamond Plate Glass Company supplied the large plate-glass windows.

The street façades were no ordinary walls, even by Chicago's rapidly evolving aesthetic standards. Although the Reliance was built using an entirely new structural system, Gothic architecture seemed the most obvious historical referent

5.03 Reliance Building under construction; from *Architectural Record* (August 1894). Utilizing the new "Chicago construction," in which the steel-frame structure is erected separately from the cladding, the contractor George A. Fuller put up the Reliance Building at breathtaking speed during a few short weeks in the summer of 1894. Used by permission from the Marquand Library of Art and Archaeology, Princeton University.

for such a tall, slender building. Its terra-cotta skin is gathered and folded to form groups of medieval-inspired pilasters around each pier. The edges where the terra-cotta walls meet the brick ones are designed in imitation of a framelike pilaster. This same pilaster is repeated where the two terra-cotta walls meet, but in this case the pilaster is folded around the corner, appearing only half as wide as its partner on the other edge. Because of this, the terra-cotta tile seems to literally wrap itself around its structure, with no pretense that it is supporting weight at its leading corner (fig. 5.05). In this way the glass and terra-cotta wall is wrapped around the two sides of the intersection, floating incongruously above Root's dark-colored base.

Donald Hoffman has suggested that Burnham and Atwood's choice of pale terra-cotta tile may have been a result of Burnham's success with the World's Columbian Exposition, an attempt to bring the beauty of those neoclassical buildings to downtown Chicago. Perhaps it was also a rejection of Root's aesthetic influence.[7] But although it is dissimilar to the Monadnock in color and construction, the Reliance is not dissimilar in its formal aesthetic. The two buildings are both tall and slender, with distinct horizontal bands at the ground and cornice levels. Both emphasize the vertical with continuous bay windows, and in both cases historic stylistic reference is reduced to a minimum. The major difference between the two buildings is that the plate-glass windows of the Reliance are enormous, even by Chicago standards—nothing like the heavy defensive walls of the Monadnock, with its small, punched window openings. In designing these walls, Atwood took full advantage of Shankland's structural expertise, and of recent technological advances in the manufacture of steel, terra-cotta, and glass.

As we have seen, terra-cotta was increasingly used in the construction of steel-framed buildings in Chicago, first as interior fireproofing and then as exterior

cladding. However, up until this moment architects used terra-cotta to simulate traditional masonry construction, brick and stone. The material was colored brown or gray, and textured to resemble these more familiar materials. At first it was used sparingly, usually in the form of ornamental elements above doors and windows or on cornices, where carved stone might have been used before. By 1890 the Northwestern Terra Cotta Co. developed a method of enameling terra-cotta tile so that its surface was less porous and consequently suitable for exposure on building exteriors, even in harsh climatic environments like Chicago.[8] Yet architects initially restricted the use of pale, glazed terra-cotta to light wells, where its light color and reflective surface helped bring daylight deep down into building interiors.

As well as exploiting recent innovations in the manufacture of terra-cotta, Burnham and Atwood also took advantage of a boom in glass manufacture in the Midwest. While "polished plate" glass had been available since the 1870s, it was extremely expensive up until the early 1890s, because it took a great deal of energy to manufacture. As Thomas Leslie has shown, new glass-manufacturing companies were established in Indiana and Ohio in 1886, when a huge repository of underground natural gas was discovered.[9] These companies supplied plate glass to the insatiable Chicago construction market at much lower costs than before (by 1896 the *Chicago Tribune* could report, with only a little hyperbole, that plate glass was cheaper than brick[10]). One of those companies, the Diamond Plate Glass Company, was controlled by Chicago business interests and represented in the city by the George A. Fuller Company. By 1889 Fuller and Diamond Plate Glass were distributing large sheets of relatively cheap plate glass throughout the Midwest. It was in Fuller's interest, then, to use as much glass as possible in his buildings, and the Reliance may have been designed as a showpiece for the new material.

While the Reliance was the aesthetic expression of a new tectonic system and new building materials, it was also designed to advertise its interior program: a department store and medical offices. Carson Pirie Scott occupied the first and

5.04 *(opposite)* "State Street Looking North from Madison Street"; Detroit Publishing Co., ca. 1900. Photograph by Barnes-Crosby. The famous pale-colored, glazed terra-cotta walls of the Reliance Building wrapped around the two street façades only. The right-hand side of this photograph shows the south-facing brick party wall, painted with an advertising slogan. Used by permission from the Chicago History Museum; ICHi-19268.

5.05 *(above)* Reliance Building, detail of façade. In his design for the Reliance, Charles Atwood took advantage of newly available "polished plate" glass manufactured by the Diamond Plate Glass Company. The solid part of the façade is a 4-foot-high horizontal spandrel panel at each floor level decorated with abstracted Gothic motifs. Six-foot-square glass panes sit between these spandrels in the bay windows. Historic American Buildings Survey, ILL, 16-CHIG, 30-3. Courtesy of the Library of Congress.

second floors of the building until 1906, when the company bought out its chief rival, the Schlesinger Mayer Company, and moved into that firm's much larger premises a few blocks south on State Street. (Substantially altered by Louis Sullivan in a florid art-nouveau style, the new Carson Pirie Scott building was as radical in 1906 as the Reliance had been in 1895.) After this move the ground floor of the Reliance was leased to the Central Drug Company of Detroit as a drugstore, and operated in this capacity throughout most of the twentieth century.[11] Meanwhile the third through sixth floors were used as salesrooms for milliners, tailors, dressmakers, and jewelers. The seventh through thirteenth floors were reserved for the downtown offices of leading doctors and dentists, and the building's tenants continued to be medical practitioners well into the twentieth century. (This part of town, easily accessible to suburban visitors, was home to a number of medical buildings, including W. W. Boyington's 1893 Columbus Memorial Building, on the southeast corner of State and Washington, opposite the Reliance.) The consulting rooms in the Reliance were initially rented out for $10 per month for one hour a day. In this way a physician could supplement his suburban practice with a city one. The owners of the Reliance advertised that their building would be operated on "strictly ethical principles," and that the tenants would be of the "best class." Through this language, they implied that the building was both physically and morally sanitary.[12]

The interior planning and decor of the Reliance reflected its genteel occupants. Hale, retired from the elevator business, instructed the Winslow Brothers metalworking company (a reorganization of his former employees) to design four efficient passenger elevators close to the main entrance. He and Atwood recycled some of Root's earlier work here—the ornate black iron elevator cages had originally been designed for use in the Rookery building (fig. 5.06).[13] Because the floor plate of the building was so narrow, no internal light well was necessary. The corridor to the south of the building is well lit by clerestory windows above the interior partition walls. The upper floors were arranged around a communal reception room staffed by pleasant and discreet female assistants. The consulting rooms were furnished with mahogany furniture and oriental rugs, and each had an independent exit for the sake of modesty.[14] The private bathrooms were lined with white Italian marble and boasted the latest in sanitary plumbing fixtures.

5.06 Reliance Building, interior of lobby after renovation in the 1990s. The interior was designed to demonstrate that commercial buildings could be artful and elegant. The design for the black-painted iron elevator cages, described as being in the "German Gothic" style, was originally used in the Rookery. Photograph by Jennifer Dickert.

There were telephone exchanges on the first, ninth, and fourteenth floors connecting all offices, and electric light and power in every room.

When the Reliance opened in 1895, it earned the description "a glazed terra-cotta tower" (fig. 5.07). It was part of a new urban aesthetic in Chicago: tall office buildings clad in pale-colored brick and terra-cotta incorporating large areas of glass in their façades. The next year Burnham's company erected another building in a similar style, the pale-pink Fisher Building on the northeast corner of Dearborn and Van Buren streets. Although it does not hold a significant place in architectural history, many contemporary critics described the Fisher as the logical extension of the design method begun in the Reliance. The *Inland Architect* labeled it a "Building without Walls."[15] Burnham and Atwood were not alone in developing this new aesthetic. Two buildings designed by Holabird and Roche and constructed by the George A. Fuller Company, the Venetian (1891–92) and the Champlain (1894–95), competed with the Reliance for attention (figs. 5.08 and 5.09).[16] All three were situated a few blocks from one another on or near State Street, Chicago's prime retail corridor, and all three were designed to accommodate medical offices above ground-floor shops.

Unlike the Columbus Memorial Building, which was dark in color, vertically oriented, and heavily ornamented, this second generation of medical buildings was pale in color, with large, horizontally oriented windows and relatively little ornament. The Venetian was of pale-beige-colored brick with matching terra-cotta trim. It was simple in design, apart from the uppermost stories that were ornamented with an oriental-style screen. The Champlain, clad entirely in pale-cream terra-cotta above a dark-brown terra-cotta base, was austere enough to earn a risqué nickname: the "Damned-Plain."[17] While the Venetian and the Champlain both had flat screen walls, the Reliance breaks out of its boxlike container with delicately undulating bay windows, in a manner somewhat similar to the Tacoma.

With these buildings Chicago architects had taken the lead in the design of terra-cotta-clad buildings, but their aesthetic effect was still highly contentious. Criticism about the plainness of the Reliance, the Venetian, and the Champlain was part of a larger argument about the appropriate use of glass in the steel-framed tall office building. Peter B. Wight wrote of the Champlain, "it is the first building in which Holabird and Roche adopted the plan of throwing the whole space between the main steel posts into single, wide windows, wider than their own height."[18] There is no doubt that the desire for copious amounts of natural light influenced the design of these and other tall office buildings in this period. Both John Root and Dankmar Adler were explicit in stating that the need for natural light dictated their choice of structure.[19]

In 1890 buildings with large areas of plate glass in their façades were viewed as expedient responses to the problem of bringing light into the building interior, but were not necessarily seen as beautiful in their own right. Until very late in the century, direct sunlight was considered harmful, far too bright for most everyday activities and only necessary for particular kinds of manufacturing work. Strong light was associated with utilitarian buildings such as factories.[20] While glass manufacturers like the Diamond Company promoted their product as a possible cladding material for the Chicago construction, even they did not propose transparent glass buildings as a desirable solution. Rather, they imagined glass being used in the form of colored or translucent panels, lending a decorative aspect to its practical advantages.[21]

INFORMAL OPENING

—OF—

"THE RELIANCE."

A TRIUMPH OF THE BUILDERS' ART—UNIQUE BUILDING CONSTRUCTION.

During the past year the old First National Bank Building, which was one of the two structures in the heart of the city that remained standing after the Chicago fire, has given place to a glazed terra-cotta tower. The circumstances under which this, the latest of Chicago's great office buildings, was erected are indeed novel.

In 1890 Mr. William E. Hale decided to construct upon the site of the old First National Bank a building fourteen stories high. The ground floor had been left free by the expiration of leases, but the three upper floors were occupied by tenants whose leases did not expire until May 1, 1894. Plans were prepared by the well-known architects, Messrs. Burnham & Root, and, without disturbing in the least the tenants of the upper floors, the old foundations, basement, and first floor were removed and replaced by the substructure of the new building. This was accomplished by supporting the three upper stories on jack screws. Immediately after the completion of this work the first floor and basement were leased by Carson, Pirie, Scott & Co. Thus, in the minimum time and with little loss of rent, the first half of the undertaking was successfully carried out.

In May, 1894, the leases of the three upper floors expired and Mr. Hale was at last free to complete the improvement. Here again was performed an engineering feat of an exceptional character. An agreement had previously been entered into with Carson, Pirie, Scott & Co. that their business should not be interfered with during the completion of the building, and this was observed to the letter. The sidewalks were roofed over with heavy timbers at so great a height that the light was but slightly obstructed, while the crowds passing and repassing this busy corner were not in the least incommoded. A temporary roof was placed over the first story and in a very short time the upper floors had been removed. Then commenced the erection of the steel-skeleton, which progressed with unprecedented rapidity. Incredible as it may appear, it is a fact that less than two days were required to run up the steel-work of each of the upper stories. The accompanying photographs illustrate this. On July 16 the steel shell had risen to the seventh floor; twelve days later preparations were being made to put in the roof structure—200 feet above the sidewalk.

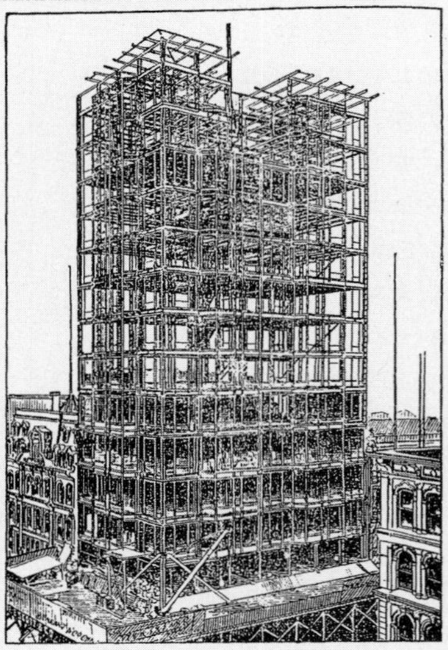

Reliance Building—August 1, 1894.

The designing and supervision of this work was entrusted to Mr. Edward C. Shankland, whose great roof trusses of the Manufacturers' Building were so much admired at the World's Fair. It is no small compliment to the engineer and contractors that the tenants of the first floor carried on their extensive business, unmindful of the great work in progress above their heads.

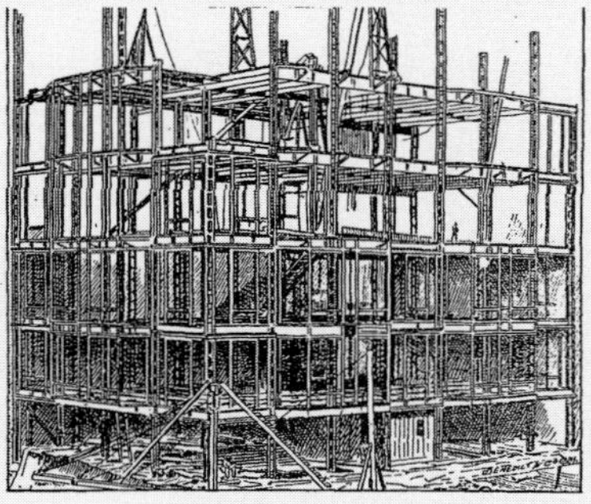

Reliance Building—July 16, 1894.

In its location on one of the most prominent corners in Chicago, it was evident from the first that the building must be of the finest construction throughout. The necessity of providing ample light in each office was pointed out to the architects by Mr. Hale, and this was fully recognized by them in making the design.

The exterior of the building is faced with enameled Terra Cotta, manufactured by the Northwestern Terra Cotta Co. of this city. This is the first work of such magnitude in this country as well as anywhere in the world. For a number of years Chicago has taken the lead in the construction of office buildings, wherein the steel skeleton was protected from fire by Terra Cotta in various colors, and no other city has so great a variety of elegant Terra Cotta fronts. It was long thought impossible to obtain the enameled material of such perfection and in such quantities, although for years it has been the desire of architects and owners to procure a surface easily cleaned as well as pleasing in color and perfectly fireproof, and a material imperishable and unaffected by the weather.

Partly on account of the failure of earlier enameled brick manufactured in this country there was an overwhelming prejudice against this kind of work, that only after the most conclusive evidence the Northwestern Terra Cotta Co. were permitted to make what was generally supposed to be an experiment on a large scale, and what proved to be a perfect success. There is no doubt but that this first example will find many imitators, and although it is doubtful if any other company will undertake a job of this kind the capacity of the Northwestern Terra Cotta Co. is such that they will be able to meet the requirements under all circumstances.

The interior of the building is in keeping with the exterior. The finest woods, marbles, and mosaics have been used on every floor. Carefully selected mahogany of superior quality and finish has been exclusively employed for the woodwork. The wainscotings and columns are of Italian marble, perfectly matched to produce veritable pictures in stone, and set by skilled workmen. The mosaic floors are beautiful in pattern and execution.

For the equipment of his own building Mr. Hale, appreciating the value of having as nearly perfect elevator service as possible, desired to obtain better elevators than had ever been built. This was not an easy task to accomplish, because the Hale Elevator already had a world-wide reputation for safety and perfection.

Having retired from the business himself and being familiar with the merits and defects of all the various elevators made, Mr. Hale adopted the Hale type, secured improvements, and gave his order and instructions to the Winslow Bros. Elevator Co., a reorganization of his former employés, who had been trained by him to appreciate the importance of building elevators in the best possible manner.

The four passenger elevators located close to the main entrance should be seen in order to be appreciated. The hatchway inclosure and the cars are of beautiful design and have been executed in iron in the inimitable way peculiar to the Winslow Bros. Co. A striking feature is immediately noticed in the double door opening—one for entrance and the other for exit—both doors being operated simultaneously by a simple arrangement of levers, with compressed air. It is, however, by the contruction of the safety devices that the attention of the practical investigator is particularly attracted. The cars are provided not only with a safety governor, through the action of which they would be brought to a perfect stop in case of the breaking of the lifting cables, or of any part of the lifting mechanism, but also with a simple, very ingenius safety friction brake, through which the operator may, by the pressure of his foot, release the powerful grips and immediately bring his car to a stop. By this device accidents will be obviated which have been frequently incident to the breaking or disarrangement of some part of the operating mechanism, or to the carelessness of passengers or operators.

Especially in the perfection of the elevator machinery the investigating engineer will find and appreciate the practical superiority of these improved Hale Elevators, and it is on account of their general construction that the elevator service will prove a most attractive feature of this beautiful building.

The Hardware is furnished by the Orr & Lockett Hardware Co. It is of special design, in genuine Bower-Barffed black iron, which was first introduced by this company for use on builders' hardware on the Rookery Office building in this city and the Midland Hotel of Kansas City. The hardware on the main entrance doors is of natural colored bronze metal to correspond with the front.

The Orr & Lockett Hardware Co. have a wonderful record for this class of work, having furnished nearly all the prominent hotels, office buildings, and railway depots, as well as the finest residences erected in Chicago since the great fire of 1871. They are now engaged upon the Hardware for the Temple of Music and the Mammoth Marquette.

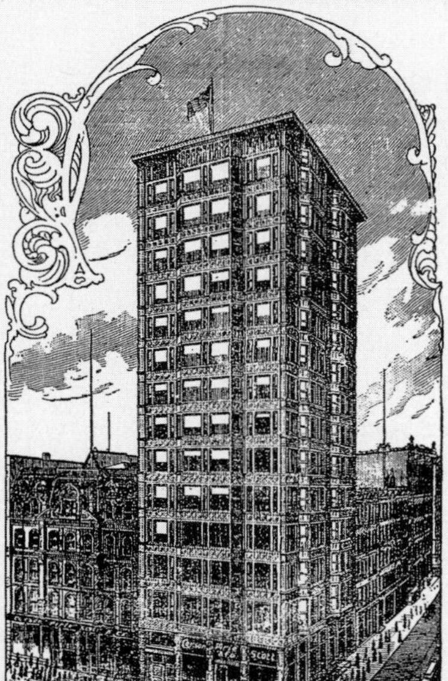

The Reliance is fitted throughout with the best sanitary plumbing, and none but filtered water is used in the building. The toilet rooms and private baths are lined with white Italian marble.

The plumbing of this building was executed by the well-known firm of J. J. Wade & Son, 276 Dearborn-st., who have done most of the work in the *large down town buildings* during the past 5 years. It consists of the latest and most improved open sanitary plumbing, and cannot be excelled.

On the first floor there is located a telephone exchange connected with all offices. At this exchange one may ascertain in a moment if the party they desire to see is in, can leave a message, or converse with him—all without going above the street level.

Similar exchanges are also located on the ninth and fourteenth floors, connecting the consultation rooms with the general reception rooms, and also with the exchange on first floor. The above mentioned telephones were supplied by the Harrison International Telephone Co.

Ventilation for all offices, halls, and closets is secured by means of a large fan in the attic, operated by an electric motor.

The heating has been carefully installed to secure the most satisfactory results. All hammering in pipes, leaking of air valves, wetting of carpets, and escape of disagreeable odors have been avoided by using the Paul exhaust system, by which a constant and free circulation is secured at all times. Electric light and power and gas also are provided in every room.

The first floor of the Reliance Building is occupied by Carson, Pirie, Scott & Co. The second floor is reserved for a large retail business. The third, fourth, fifth, and sixth are divided into salesrooms for tailors, milliners, dressmakers, jewelers, and others. The seventh, eighth, tenth, eleventh, twelfth, and thirteenth floors are devoted to the purposes of physicians, dentists, and others desiring large suites of offices.

OFFICE HOURS.

The ninth and fourteenth floors are fitted especially for physicians and surgeons who desire office accommodations during only a few hours of each day. All of the offices on these floors are completely furnished by the owner. On each floor is a large, general reception-room, managed by lady attendants. About this and connecting with it by telephone are grouped the private consultation rooms, each of which has its independent exit; it is thus unnecessary for patients to pass out through the reception-room. The offices are rented at very low monthly rates for as many hours per day as the physician may desire. The rental includes use of room, furniture, light, heat, power, etc. The physician is subject to no expense for attendants nor anything else but the one charge for rent, which averages $10 per month for use of an office one hour daily. Physicians may thus at very small expense supplement their home practice and enjoy the advantages of an office in the very heart of the city.

These reception rooms are most luxuriously furnished, the services of Messrs. J. A. Colby & Sons of Wabash-av. having been requisitioned for this work. The tables, chairs, and lounges are of solid mahogany, and of a most unique pattern, constructed from special designs by Mr. L. F. Crosby, the above named firm's superintendent and manager. The floors are covered with rich Wilton and Oriental rugs, which at once impart style and comfort to the rooms.

The building will be operated on strictly ethical principles, and no tenants will be admitted who are not entitled to position with the most particular classes. As the space is limited, and all appointments are of the best, it is believed there will be enough tenants of the best class to always keep it full.

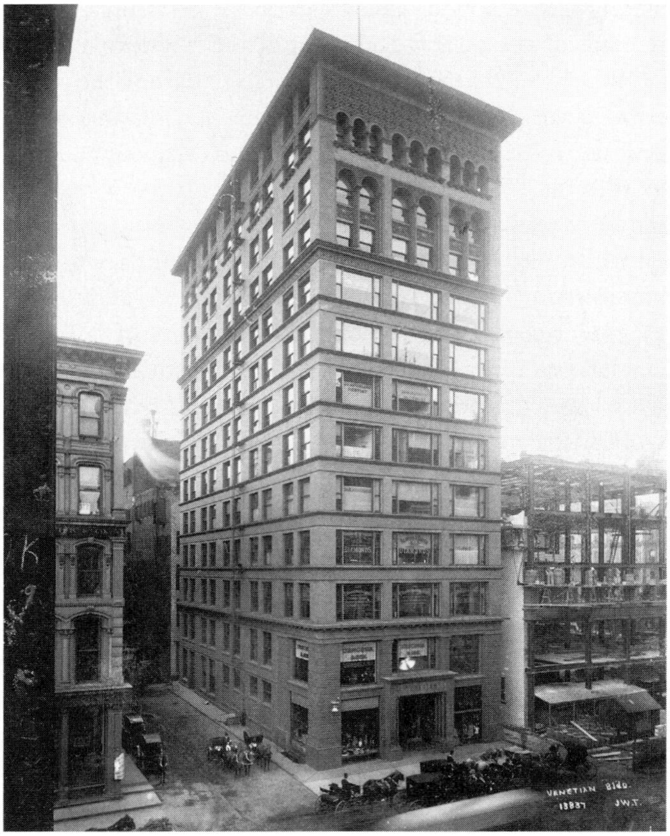

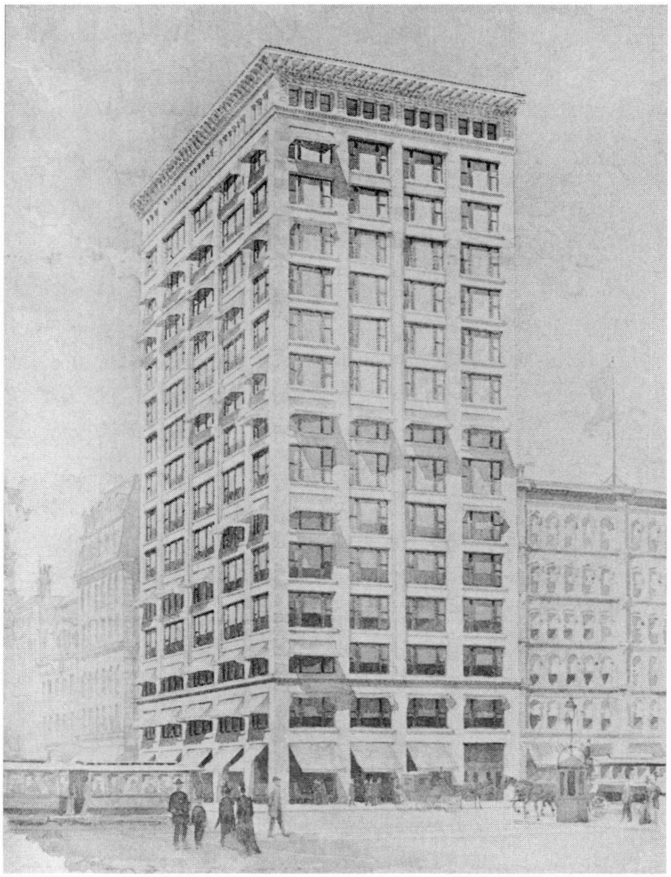

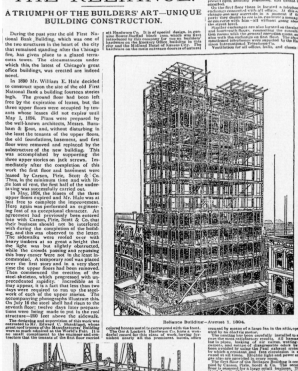

The Reliance received mixed reviews. Soon after it was built it received a positive notice in a review of the year's construction in the *Chicago Tribune*. While Burnham and Root had approached the design of the Monadnock from a "utilitarian point of view," said the reviewer, "in the Reliance building, from the same office, there was a radical departure. A very pleasing style of gothic was adopted as the style, and the material was glazed terra cotta, almost white. The effect is agreeable and the maximum amount of light is obtained."[22] But popular acceptance did not always mean critical success. Architectural critics outside Chicago were unconvinced by the novelty of the Reliance, seeing its apparent fragility as a sign of the aesthetic poverty of the industrial age. Commenting on the novelty of a façade made entirely of glass and pale terra-cotta, the critic for the *American Architect and Building News* wrote in 1895, "The effect is not so startling as it might seem, but, most assuredly, treated as the material is in this mammoth sky-scraper, it is possessed of few charms."[23] In the same year the British publication *Engineering* chose to illustrate the Reliance because of its unusual construction method and innovative structure, while claiming that "in its external appearance, it is not admirable" (figs. 5.10 and 5.11).[24] When the New York–based architecture critic Montgomery Schuyler assessed the not-yet-complete Reliance as part of an 1894 review of Daniel Burnham's work, he found it highly disturbing: "The real structure of these towering buildings, the 'Chicago Construction,' is a structure of steel and baked clay, and when we look for an architectural expression of it, we look in vain. No matter what the merits or demerits may be of the architectural envelope of masonry, it is still an envelope, and not the thing in itself, which is nowhere, inside or out permitted to appear."[25] Schuyler wondered if walls could truly be called architecture if they were no longer load bearing.

The surfaces of the Reliance as well as the Tacoma, the Champlain, and the Venetian were notable not only for their glass and terra-cotta façades but also for the shiny gold signs painted on their windows. The street-level windows of the Reliance acted as giant advertisements for the Carson Pirie Scott store inside. Contemporary photographs reveal elaborate displays of dresses and linens behind the glass, as well as large gold-lettered signs painted on the upper windows advertising the services of the doctors and dentists within. This signage was repeated almost all the way up the height of the building. Gilt lettering was popular, because its reflective surface meant it could be seen from far away, but it was also looked down upon as cheap and tawdry. The electric sign, a recent innovation, was considered even worse. A 1901 article on "skyscraper signs" published in the *Chicago Tribune* noted disapprovingly that the Reliance Building and the Chamber of Commerce on LaSalle Street carried the greatest amount of lettering in proportion to their wall area of any buildings in downtown Chicago. By contrast the Monadnock, "the greatest office building in Chicago," had the fewest lettered surfaces.[26] (At this time there were no restrictions as to the amount and size of window signs on exterior walls and windows in Chicago. Inside, however, building managers usually dictated and restricted the style and size of lettering. For example, the signage on the plate-glass windows inside the Masonic Temple was restricted.)

To many contemporary critics, the Reliance Building was a response to a series of pragmatic needs—height, daylight, and advertising—rather than a true piece of architecture. Along with other buildings designed in the same manner, it troubled those concerned with civic beauty. But although it was regarded as structurally insubstantial and aesthetically questionable, some critics did credit the

5.07 *(opposite, left)* "Informal Opening of 'The Reliance.' A Triumph of the Builder's Art—Unique Building Construction," *Chicago Daily Tribune* 54, March 16, 1895, p. 8.

5.08 *(opposite, top)* Holabird and Roche, Venetian Building (1891–92), Washington Street east of State Street. Like the Reliance, the Venetian was designed to accommodate medical offices. The façades were clad in pale-colored brick with horizontally oriented windows. The only concession to architectural precedent are the top few stories, which are in the Venetian Gothic style. Used by permission from the Chicago History Museum; ICHi-14372.

5.09 *(opposite, bottom)* Holabird and Roche, Champlain Building, Northwest Corner of State and Madison, Chicago; from *Inland Architect* 22, no. 4 (November 1893). Like the Reliance and the Venetian, the Champlain was designed to have very long windows spanning almost the whole distance between the columns. The two street façades of the Champlain were originally to be clad in thin sheets of a gold-colored alloy called "aluminum bronze." It was eventually built in pale-colored terra-cotta. Used by permission from the Avery Architectural and Fine Arts Library, Columbia University.

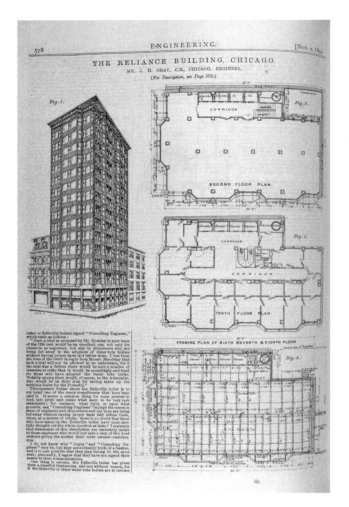

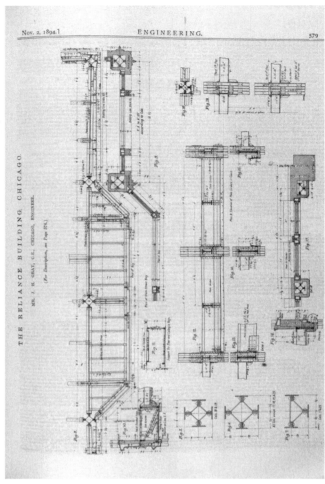

Reliance with one particular benefit. Its pale, terra-cotta and plate-glass façades were considered an entirely appropriate and practical response to the problem of urban sanitation.

THE SKYSCRAPER AND THE QUEST FOR URBAN SANITATION

What little praise the Reliance Building received at the time it was built was due to its apparent "washability," the association made between pale, glazed-terra-cotta building façades and the sanitary porcelain used in bathrooms, kitchens, and hospitals. In 1894 the Chicago-based real estate journal the *Economist* wrote that the Reliance was as "indestructible and as hard and smooth as any porcelain ware. It will be washed by every rainstorm and may if necessary be scrubbed like a dinner plate."[27] In an 1895 review of the building for *Architectural Record*, the critic Charles Jenkins echoed this theme. "The idea of being able to wash your building and have it as fresh and clean as the day it was put up must undoubtedly attract people to the use of this material," he wrote.[28] Even Montgomery Schuyler called terra-cotta "a very eligible material in the atmosphere of Chicago."[29] This criticism deserves further examination as a way to understand the contemporary reading of the Reliance. Apparently the pale-colored, terra-cotta and glass building could only be accepted as aesthetically pleasing in relation to a larger discussion about urban hygiene (fig. 5.12).

The Reliance was at the center of efforts to protect the health of the city around it. In 1895 the Cook County Medical Society held a meeting in the newly completed building to discuss ways to oversee and regulate the sanitation of the city.[30] The society recommended that the local board of health employ a superintendent in each of Chicago's wards to oversee the sanitary aspects of building construction, including fire prevention, ventilation, and plumbing. It also suggested that policemen be educated in matters of health so that they could properly enforce sanitation laws. Since many doctors had their office in the Reliance, it was no doubt a convenient location for such a meeting. But the building was a suitable site for this

5.12 "Chicago Is Enveloped in Smoke. Dirty, Black Clouds from Downtown Chimneys Hang over the City Like a Pall," *Chicago Daily Tribune*, December 2, 1898, p. 3. This article drew attention to the atmospheric pollution produced by burning soft coal. As the tallest building in Chicago, the Masonic Temple was the ideal vantage point from which to survey the problem. Civic reformers claimed that the increasing number of tall office buildings was a threat to public health, because these buildings led to overcrowding and pollution.

discussion in other ways. The Reliance represented a new vision for a future sky-scraper city, one in which pale-colored, glazed-terra-cotta and glass walls were employed to counter new threats to the public: pollution and germs.

The Reliance was an example to a filthy city. From the 1830s to the turn of the twentieth century, Chicago grew in size and population at an incredible rate. But as Harold Platt has shown, urban expansion came at great environmental cost.[31] Factories poured thick, black coal smoke into the air, and the streets were filled with garbage. Wastewater flowed directly into rivers and lakes. Hundreds of new immigrants arrived every day with nowhere to live but overcrowded tenement houses. Epidemic diseases ravaged working-class neighborhoods. By the 1860s some kind of health regulation was clearly needed if the city was to continue to function properly. The medical community and a growing body of "sanitarians" argued for stricter control over the urban landscape. The Chicago Department of Health was founded, charged with the oversight of all building construction in the city. Suddenly the architecture profession was held accountable for public health. From its inception in 1883, the *Inland Architect* was filled with articles discussing sanitation. In its pages architects considered the design of the tall office building in Chicago not only in relation to aesthetics and function but also in relation to contemporary theories of hygiene.

When John J. Flinn described Chicago in his 1892 guidebook, he wrote of an organic connection between the strength of the people and the site of the city: "Many thoughtful persons attribute the wonderful growth of the city to the stimulating atmosphere which arouses all the latent energy in the human system, and makes possible the hard mental and physical labor of the people."[32] But while boosters like Flinn argued for Chicago's supposed natural geographic advantages, the topography of city was of growing concern from the mid-nineteenth century onward. Its low-lying clay soil had a high water table, leading to muddy conditions most of the year. The natural water supply was soon polluted by industrial activity. The rapidly growing city suffered successive years of cholera and dysentery epidemics.

Though comprehensive city planning was not established as a discipline in the United States until the turn of the twentieth century, ideas about public health began to alter the ways American cities were built at least fifty years earlier.[33] In the 1840s European and American doctors believed that disease-laden air, sometimes called "miasma," was the source of epidemic disease, and that this foul air was produced by particular landscapes and climates. Medical surveys, or "topographies," of cities confirmed the correlation between environmental features such as standing water, moist soil, poor air circulation, high population densities, and decaying organic matter, and the spread of diseases like cholera and typhoid. Following the Civil War most American cities established a sanitary infrastructure to deal with these problems. Doctors, engineers, and sanitary reformers proposed a variety of solutions to increase the flow of fresh air and water, to reduce overcrowding, and to prevent the spread of disease. These included the segregation of noxious industries, systematic drainage systems and garbage collection, the planting of trees, and the creation of wide streets and public parks. At the same time, local authorities established laws regulating building, plumbing, and other public-health safeguards.

Chicago was subjected to a number of large-scale infrastructural interventions in order to render the city healthier and more pleasant to live in. In an unprecedented effort, between 1852 and 1858 the entire city, streets and buildings, was raised up between 4 and 7 feet to improve drainage conditions and widen the streets. The Chicago park system, a ring of green spaces around the city, was established in 1869, with the aim of providing fresh air and contact with nature for the growing population. In 1887 a drainage and water supply commission proposed that the direction of the Chicago River be reversed so that the city's waste would not flow into Lake Michigan and contaminate its water supply. This work, which involved digging a new canal south of the city, was completed in 1900.[34]

Like other large American cities, Chicago instituted a public health bureaucracy to oversee these physical improvements. In 1865 the city council appointed a committee to make a sanitation survey of the city in response to the threat of another cholera epidemic. In 1867 a board of health was established under the leadership of John Henry Rauch, a doctor and prominent sanitarian. This board appointed sixteen new sanitary inspectors and began a vigorous cleanup campaign. In 1876 the city established a permanent Department of Health with its own commissioner, Dr. Oscar C. De Wolf. De Wolf's first act was to institute inspection of slaughterhouses and meatpacking plants, and to survey the "tenement house problem." While business and property owners at first resisted his efforts at oversight, seeing them as an unwarranted public intrusion into the private sphere, they gradually accepted them as a necessary means to protect the health of the city as a whole. By 1889, when the Chicago Sanitary District was formed, the Department of Health had nearly fifty health inspectors, including meat and medical inspectors, along with a corps of "sanitary policemen" responsible for visiting factories and tenement houses in order to enforce public health laws. By 1890 the link between public health and the built environment was firmly established.[35]

The *Inland Architect* continually reminded its readers that the architecture profession was at the forefront of efforts to police public health. The architect ignored the field of sanitary engineering at his own peril, the magazine emphasized, because the new profession had a growing influence on the process of building through the introduction of new technologies and practices, and through building regulation.[36] Dr. De Wolf himself was a frequent contributor to the magazine. In an 1886 article entitled "The Relation of State Medicine to the Profession of Architecture," he argued that the state's efforts at controlling the health of the city, including quarantine and vaccination programs, must be supported by the profession through the protection of water supplies, the provision of adequate ventilation, and the implementation of fire prevention measures. Above all, he stressed, healthy citizens must be protected from air tainted by dirt and organic waste.[37]

In discussing urban sanitation the *Inland Architect* emphasized two main problems, both involving atmospheric pollution: the noxious gases given off by decomposing organic waste and the smoke produced by thousands of boilers used to produce heat and power. In an 1884 article, "The Sanitation of Cities," the sanitary engineer Alex Murray described the urgent need for an instrument to measure the purity of the atmosphere, in the same way a thermometer measures temperature.[38] The most impure air of all was the dreaded "sewer gas," an urban legend that dominated medical and popular literature. This putrid gas supposedly lurked in the soil beneath houses and other buildings, permeating basements and rising up to choke the unsuspecting occupants of higher floors. Strangely for a magazine that extolled the virtues of nature, the *Inland Architect* continually warned that direct contact with the soil was to be avoided at all costs. For example, in 1891 the architect Frederick Baumann described the dangers of basements and damp earth, and the efforts that architects must make to protect their clients from the ground.[39] Another article from the same time warned that one open sewer might infect an entire neighborhood.[40] In an era of frequent epidemics and high infant mortality, this apparent danger held powerful sway over architects, doctors, and parents alike.

Dirt was not only a real sanitary concern, it operated as a metaphor for other dangers lurking within the metropolis.[41] The campaign for a clean city through the containment of dirt and odors was an extension of a larger effort to control the industrial city and its inhabitants. Public health reform was a way to reinforce race and class distinctions in a society where they seemed increasingly eroded. Tropes of dirtiness and cleanliness informed attitudes toward the poor and the working class, especially immigrants, who were widely seen as carriers of disease. In *The Cliff-Dwellers* (1893), set in a Chicago office building, the novelist Henry Blake Fuller described the "human maelstrom" of different ethnicities to be found in the Chicago Public Library, where his protagonist sought shelter during a sudden rainstorm: "The down-pour without seemed but a trifle compared with the confused cataract of conflicting nationalities within, and the fumes of incense that the united throng caused to rise upon the altar of learning stunned him with a sudden and sickening surprise—the bogs of Kilkenny, the dung-heaps of the Black Forest, the miry ways of Transylvania and Little Russia had all contributed to it."[42]

This all-too-common view of immigrants as carriers of disease had specific architectural consequences. For example, S. S. Beman's Wisconsin Central Depot Railroad Station, completed in 1890, was designed to keep arriving immigrants entirely isolated from other users of the building in a large waiting area equipped with separate bathrooms. "The immigrant who has just passed through Castle Garden, New York, carrying all sorts of latent diseases in his clothes and about his person can sit alongside anybody in the world at many large stations, but not so at Wisconsin Central Depot," ran a contemporary description. "The train containing the immigrants can be pulled up to the entrance, its cargo unloaded, and another taken on without any of its passengers rubbing against the travelers of the first class."[43] In this way architecture was an instrument used to separate the recent arrivals from the rest of the population, the unclean from the clean.

In the early 1880s the emergence of the germ theory of disease changed discussions of architecture in relation to public health.[44] Devised by Louis Pasteur and Joseph Lister, it replaced the older idea of "miasma," or tainted air. Instead, the danger lay in bacteria, microscopic particles transmitted by direct human contact. The English physicist John Tyndall's book, *Essays on the Floating Matter of the Air in Relation to Putrefaction and Infection* (1881), explaining the existence of bacteria, was particularly influential in the United States. In it Tyndall described the process of putrefaction, emphasizing the importance of the skin as protection from bacteria-laden air. In response to the germ theory of disease, sanitarians expanded their efforts at environmental control to include the reform of personal behavior. Voluntary groups of sanitary reformers, often women, redoubled efforts at education. While the Department of Health emphasized providing running water and bathrooms in tenement houses, as well as restricting overcrowding and ensuring adequate exposure to sunlight and fresh air, philanthropic groups began campaigns to build public bathhouses and to teach working-class children the importance of personal hygiene.[45]

The germ theory of disease had an almost immediate impact on architecture, because it implied that everyday surfaces and furnishings could potentially harbor bacteria.[46] Citing Tyndall, Dr. De Wolf wrote of the danger of contagious diseases, and the role that architecture played in transmitting them. For De Wolf, the plush and porous surfaces of the domestic interior presented a special risk. "The solid particles of these contagia—dried up into a mere dust, absorbed by porous bodies, attached to adhesive surfaces—retain their poisonous properties for varying periods, some of them for a practically unlimited time," he said. They "may remain potent in the plaster of a wall or ceiling, or in the woodwork of a room."[47] In other words, disease was very likely embedded within one's everyday surroundings. In response architects and sanitary engineers began to promote new standards for interior design. Popular household manuals spread the message that dust and dirt were to be purged as part of a campaign for domestic cleanliness.[48]

The first casualties of the new campaign were thick carpets, elaborate draperies, and heavily ornamented furniture. The rules dictated by the English architect Charles Eastlake in his wildly popular interior design manual, *Hints on Household Taste in Furniture, Upholstery and Other Details* (1868), were overthrown. Where Eastlake abhorred anything shiny or reflective, upholstered furniture now lost its popularity in favor of leather and varnished wood, materials that could be easily washed. Linoleum replaced carpet in heavily trafficked hallways and kitchens. Separate bathrooms lined with white porcelain tile were established to contain the dangerous activities of washing and bathing.[49] Lastly, Eastlake's beloved deep reds, browns, greens, and blues went out of fashion, abolished for fear that they could harbor unseen dirt; they were replaced by pale-colored fabrics and wallpapers, and by white paint. Another English architect, Robert Edis, promoted new standards of household taste in a book called *Healthy Furniture and Decoration*, published in conjunction with the International Health Exhibition held in London in 1884. Edis banished heavily carved ornaments, fitted carpets and curtains, which might harbor "bad effluvium and infection."[50] Influenced by concerns for hygiene, fashion now dictated the use of pale colors, simple forms, and shiny, nonporous surfaces.

These developments in medicine and consequently aesthetics are reflected in the design of the Reliance Building. At the time the Reliance was begun, Daniel Burnham, the consummate professional, had already made his interest in sanitation plain. In 1887 he had participated in a symposium on the potential of glass as a building material, in which he emphasized its hygienic character.[51] The vision of a future glass architecture as presented by Burnham fit squarely into an American tradition of experimentation with glass for hygienic purposes that had existed since at least the mid-nineteenth century.[52] In his talk he described two applications for the extensive use of glass in architecture: the hospital and the private house. Glass was a superior material, he claimed, because it let in large amounts of health-giving light, and at the same time kept out the germs that carry disease. Echoing De Wolf's essay on the dangers of "contagia," he described a house where "impenetrable surfaces of floors, ceilings, and walls would all be made of polished glass, from which every extraneous material could be most easily removed." Burnham also described in some detail a recent patent application for a hospital with glass walls, opaque to the north and transparent to the south. This polished-glass facility would be impervious to germs, letting in only "the glowing health of the sun's warm rays to mend up the failing tissues of the body and the despondent minds of the patients." Referring to the newly devised germ theory of disease, Burnham said, "the large sheets of this material would leave few and exceedingly fine joints in which the microbes of fever could lurk . . . a house thus built will protect its occupant more thoroughly than any other from dust, dirt and permeation of gases, and thus from the seeds of disease and death."[53]

Burnham believed glass architecture could be beautiful as well as sanitary. He concluded his talk by addressing the aesthetic possibilities of the material. Glass might be used structurally and decoratively, he claimed, as a cheap alternative to granite and marble, and in time it might also inaugurate a new style of architecture. "We may live to see many a building built of glass from grade to roof-tree, the walls, the ornaments, the gutters, the ridges, the tiles, the chimneys, in short, the whole exteriors," he declared. "Nor will its use stop here: for why may it not become the best of partitions, ceilings, stairs, balustrades, fireplaces and baths?"[54] Even excusing his rhetorical flourish, Burnham was clearly convinced that it was only a matter of time before Americans favored glass architecture.

This essay, combined with Burnham's extensive knowledge of tall office building design, hints at the possibility of a glass skyscraper designed for both hygiene and beauty. These are the concerns reflected in the design of the Reliance Building. As contemporary critics noted, the Reliance appeared to be the urban application of an established domestic truth that shiny white surfaces are easier to keep clean. As in the fashionable houses to the north of the city, dull reds and browns were abolished in favor of shining white in the design of the downtown skyscraper.

THE SMOKE NUISANCE

In the foul atmosphere of Chicago, any practical attempt at the reform of urban sanitation had to start with the smoke problem.[55] No program for public health or civic beauty could succeed without first clearing the air. When contemporary critics commented on the Reliance's "washability," they understood that this was no small benefit. John Wellborn Root himself noted in his essay on the tall office building, "A Great Architectural Problem" (1890), that the external aspect, or appearance, of such a building is dictated by two things: the need to represent the face of business, and the fact that "dust and soot are the two main ingredients of our native air."[56] Terra-cotta cladding seemed to be the answer to the problem. As Charles Jenkins wrote, "Should enameled terracotta prove to be what is claimed for it, if it stands the test of Chicago's severe winters and changeable climate, there can be no possible doubt but that as a material for exterior construction it will be largely used in such cities as are afflicted with a smoky, sooty atmosphere."[57]

The windows of the city's tall office buildings, including the famous "Chicago windows" designed to maximize light and ventilation, were mostly shut tight against thick smoke. The city suffered not only from tainted water but also from severe air pollution. Slaughterhouses, factories, and tanneries belched out disgusting organic and chemical odors. Trains, boats, office buildings, and warehouses emitted huge amounts of heavy coal smoke that blackened the sky. The problem had a predictable daily cycle. It started when the chimneys were fired up at 4:00

a.m., and worsened at 4:00 p.m., when electric-light generators were turned on, causing another "volcanic eruption."[58] In an 1892 article on Chicago architecture, the New York critic Barr Ferree wrote, "The smoke from the soft coal in universal use soils the buildings and the people in an incredibly short time, and in a most unpleasant manner. In the downtown districts there is no perspective, for the streets are continually veiled with a dark cloud from morning to night."[59] This smoke, produced by thousands of heat and steam generators burning soft coal, was so dense that it settled on streets and buildings as thick ash, and released dangerous amounts of sulfur dioxide, carbon monoxide, carbon dioxide, and other gases into the air.

While the health risks of these gases were not fully comprehended at the time, Chicagoans knew that their clothes and faces would become coated with soot after only a few minutes spent outside. Storekeepers knew that their window displays must be changed regularly to remain clean. Businessmen and clerical workers knew not to leave papers close to a window. Architects knew that pollutants would erode soft stone, and that the ornament on their carefully designed façades would soon become invisible under a layer of grime. Everyone knew that the city seemed to lurk beneath a perpetual dark cloud, illuminated only by coal fires, even on sunny days. In 1901 Frank Lloyd Wright anthropomorphized Chicago as a "monster Leviathan" with "fetid breath, reddened with the light from its myriad eyes everywhere blinking."[60]

The smoke problem predated the erection of tall office buildings. In 1874 the Citizen's Association, a voluntary society concerned with public welfare, began lobbying for smoke control legislation. However, this group had little success. An 1881 city ordinance banning the release of dense smoke was widely ignored; the city could not afford to police its own regulations, so the law had little effect. But lobbying against the smoke nuisance continued. The *Inland Architect* supported efforts to curb Chicago's air pollution.[61] In 1887 the magazine editorialized on the need for an alternative fuel to coal. "Chicago and its environment is one vast manufacturing plain and the use of our common soft coal constantly emits volumes of smoke which is proving not only to be obnoxious but deleterious, and of a permanent injury to residence property [*sic*]," the editor opined.[62]

When tall office buildings appeared, they offered particularly obvious examples of the smoke problem. Advanced technology was called into play to catch the culprits. In an extensive series of articles published in the *Building Budget* in 1888, the civil engineer William MacHarg used photography to find the location and direction of the smoke plumes violating the atmosphere of Chicago. Placing a camera on the roof of the Monadnock, MacHarg made a panoramic record of the skyline, recording the worst smoke offenders.[63] The *Chicago Tribune* took up the cause and it too used photography to make its case. "Chicago Is Enveloped in Smoke" was the title of an 1898 article, accompanied by dramatic photographs of the skyline. "Dirty, Black Clouds from Downtown Chimneys Hang over the City like a Pall," read the subtitle.[64] This article illustrated several of the worst offenders, including the Masonic Temple, a popular source of complaints because its highly visible chimney with its plume of black smoke could be seen for miles around (fig. 5.13).

The men who built tall office buildings were among the first to try and solve the smoke problem. After all, clean air was in the city's economic interest. Attempts

5.13 "Cityscape view east from the roof of the County Building toward the Masonic Temple (tallest building on left) with smokestacks on the roofs of buildings in the foreground, Chicago"; glass negative, from the *Chicago Daily News*, 1907. The Masonic Temple can hardly be seen through clouds of coal smoke. Used by permission from the Chicago History Museum; DN-0004956A.

to address smoke pollution became especially important after 1890, when Chicago was awarded the World's Fair. In 1891 a number of the city's business leaders organized the privately funded Society for the Prevention of Smoke in order to persuade building owners to voluntarily install smoke control equipment on their boilers, and to tend them in such a way as to reduce the amount of smoke they produced.[65] The society established an office at the top of the Monadnock building, from whence it could oversee the problem.[66] Owen F. Aldis, Peter and Shepherd Brooks' Chicago agent and a prominent real estate developer, was a founding member of the group. An early advocate for smoke reform, he earned special praise from the *Chicago Tribune* for successfully abating smoke at the Venetian Building, of which he was part owner, as well as at buildings he managed.[67]

Through their efforts at collective action, building owners largely succeeded in policing themselves. The Society for the Prevention of Smoke was more aggressive in pursuing its goal than the city government, hiring a staff of five engineers to inspect the nearly five hundred buildings not in compliance with the ordinance banning excessive smoke. These engineers issued reports on each building, advising owners how to reduce the smoke produced by their boilers. In the same year the society hired a lawyer who began vigorously prosecuting violators, sometimes more than once if they refused to pay their fines. While the society's goal of a smoke-free Chicago in time for the World's Columbian Exposition was not achieved, by 1892 it had succeeded in reducing smoke emissions in 40 percent of its targeted buildings.[68]

Rather than foreshadowing the modernist ideal of transparency, the Reliance was designed to resist penetration by the noxious environment outside, acting as an impenetrable barrier to smoke and air-borne germs. Though it did not solve the smoke problem, it drew attention to the problem of urban sanitation. At a time when skyscrapers were criticized for polluting the air with thick coal smoke and for casting the surrounding streets into perpetual shadow, the Reliance seemed to reverse this negative impact. Subject to new restrictions on smoke emission put in place by the Society for Smoke Prevention, and clad in the same pale, non-porous tiles used for sanitary purposes in hospitals, kitchens, and bathrooms, it was designed to convince the world that the skyscraper was not a threat to the city after all. While the practical sanitary effect of the Reliance is questionable, its symbolism is not. Along with the World's Columbian Exposition, it foreshadowed Daniel Burnham's early twentieth-century vision of a shining urban vista where poverty, disease, and class conflict were banished.

CHICAGO 1900

6

CHAPTER

THE CITY BEAUTIFUL MOVEMENT AND THE DECLINE OF THE SKYSCRAPER

Completed in 1895, the Reliance Building sits at the nexus between utopian visions of future skyscraper cities of the early 1890s, and the City Beautiful ideal that took shape around 1900. Though Chicago architects were only just beginning to imagine the reform of the city in terms of large-scale urban planning (the relationship of the skyscraper to its surroundings, for example), through buildings like the Reliance they presented an alternative vision of the skyscraper: not as an ominous dark tower billowing poisonous smoke but as a shining beacon of light. Chicago encouraged a slew of enthusiasts to predict that the skyscraper would be the future of the American city. Inspired by Edward Bellamy's enormously successful *Looking Backward: A.D. 2000–1887* (1888), a novel of time travel set in Boston in the year 2000, a number of futuristic works promoted the skyscraper as a model of urban organization (fig. 6.01). The authors of these books rejected the early nineteenth-century agrarian utopia in favor of an urban, technological one.[1] But while elaborate visions of futuristic high-rise cities dominated popular literature, in academic and professional discussions the recently established building type seemed doomed as an experimental but ultimately unsatisfactory solution to the problem of rapid urban growth. Many critics argued that the skyscraper was inherently ugly, unsafe, and unsanitary.

Turn-of-the-century architects and social activists associated with the City Beautiful movement had very much the same desires for the future of the city as the authors of utopian literature. They wanted community, prosperity, health, and beauty. They believed all Americans should be surrounded by art and culture, even as they took advantage of everything that advanced technology had to offer. They agreed on the value of large and easily accessible parks; broad, straight streets laid out in a logical manner; and the grouping of important public buildings within organized government centers. Above all they agreed on the necessity for comprehensive city planning in the service of all, directed by newly minted city planning professionals. But unlike utopian writers, they were not convinced of the value of the tall building as "social condenser."[2]

The skyscraper boom was in decline by the mid-1890s. Following a downturn in the national economy, the tall office building was no longer a sound business investment. Inspired by the World's Columbian Exposition of 1893, the city was reimagined in terms of horizontal rather than vertical extension. By 1909, when Daniel Burnham and Edward Bennett's grand scheme for the reshaping of the Chicago region was published, the skyscraper seemed defeated as an urban solution. How, then, did it lose the place it had so recently claimed as an inspiring symbol of urban progress?

THE BATTLE FOR BUILDING HEIGHT RESTRICTIONS

In 1890 the skyscraper stood as a symbol of everything good and bad about the American metropolis. It stood for prosperity, technological achievement, and national progress. But it also stood for economic inequity, overcrowding, and the loss of traditional forms of community in an industrial economy. Efforts to restrict its vertical growth reflected ambivalence about the future of the industrial city and about the quality of city life. Between 1892 and 1910, building owners, architects, contractors, civic reformers, politicians, and social commentators fought a fierce battle to introduce building height limits in large American cities.[3] In 1893, when the standard height for new commercial construction was around 200 feet, or sixteen stories, the Chicago City Council applied a height limit of 130 feet, or about ten stories.[4] Under this new law, buildings as tall as the Monadnock, the Masonic Temple, and the Reliance were no longer allowed. (Although it exceeded the new limit, plans for the Reliance were filed before the law went into effect.) Arguing that it was vitally important not to check economic growth, building owners and some of Chicago's most prominent architects and contractors immediately challenged this restriction. For the next twenty-seven years they fought a battle over building heights in public meetings, in civic chambers, in the courts, and in newspapers. In answer to pressure from one side or the other, the city council revised its initial ordinance many times. Although the height limit in Chicago varied from 130 to 264 feet between 1893 and 1920, the era of unlimited growth was definitely over.

Calls for building height restrictions appeared in Chicago in the early 1880s, at the same moment that tall office buildings were first constructed. In 1884 the *Inland Architect* reported on a height restriction ordinance put forward by a city alderman.[5] Since very few office buildings were taller than six stories at this time, either the definition of excessive height was relative, or critics were anticipating a vertiginous urban landscape not yet realized. Nationally, concern over building height centered on four general areas: aesthetics, economics, public health, and social harmony. While aesthetics were not much of an issue in Chicago (after all, its citizens believed this new building type was the spontaneous organic creation of their particular city), the other three factors were in play. Some city council members argued that the construction of tall buildings in the Loop concentrated business downtown at the economic expense of outlying areas (fig. 6.02). In 1894 the

6.01 King Camp Gillette, plate 5, *Apartment Building*; from *The Human Drift* (1894). In his utopian proposal for a future collectivist society, the Chicago-born Gillette (who later became a safety-razor tycoon) proposed a large city near Niagara Falls, made up entirely of gargantuan residential skyscrapers clad in glass and ceramic tile.

6.02 "One of the Busiest Streets in the World—State St., Chicago, Ill. (18 Miles Long), North from Madison." Stereo card by Underwood and Underwood, ca. 1903. Critics of the skyscraper claimed it concentrated too many people in the center of the city, causing unhealthy overcrowding. Courtesy of the Library of Congress; LC-USZ62-51769.

Chicago Tribune summarized the health concerns associated with the skyscraper: "It has been asserted that the imposing piles shut out the light from the streets, interfere with the free circulation of air, and are general disease breeders."[6] The higher the building, the deeper the shadow it threw onto the surrounding streets, and the larger the barrier it presented to natural breezes. The longer those streets were in darkness, and the more they were hemmed in, the less chance that potentially dangerous damp air could be evaporated by sunlight and blown away by the wind. The more tall buildings were constructed, the more smoke they would produce to pollute the atmosphere, choking the city with their poisonous emissions.

The equation between urban hygiene and social harmony, between dirt, crime, and revolutionary fervor, was also made at an early date. In "The Sanitation of Cities," an essay published in the *Inland Architect* in 1884 at the height of social unrest, the sanitary engineer Alex Murray described the necessity for wide streets so that sunlight and air might penetrate crowded thoroughfares. He also called for building height regulations. Like other social reformers, Murray believed that darkness breeds crime and immorality: "All know that filth, ignorance and crime are inseparable. To remove filth is to remove a potent provocative of degradation; a degradation which fills our infirmaries, prisons, which makes bad citizenship."[7] For Murray as for other urban reformers, healthy cities made healthy citizens.

Despite these concerns, and the enthusiasm with which they adopted other principles of municipal reform, Chicago architects were understandably partisan toward the high buildings that had made their fortunes, and made their city famous. Though the *Inland Architect* published many articles such as Murray's calling for urban reform, it also opposed calls for an absolute height restriction and made the case for the health benefits of the skyscraper. Chicago architects argued that tall buildings were far superior to those they replaced in terms of structural soundness, hygiene, and fire protection. An article reprinted in the compendium *Industrial Chicago* was quick to praise the hygienic advantages of the new type: "The advantages of the altitude as regards fresh air, freedom from the noise of the streets and practical exemption from smoke, are so well known and thoroughly appreciated, that it is unnecessary to comment upon them here."[8] In other words, skyscraper-dwelling was actually beneficial, not harmful, to public health. A 1902 *Inland Architect* article entitled "High Building Construction Should Not Be Restricted" claimed that tall office buildings greatly improved the lives of those working in them, people who would otherwise be housed in the low and mean buildings constructed during Chicago's early industrial era.[9]

But this argument in favor of the skyscraper seemed to benefit only a few. The tall office building seemed all the more egregious because it stood in stark contrast to the poorly built and maintained tenement houses immediately surrounding it. These buildings, home to huge numbers of immigrant workers, lacked basic hygiene and sanitation. As we have seen, labor leaders used the disparity between the skyscraper and the slum as a key image in their revolutionary rhetoric. The demonstrations planned in the slums, culminating in the disastrous Haymarket bombing of 1886 and the building trades strikes of 1887, seemed to signal a chronic and incurable social malaise that the skyscraper could only exacerbate. By the late 1890s, many Chicago architects came to believe that the laissez-faire construction of skyscrapers might be contributing to the city's social problems. The desire for a visible urban order gained momentum. The vertical skyline, once seen as the organic product of western expansion, the spontaneous eruption of an indigenous American style, was now seen as evidence of harmful individualism and materialism. Though the *Inland Architect* continued to oppose absolute height restrictions, it also printed many articles supporting the growing City Beautiful movement, a movement that would momentarily halt the popularity of the skyscraper as an urban solution.

CHICAGO AND THE CITY BEAUTIFUL

Starting in the final years of the nineteenth century, a nationwide campaign for civic beautification supplemented the challenge to the skyscraper on the grounds of public health.[10] For adherents of the so-called City Beautiful movement, unrestrained urban growth had negative rather than positive consequences. Their philosophy was disseminated among Chicago architects in a series of articles published in the *Inland Architect* between the late 1890s and the magazine's closure in 1908. Most were written by easterners known nationally for their expertise in municipal improvement. They included the Boston architects C. Howard Walker, T. M. Clark, and Ralph Adams Cram, and the Philadelphia architect Albert Kelsey. However, Chicago had its own proponents of the City Beautiful. Following his success with the World's Columbian Exposition of 1893, Burnham was considered one of the country's foremost experts in city planning, and the *Inland Architect* followed his national and international projects closely. William Le Baron Jenney and Peter B. Wight also wrote on the topic for the magazine, as did Lucy Fitch Perkins, a designer and faculty member of the Pratt Institute in Brooklyn, New York, before she married the Chicago architect Dwight Perkins, one of Burnham's employees. Together these writers summarized the national debate about city planning for a Chicago audience.

The formal and aesthetic wing of the municipal reform movement, to which these authors belonged, maintained that the unplanned growth of American cities had resulted in ugly, disorganized, and unhealthy urban landscapes, of which Chicago was a prime example. For the sake of efficiency and prosperity as well as beauty and hygiene, the city must be seen as an ordered whole to be designed and controlled by experts rather than as an agglomeration of individual parcels of land, each developed without reference to its neighbors. Influenced by the recent grand-scale urban renovations of Paris and Vienna, advocates of the City Beautiful believed the time had come for the same artful planning to be applied to American cities. They lobbied for both physical improvements and the legislation needed to enact them.

The organic metaphor so important to nineteenth century architects also informed ideas of city planning. Walker, a painter and critic in addition to being an architect, was one of the many experts on municipal reform who published in the *Inland Architect*. In 1901 he wrote, "A great city resembles an articulate animal. It is made up of a number of parts jointed to each other. It grows in that way."[11] In a 1905 article, "Municipal Improvements," Kelsey compared the American city to "the savage man [who] has the same faculties as his civilized brother, but these faculties are less developed. The savage man is unkempt, shaggy and dirty."[12] Just as the savage man learned to wash and clothe himself, he said, the primitive city would learn the value of cleanliness and grooming. In organic theories of architecture and urbanism, aesthetic pleasure is derived from the elegant fulfillment of function. In a 1908 essay entitled "Civic Development," Cram wrote, "A beautiful thing is a thing done right, and an ugly thing is a thing done wrong." He believed that American cities were ugly because they did not follow a pre-planned scheme: "like Topsy, they have 'just growed' and 'growed' wrong."[13] The organic metaphor demanded order in place of chaos.

As in other American cities, municipal reformers in Chicago argued for a connection between harmonious urban planning and a harmonious citizenry. Magnificent new civic buildings would stand as reminders of the common goal of American democracy while commodious parks would provide amenities for new citizens otherwise crowded into factories and tenement dwellings. Lucy Perkins's 1899 essay, "The City Beautiful: A Study of the Artistic Possibilities of Chicago," one of the first to address the plan of Chicago from a City Beautiful perspective, took on this issue directly. While the City Beautiful movement was largely a middle-class one, in which the needs and desires of the working classes were referred to only indirectly, Perkins had strong opinions about the role of design in the improvement of class relations. She was one of the few authors published in Chicago's premier architectural journal to describe the need for improved housing for the poor. She also believed that the working class should be directly involved in the practice of city beautification: "The universal hunger to put ourselves into our work, to produce something of lasting value and meaning to others, has a bearing upon industrial problems, and we see that man can provide work for the growing race only by the industries and arts which minister to the spirit as well as to the body."[14] She believed the production of art as well as the objects of necessity would nourish the spirit of the worker. If the worker could look around and see a beautiful city that he had helped create, he would be reconciled to its progress rather than alienated from it.

Civic reformers frequently argued for a link between civic beauty and commercial prosperity. The support of the powerful business community was necessary in order to implement change. It was often noted that a public improvement to one area of the city increased the value of all private properties in the vicinity. In 1904 the *Inland Architect* noted that this was the case when the streets around the New York City Public Library, between Fortieth and Forty-second streets, were widened.[15] New highways, beautiful vistas, landscaped parks, and artfully arranged public buildings and squares would rationalize the circulation of people and goods throughout the city and attract foreign interest and investment as well as improve the health and well-being of all citizens.

While at least one author cited the English reformer Ebenezer Howard's recently published *Garden Cities of Tomorrow* (1898) as a source of inspiration, the precedents referred to in essays on municipal improvement published in the *Inland Architect* were largely real cities, not ideal ones.[16] Proposals for Washington, DC, which took Pierre L'Enfant's original plan of 1791 as a guide for future development, attracted the most attention, especially as Daniel Burnham was chairman of the planning commission in charge of the project.[17] The magazine also took note of plans to redevelop New York City's City Hall area into a civic park surrounded by a series of gargantuan new skyscrapers housing the functions of city government (fig. 6.03).[18]

But despite references to these American examples, European cities were the favored points of comparison. The Old World was the model for the new one where civic improvement was concerned, because it seemed to have a historic authenticity that American cities lacked. Paris, Vienna, and London, along with Berlin, Rome, Madrid, Budapest, Brussels, Frankfurt, and Prague, served as paradigms of elegant city planning in the pages of the *Inland Architect*. Views of their wide avenues and imposing public squares were reproduced over and over again, amounting to a European pattern book for modern American urban design. The fact that such different cities could be praised implies that Americans were interested less in specific planning strategies than in an abstract sense of old-world charm.

Americans envied European urban design not only for its elegance but also for the absolute power with which it was implemented. The modern improvements put in place by Napoleon III in Paris and the emperor Franz Joseph in Vienna were the supreme examples of modern city planning for Americans. In a 1902

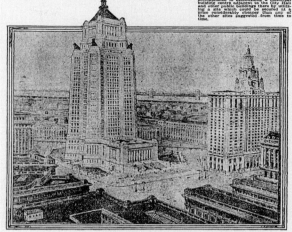

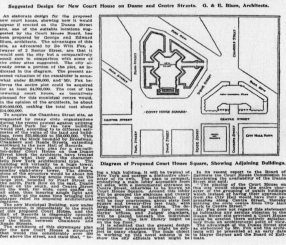

6.03 "Suggest Skyscraper for Court House to Typify Architecture of New York," *New York Times*, June 26, 1910, p. X10. Large municipal skyscrapers were often proposed in American urban planning schemes around the turn of the twentieth century. This tower was to provide a "great municipal center" for New York City.

article entitled "Beautiful Vienna" reprinted in the *Inland Architect* from the *Chicago Record-Herald*, Burnham's friend William E. Curtis went so far as to remark, "It is a pity that Mr. Burnham's commission recently appointed to prepare a plan for the beautification of Washington could not have the support of an autocrat with the taste of Francis Joseph [*sic*] to do here what was done there . . . However much we may appreciate the blessings of civil liberties and self-government they have their disadvantages when great national enterprises are to be undertaken."[19] While America lacked the autocratic leadership of an emperor, civic reformers hoped to replace imperial rule with an equally powerful civic bureaucracy. For the sake of health and beauty, all aspects of the city, including buildings, parks, roads, and highways, were to be controlled via a central city planning authority and strict building legislation.[20]

If city planning was to be efficient, it needed to become a science with the same kinds of quantitative methods of analysis as other sciences.[21] The new discipline depended on the collection of vast amounts of information about property ownership, demographics, rents, disease, and crime among many other things, data that had never been gathered before, let alone systematically organized for easy retrieval and comparison. Civic reformers also argued that city management needed to be separated from the expectations of political patronage. It is no coincidence that in the first decade of the twentieth century, articles in the *Inland Architect* encouraging centralized city planning coincided with Chicago's charter reform movement. In an effort to detach the city government from state politics and make it more accountable, a number of middle-class civic associations tried to convince the Illinois legislature that Chicago needed its own separate charter for much greater authority over its affairs. While this effort was ultimately unsuccessful, it stimulated a lengthy conversation about the role of city government in city planning.[22]

In opposition to the organic ideal of unrestricted urban growth, city planners began to imagine the urban environment as a design problem to be solved. They approached it in much the same way that Frederick Law Olmsted and Calvert Vaux approached the planning of Central Park in New York City: as a natural landscape to be enhanced through careful editing and enhancement. Reformers argued that a city's topography, or "natural aspect," should form the basis for its design. Natural features such as hills, rivers, and lakes were to be appreciated and improved as aesthetic assets as well as manipulated for utilitarian purposes. There was widespread dismay in Chicago at the way the city's two natural assets, its river and lakefront, had been despoiled by commercial shipping, rail transportation, and other industrial uses. The river had long been polluted by waste from nearby meatpacking plants and factories, and a railroad company had sole possession of the lakefront to the south of the city. In 1887 the *Building Budget* criticized Chicago for its lack of a real center, and for giving over its shoreline to the railways. "Chicago Is Not Yet Paris" was the title of the article.[23] Inspired by the charming street scenes depicted in modern French painting, reformers like Perkins believed that the Chicago River should be enhanced with stone embankments and beautiful bridges, with tree-lined boulevards and grand hotels (fig. 6.04). Similarly, she argued that the lakeshore should be landscaped as an enormous public park. In this way, Chicago's waterways, the source of the city's economic power, were to be transformed from industrial infrastructure into a series of urban landscapes dedicated to leisure.[24]

5381. Chicago's Pride, Her Boulevard. U. S. A.

Plans for picturesque cityscapes almost always began with a series of urban parks intended to bring the benefits of fresh air and open space to city dwellers.[25] Extensive parks were already in place in many late nineteenth-century American cities thanks to the influence of Olmsted and the park systems he had established in New York City and Boston. In Chicago a park system was initiated in the late 1860s, under the stewardship of Olmsted, Jenney, and the Chicago doctor John Rauch, and open land had been set aside for future parks in the rapidly developing areas to the south and west of the city. By 1871 Humboldt, Central, and Douglas parks were established to the west, adjacent to commuter rail lines and complementing Lincoln Park to the north and Washington and Jackson Parks to the south. Closer to the center of the city, the construction of Grant Park was begun in the 1890s, offering the city more pleasant lakefront scenery than the existing Illinois Central Railroad tracks.[26] Municipal reformers like Perkins wanted the whole lakefront from Jackson Park in the south to Lake Forest in the north to be a continuous landscaped shoreline that would complement the existing parks to the west. "Why should we not make a park of our whole city?" she exclaimed. "Why should not every street have a border of well-kept grass and be lined with trees?"[27]

While the addition of parks undoubtedly improved urban life, reformers believed the underlying structure of Chicago constituted its biggest problem. They blamed many of its ills on the one template of comprehensive planning that did exist, the grid. By this time the eighteenth-century democratic rationale behind the grid plan was far outweighed by its lack of aesthetic appeal. In an era when the picturesque garden suburb was in bloom on the outskirts of American cities, the grid was condemned for its endless straight streets without destination, and for the kinds of building it encouraged on the outskirts of the city: mile upon mile of private development, with little opportunity for larger public buildings or open spaces (fig. 6.05).[28]

For those Chicagoans who hated the grid, the great fire of 1871 represented a moment of great potential sadly unrealized. At that time, Curtis wrote,

Chicago had the greatest opportunity ever offered to any city of size, and if its municipal government in October 1871 had purchased the entire burnt district and appointed a commission of architects, artists and landscape gardeners to lay out a series of broad avenues, parks and public gardens, to erect public buildings, opera houses and theaters

6.04 "Chicago's Pride, Her Boulevard, U.S.A. (South Michigan Avenue)." Stereo card by B. W. Kilburn, ca. 1890. City Beautiful reformers argued for the construction of new landscaped boulevards like these as antidotes to the narrow crowded streets of the grid. These wide streets were not only for traffic circulation but also for leisure activities, as the recreational cyclists in this picture demonstrate. Courtesy of the Library of Congress; LC-USZ62-124290.

of monumental character, and then sold the remaining space to private parties who were required to observe rigid regulations in the erection of buildings it would have furnished a parallel to the recent history of Vienna.[29]

In this way the rebuilding of the city after the fire, once celebrated as a triumphant rebirth, one that led to the creation of Chicago's greatest architectural feature, the skyscraper, was now mourned as a failure, a great lost opportunity for city planning.

Municipal reformers hoped to replace of the uniformity of the grid with a hierarchically ordered system of avenues and streets, private and public buildings. Wanting to eliminate the seeming randomness of the grid, they believed street vistas should terminate at groups of public buildings artfully arranged at the center of public squares. The design of such complexes was discussed in *Inland Architect* articles such as C. Howard Walker's "The Grouping of Public Buildings in a Great City" (January–February 1901), and in numerous editorials with titles such

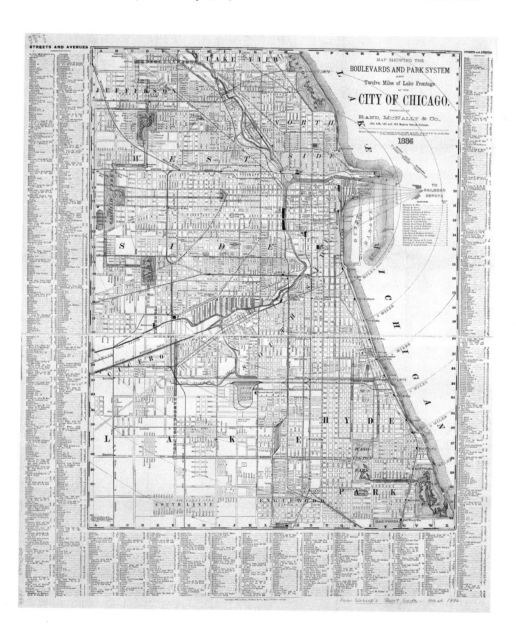

6.05 "Map Showing the Boulevards and Park System and Twelve Miles of Lake Frontage of the City of Chicago," Rand McNally and Co., 1886. The original 1830 grid stretched for miles as the city grew, dictating the pattern of development far beyond the city center. In the 1890s Chicago architects began to criticize its rigid and unrelenting orthogonality. Used by permission from the Chicago History Museum; ICHi-31337.

as "The Grouping of Public Buildings" (May 1905) and "Progress in Grouping of Buildings" (August 1905). The main point of these essays was to differentiate public buildings from private ones by arranging them as urban ensembles rather than as isolated objects. Walker argued from the point of view of aesthetics as well as convenience. Public buildings should be grouped together so that they can have "the most practical relations to each other," he said. "Buildings of any description gain in effect by being grouped, and . . . isolated buildings of whatever individual merit, are insignificant in comparison to massed constructions, even if this latter be comparatively mediocre in quality."[30] Along with other critics, Walker saw the World's Columbian Exposition fairgrounds as a positive example of future urban design. Early twentieth-century architects and critics, including Louis Sullivan and Montgomery Schuyler, notoriously criticized the buildings of the fair for their lack of artistic imagination. However, as Walker's comment implies, they were always considered less important as individual objects than as examples of unified city planning. The true art of the fair was to be found in its plan, not in the design of individual buildings.

In discussing the composition of cities, American architects and critics employed a new language of abstract form, imagining the city itself as a sculptural whole. "A fixed ratio should exist between the voids and solids of all quarters of the city," noted Albert Kelsey, "whether such quarter be one of lofty buildings or of modest two or three story residences."[31] The voids of the great avenues should be balanced by masses of grouped public buildings at either end, and by smaller private buildings in between. Here the same logic that John Wellborn Root had applied to the design of the Monadnock was applied to the design of a city: perception of individual parts (whether ornament or buildings) must give way to the perception of the whole (whether a building or group of buildings) if the object being viewed is to be seen as an aesthetic object in itself. If municipal reformers had their way, the city would surpass the skyscraper as the pinnacle of municipal art.

What happened to the tall building in plans for the municipal reform of Chicago made in the first decade of the twentieth century? Was it to be incorporated into the comprehensive plan for the city as one of the many "centers of interest," or abolished altogether as an ugly and unsanitary construction dictated by business and not art? There was no clear agreement as to its fate. Despite the success of buildings like the Masonic Temple, the potential for the tall building to serve civic rather than purely commercial functions was not universally embraced. When this building type was mentioned, it was still usually identified with the program of business. If commercial and industrial interests were to be subordinate to public interests in the new city (at least visually if not practically), then the tall office building was an awkward reminder of a past age of individualism. The haphazard skyline of Chicago seemed to epitomize a basic lack of order on the ground—skyscrapers were built in a seemingly random manner within the Loop, dictated by invisible economic forces, not visible aesthetic ones.

Despite the potential of the skyscraper for urban reform imagined by architects and writers around 1890, by 1900 civic reformers were nervous about its replication. They foresaw not rational grids of skyscrapers, each related to the other, as Bellamy did in his utopian fantasy, *Looking Backward*, but the kind of rampant "Manhattanism" later celebrated by the architect Rem Koolhaas, the autonomous development of miniature skyscraper cities on adjacent blocks with little or no relation to one another, and with no consideration of the streets surrounding them. Rather than continuing the design experiments of earlier American architects, municipal reformers borrowed their urban ideal from European cities. They emphasized the ordered, decongested, horizontal growth of Europe over the dense, random, vertical development of the laissez-faire American urban landscape.

Strangely, in spite of these concerns, the quantitative height of buildings was not often directly addressed in writings on municipal reform. While Parisian laws restricting buildings to six stories were often quoted with approval, American architects and planners were more interested in achieving a uniform height than in dictating what that height should be. Most writers on the subject agreed that important public buildings should be protected from the erection of large, unsightly buildings in close proximity, but did not abolish the idea of high buildings altogether. In 1899 Lucy Fitch Perkins argued that Chicago's existing tall buildings were of sufficient artistic merit to survive the planner's axe: "The commercial architecture of Chicago stands in proud preeminence, for our office buildings lead the world," she declared. "Structurally the world looks to us. The tall buildings are justified on business rather than artistic or sanitary grounds, but that they need not themselves be ugly is proven by the Masonic Temple, the Marshall Field Wholesale, Monadnock, Woman's Temple and other buildings."[32]

Yet overall, the subject of tall buildings received surprisingly little attention in writings on civic reform published in Chicago around 1900. Perhaps the skyscraper was condemned less stridently than one might have expected, because this building type had been economically successful, at least up until that moment. Reformers depended on business interests to support their ideas, and calls for the wholesale abolition of the tall building might alienate this powerful group. Or perhaps these reformers believed that tall buildings, along with slums, congested streets, disease, and crime, were the natural result of bad planning, and that the implementation of good urban design would preclude the need for very high buildings altogether.

THE 1893 WORLD'S FAIR AND THE 1909 *PLAN OF CHICAGO*

The articles on municipal reform cited here are reflections of the City Beautiful philosophy that dominated American city planning in the first two decades of the twentieth century. Printed in the *Inland Architect*, they represent the ambitious plans architects and reformers held for Chicago, plans that overturned the skyscraper as the vertical icon of progress in favor of an ordered horizontal expansion. Following the success of the 1893 World's Columbian Exposition and spurred on by the national movement for urban reform, Chicago tried to realize these ambitions through a comprehensive plan for the city developed by the Commercial Club, a powerful organization of businessmen, and drawn up by Daniel Burnham and his employee and collaborator, Edward H. Bennett. After three years of work, this plan was published in 1909. It converted the lakeshore to a pleasure grounds, dictated the construction of more parks and open spaces, imposed a radial street plan on the existing grid, encouraged the grouping together of important civic and cultural buildings around a new city center, and rationalized all other buildings to conform to the scheme for the greater whole. Burnham's visionary plan was never realized completely, nor could it have been. Its scope was simply too vast to be accomplished by state and local government authorities, even with the support of business leaders. However, it dictated the way Chicago grew between 1910 and the late 1920s, when new roads and parks were built conforming to its general outline. Burnham's power and influence were such that he could claim to have successfully molded the city into a new form, one in which the singular iconic skyscraper, the symbol of individualism, seemed almost to disappear.

Daniel Burnham's struggle with the future of the skyscraper came after his early success with tall building design. His practical involvement with city planning began with the World's Columbian Exposition of 1893. Ostensibly built to celebrate the four hundredth anniversary of Christopher Columbus's arrival in North America, the fair was designed by a group of American architects under the directorship of Burnham to showcase the United States as an equal partner to Europe in terms of cultural as well as economic development, and to establish Chicago as the new focal point of American civilization. Built 7 miles to the south of the Loop on the shore of Lake Michigan at Jackson Park, it was a vast display of international art, science, and industry contained within a carefully orchestrated complex of neoclassical buildings, with only a few symbolic domes piercing the skyline.[33]

The fairgrounds, open and spacious, surrounded by lagoons and trees, presented a dramatic contrast to the streets of the Loop (fig. 6.06). The view across the central lagoon and the Court of Honor was an American version of an ideal city borrowed from Paris and Venice, a horizontal urban landscape with wide streets for leisurely strolling and monumental buildings set in spacious landscaped grounds. The major exhibition buildings were grouped symmetrically around Richard Morris Hunt's Administration Building and a central lagoon complete with gondolas. Extending westward away from the lake, the grounds connected to the system of parks created by Frederick Law Olmsted, via the tentaclelike extension of the mile-long Midway Plaisance, the fair's dizzying pleasure grounds. Though built using the same Chicago construction as the buildings downtown, these temporary buildings imitated a neoclassical ideal, providing a stylistic homogeneity and a unity to the entire composition that the Loop skyscrapers lacked.[34]

While Chicagoans hoped their World's Fair would compare favorably to the celebrated Paris Exhibition four years earlier, there was one Parisian element they did not wish to replicate: Gustav Eiffel's tower. At the beginning of the planning

6.06 The Chicago World's Fair of 1893. The carefully orchestrated landscape of the fairgrounds, with its low-lying, neoclassical buildings surrounded by gardens and lakes, served as a model for urban development of Chicago in the early years of the twentieth century. Courtesy of the Library of Congress; LC-USZ62-128873.

process for the fair, numerous proposals were made for a tower to compete with this infamous construction, but in the end they were all abandoned.[35] Unlike France, which was eager to prove its technical prowess on a world stage, Chicago had a different set of aspirations. While the French were increasingly curious about the possibility of tall buildings (the *Inland Architect* published the results of an École des Beaux-Arts competition for "Une maison à quatorze étages" in May of 1892), Americans were not anxious to make the skyscraper the central attraction of their World's Fair.[36] Chicago's famous verticality was celebrated in one structure only, and it was not really a building but an object of entertainment. Where Paris had the Eiffel Tower, Chicago had the Ferris Wheel.

Following the success of the World's Columbian Exposition, Burnham cast his sights northward toward the city itself. In 1896, influenced by plans put forward by the South Park Commissioners, he presented a scheme for the improvement of the lakeshore from Jackson Park to Grant Park at the mouth of the Chicago River. This scheme called for the reclamation of the whole lakeshore as a recreation area, with a series of landscaped parks, lagoons, and beaches included. The members of the Commercial Club to whom Burnham submitted the proposal received it with enthusiasm, and very slowly made plans for its implementation. In 1906, at the behest of the Commercial Club and the Merchant's Club (another business group with which it soon merged), Burnham, the champion of western organicism, the man who had made his name with the tall office building, took up the challenge to remake Chicago anew following the model of the fair. Assisted by his longtime employee Edward H. Bennett and the Chicago Plan Committee, which was made up of members of the two clubs, he completed the task in 1908. The Commercial Club published *The Plan of Chicago* in 1909. It was edited by Charles Moore, who had previously written the text describing the plan for Washington, DC, and accompanied by a series of sumptuous watercolor illustrations by Jules Guerin.[37]

The Plan of Chicago begins with a repudiation of organic urban growth. "Men are becoming convinced that the formless growth of the city is neither economic or satisfactory," it claims, "and that the overcrowding and congestion of traffic paralyze the vital functions of the city . . . Chicago, in common with other great cities, realizes that the time has come to bring order out of the chaos incident to rapid growth, and especially to the influx of people of many nationalities without common traditions or habits of life."[38] The desire for an ordered and harmonious city now outweighed the value of unfettered growth celebrated by Chicago architects twenty years before. Burnham's goal was nothing less than the rationalization of the whole region. The 1909 plan was not only much larger in scale than the World's Columbian Exposition; it was also far larger than the existing city.

Because of the expansive horizontal reach of the 1909 plan, one of the principal arguments for the skyscraper—that it was an economic necessity where cities were restricted by insurmountable natural features like rivers, lakes, and harbors—was put to rest before any specific planning had even begun. Burnham and Bennett's scheme imagined all the functions of the city spread out over a vast metropolitan area connected to, but not dependent on, the central business district of the downtown Loop (fig. 6.07). In this way the form of the city would be dictated by the economic good of the region, not by the economic need of landowning individuals. Recalling the city's motto, *Urbs in horto*—city in a garden—the plan aimed to transform the existing city of centralized towers surrounded by miles of untidy ex-urban development into a unified urban landscape in which low buildings alternated with parks, all linked by an ordered series of broad tree-lined avenues.

In their efforts to control the horizontal expansion of the city and limit its vertical growth, Burnham and Bennett imposed on the flat prairie landscape two things Chicago had never had before: a center and an edge. While the Loop functioned as the commercial and civic center of town, it lacked a central monument to define it precisely (although City Hall technically occupied this position, it was not visually distinct from the buildings surrounding it). From the Loop the streets of the grid spread outward to the north, west, and south, with little guidance or restriction beyond unrelenting orthogonality. To remedy this, Burnham and Bennett drew a large arc representing a wide landscaped boulevard around the city, starting from a spot to the southwest of the existing business district. This boulevard connecting the north, west, and south was described as an "elliptical avenue" along the lines of the Ringstrasse in Vienna. It established a new boundary for the city and encouraged westward expansion instead of north-south linear growth along the lakeshore.

To increase the value of the land far from the Loop, the authors of the plan placed three new parks along the arc, one each to the north, west, and south. In addition a series of smaller neighborhood "play" parks were to be built, especially in the more congested areas of the city. Complementing the three large parks, Burnham extended his 1896 proposal for a landscaped lakeshore northward, so that the shore of Lake Michigan would become a continuous park from north to south. Together with the new boundary avenue, these would form an unbroken landscaped edge around the city 100 miles in length.

In an effort to expand the city horizontally rather than vertically, Burnham and Bennett hoped to decongest the crowded streets of the Loop by extending the center of the city toward the southwest. The old center would be transplanted to a new one at the meeting point of all the radial avenues. In one audacious move, the north-south orientation of the existing city was rotated east-west by the creation of a vast landscaped public plaza along a widened and extended Congress Street from Michigan Avenue to Halsted Street. This new district, likened to Saint Peter's Square in Rome and the Piazza San Marco in Venice, was anchored by a monumental new civic center to the west and a cultural center to the east. At the western end of this plaza was a magnificent central administration building, "surmounted by a dome of impressive height, to be seen and felt by the people, to whom it should stand as the symbol of civic order and unity"[39] (fig. 6.08). This new city hall was surrounded by three groups of buildings representing municipal, state, and federal authorities. All the buildings in this complex, and those surrounding it, were to be designed with a common architectural theme, shown in the illustrations as an abstracted neoclassicism. They were also to be a common height, so as to present a unified backdrop to the plaza and to city hall.

Burnham and Bennett had remade Chicago, at least on paper. To the best of their ability they transformed the entire formal logic of the city from a grid into a radial design. Upon cursory examination, it seems that the plan allowed for no tall buildings except for a single monumental civic development. The pinnacle of the whole design, this unique edifice dominated all the other buildings, which were represented as repeated units of the same abstract block, a low rectangle pierced by light wells. But does that mean that the plan did away with the tall building altogether, except in exceptional circumstances? A closer examination of

6.07 *(right)* "Chicago. General Map Showing Topography, Waterways and Complete System of Streets, Boulevards, Parkways and Parks"; from Daniel Burnham and Edward H. Bennett, *The Plan of Chicago* (1909). Burnham and Bennett imagined Chicago in regional terms, as part of a larger organized system of towns around Lake Michigan and the Great Plains. It was no longer one point on a universal grid but the center of a vast network. Used by permission from the Chicago History Museum; ICHi-39070_3w.

6.08 *(above)* *Civic Plaza*; from Burnham and Bennett, *The Plan of Chicago* (1909). Burnham and Bennett's plan provided Chicago with the center it never had. This center, dedicated to civic life, not commerce, was carefully composed in elevation as well as in plan. The new city hall was to be the tallest building, with all others stepping down from it in height, according to their importance in the bureaucratic hierarchy. Used by permission from the Chicago History Museum; ICHi-39070_7r.

Guerin's illustrations reveals that the abstract building blocks, the basic fabric of the city, are not as small as they at first appear. They vary from around eight stories to around thirteen stories in the area surrounding the civic center. It is only the vast scale of the proposal that makes them seem short.

Interestingly, building height is barely mentioned in the text of *The Plan of Chicago*, except for vague references to the need for harmony in design, and matching cornice lines as in Paris. The possibility of height regulation is referred to specifically only in an appendix entitled "Legal Aspects of the Plan of Chicago," written by Walter Fisher, a lawyer who acted as counsel for the Plan Committee of the Commercial Club. Fisher noted that there was no question that the city was vested with the authority to "regulate the height of buildings with a view to health and public safety."[40] At the time the plan was published, Chicago had a universal height restriction of 260 feet, or around ten stories. However, neither Fisher nor anyone else associated with the plan specified what the future height limit ought to be. Considering the audacity of the plan, this seems a strange omission.

One of the principal concerns in making the 1909 plan for Chicago was the desire to reduce congestion in the central city, and there is no doubt that the authors also wished to control the construction of tall office buildings in the Loop. However, their solution to the problem of overcrowding was not to restrict building height. Rather, they hoped to encourage the dispersal of commercial building over a much wider area. Ironically, at least as it is represented in Guerin's illustrations, the plan appears to do nothing at all to decrease the overall height of the city's buildings. Since so few of the existing buildings reached higher than four or five stories, replacing them with block after block of eight- or ten-story buildings would dramatically *increase* the vertical scale of the city. In other words, tall buildings were far from discouraged: they were actually an integral part of the proposal, as long as they were planned as units of a whole, not individual monuments.

Given the apparent contradiction between Burnham's desire for horizontal rather than vertical expansion and the dramatic increase in tall buildings suggested by the plan's illustrations, how did the plan actually affect the city? While he emphasized that his design was intended to lay out the basic direction of future work without dictating it in any detail, Burnham worked actively to have it implemented. The incredible growth of the city since the mid-nineteenth century, which he had lived through, made such a vast undertaking seem entirely feasible: between 1850 and 1900 the grade of the city was raised several feet, the great sanitary canals were built, the skyscraper and the park system were created, and the World's Columbian Exposition was constructed. Following the publication of the plan, the Chicago Plan Commission, a group of influential private citizens, was established to lobby for its implementation. In 1910 voters approved it as the official guide to future growth, and soon afterward the commission became a public body appointed by the mayor. In 1917 the plan was adopted by the city council as the official plan for Chicago. However, despite this official mandate, it exists today in only a few fragmented sections of the city. Some of the lakefront development and a few partial sections of the radial roadway, including Ogden Avenue, were realized more or less in the form Burnham and Bennett proposed; the three large parks, the peripheral boulevard, and the relocation of the civic center were not. Ultimately, the plan required more intervention than state and city legislature could provide, and a higher rate of economic growth than the city could sustain during the years of the First World War and the Great Depression.[41]

But despite the failure to implement a comprehensive plan for Chicago in the first decades of the twentieth century, the radical reimagining of the city that took place in this period resulted in a new way of thinking about the tall building. The skyscraper was reconceived as part of a larger streetscape rather than as an individual monument. And although Congress Parkway never became the grand boulevard that Burnham hoped it would, his plans for Michigan Avenue did eventuate (fig. 6.09).[42] In 1920 the street was widened and extended north across the Chicago River via the Michigan Avenue Bridge, creating a major thoroughfare between the commercial district developing north of the river and the older business district to the south. As Burnham had proposed, it was partially elevated, with a separate level for commercial traffic below and a landscaped boulevard above.

In the early twentieth century, Michigan Avenue, lined with light-colored skyscrapers and elegant stores, replaced the dark-brown buildings of State Street as the center of commercial activity.[43] Prompted by Burnham, Chicago architects

6.09 Jules Guerin, proposed boulevard to connect the north and south sides of the river; from Burnham and Bennett, *The Plan of Chicago* (1909). The realignment and extension of Michigan Avenue north of the river (a project that predated the 1909 plan) was realized, while much of the rest of the plan was not. Used by permission from the Chicago History Museum; ICHi-309070_6t.

(especially William Holabird and Martin Roche) developed an aesthetic of pale, terra-cotta-clad, tall office buildings for this fashionable boulevard. The famous Wrigley Building was completed in 1924, followed by the Allerton Hotel and the Tribune Tower in 1925, and the Medinah Athletic Club and 919 North Michigan Avenue in 1929 (fig. 6.10). These buildings, modern abstractions of the classical and Gothic styles, represented the new face of Chicago. They were celebrated not for their tectonic innovation but as icons of a new urban order. The Tribune Tower in particular signaled a new age for the heroic skyscraper.[44]

The skyscrapers lining north Michigan Avenue represent the culmination of thirty years of architecture and urbanism in Chicago, the confluence of Daniel Burnham's plans for the skyscraper and for the city. When the tall office building appeared in Chicago in the early 1880s, it took the form of a high building block of around ten stories, designed to be seen as a decorative façade rather than as a singular object, supported by three utilitarian party walls that remained invisible. Around 1890, spurred on by the real estate boom, a new form appeared, one much higher and more experimental in its design than its predecessors. Built around that moment, the Stock Exchange, the Monadnock, the Masonic Temple, and the Reliance represent four very different experiments in what the tall office building could be. Each was imaged as a singular tower to be seen from more than one side, not as a uniform part of the city block. With these buildings, Dankmar Adler, Louis Sullivan, John Wellborn Root, Daniel Burnham, and Charles Atwood presented aesthetic reflections of the state of the city. Then, in the wake of the 1893 real estate bust, a powerful new idea of city planning took hold, halting at least temporarily the proliferation of skyscrapers designed as autonomous monuments.

Around 1900 the skyscraper as a work of civic art was replaced by a vision of the city itself as a work of art. Building height limits were instituted and the design of individual buildings was made subservient to the design of large-scale urban compositions. The skyscraper as a heroic figure was demonized, while at the same time the tall building became familiar and ubiquitous. Though they were just as tall or even taller than their predecessors, the second generation of Chicago skyscrapers, erected between 1900 and 1920, was imagined in a new way, not as a series of isolated buildings but as units of a larger whole. Through the rhetoric of the municipal reform movement, the tall building was redefined, not as a monument standing alone on the skyline, but as a sober building block designed in concert with its neighbor. Just as Sullivan had wrestled aesthetic control of the tall office building from the mason, between 1900 and 1920, aided by the immense power and influence of Burnham, the burden of civic representation momentarily shifted from the architect to the city planner. This condition prevailed in Chicago until 1922, when the Tribune Tower competition inaugurated a third generation of Chicago skyscrapers. In this fertile integration of American and European ideas about the future of the modern city, the heroic skyscraper reappeared as both an object and an idea.

6.10 "North Clark Street Bridge and the Wrigley and Tribune Buildings, Chicago, c.1925." North Michigan Avenue, Chicago's "Magnificent Mile," represents the convergence of Burnham's early work with Root and Atwood in developing an aesthetic for the tall office building, and his later work with Bennett on city planning. Michigan Avenue is an organized urban vista made up of iconic skyscrapers, most famously the Wrigley Building (1924) and the Tribune Tower (1925). Courtesy of the Library of Congress; LC-USZ62-104114.

POSTSCRIPT
"THE ARCHITECTONIC ANTICIPATION OF THE FUTURE"

In his book *Delirious New York* (1978), the architect Rem Koolhaas described Manhattan as a "mountain range of evidence . . . without a manifesto."[1] Between 1900 and 1939, he claimed, the prodigious growth of the city operated according to a logic of both hyperrationality and outrageous fantasy. Chicago has always stood as the counterexample to New York, and indeed the problem with Chicago is that while many manifestoes have been written about it, few authors recognize these same contradictory traits at work within it, albeit a generation earlier. For twentieth-century architects and critics alike, the Chicago skyscraper came to represent the highly rational manifestation of technology, modernity, and capitalism. Yet complex, contradictory, and often irrational agendas drove its creation, as the multiple contemporary debates surrounding it reveal. This book has focused on reconstructing those debates. To this end I have used the *Inland Architect*, the professional journal published between 1883 and 1908, as the chief source of information, although I have also referred to discussions of the new building type in other architectural journals (both American and foreign), local real estate magazines, building manufacturers' publicity pieces, labor publications, and contemporary newspapers—in short, the printed media in which the public discourse around the subject can be found. Though it does not include the views of all those who commissioned, designed, built, worked in, or visited the tall office buildings in Chicago, this literature refers to a wide selection of opinions. This is where the people of the city established what the new urban landscape meant to them.

The idea of the skyscraper in Chicago in 1890 was not singular but multiple. It encompassed diverse thoughts about economic, social, and aesthetic value. While many of the issues described in these magazines—including triumphant claims of technological innovation, passionate debates about aesthetic expression, and the definition of professional responsibility—are particular to the architecture profession, many—including arguments about the effects of industrialization on class relations, and warnings about the causal relationship between rapid urban growth and the health of the population—are not. Debates about the skyscraper are inherently architectural and at the same time embedded within the broader social questions of the day. Implicit in discussions of its form and that of the industrial city are the desire of those who identified themselves as "westerners" to establish themselves as a strong and independent people with their own forms of cultural expression; anxiety over social inequity in the face of industrial progress; fears about potential social revolution; the need to balance commercial prosperity with civic community; and concerns about environmental health.

These parochial matters are not always reflected in more distanced readings of the Chicago skyscraper, readings that are made in the service of different questions and different rhetorical objectives. Arnold Lewis has described the way in which European critics used Chicago architecture as a lens through which to view Europe's own urban and architectural future.[2] Through an analysis of British, French, and German journals, he shows that these critics described Chicago architecture as the unconscious reflection of commercial programs and industrial methods of construction. Although they were initially extremely ambivalent about the aesthetic effects, this way of thinking paved the way for the functionalist philosophy that dominated European architecture in the 1920s. In this view, which we might call the modernist one, Chicago buildings were dislocated from the place and time of their construction and sited within a linear history of building technology. In this new history certain structures became important touchstones, while others considered important at the time they were built receded into obscurity. Despite its insistence on objectivity and its narrow focus on the material facts of building, this modernist history was deeply ideological. In the early years of the twentieth century, following the deep and traumatic wounds inflicted on Europe by the First World War, architects equated the development of building technology with social progress, believing that the discoveries of the nineteenth-century scientific and industrial revolutions could be harnessed to raise the standard of living for everyone. And although they celebrated the achievements of Chicago architects, they did little to uncover the social debates surrounding the origins of the skyscraper in the United States.

As we have seen, late nineteenth-century Chicago architects believed in industrial progress. They were proud of their technical achievements, seeing them as evidence of the advance of American civilization. In their dependence on the philosophy of organicism, they helped promote the dominant modernist idea that the exterior form of a building should reflect its interior functions and construction. However, the literature examined in this book reveals that the late nineteenth-century discussion of the tall office building in Chicago differed from early twentieth-century interpretations in at least two important ways. First, the equation made between technical and social progress was still highly contentious. Second, Chicago architects believed they were responding to a specific regional and urban context with their designs. They did not imagine their solutions to be universal ones.

By way of conclusion, this postscript examines the meaning of the Monadnock and the Reliance Building for modernist architects, critics, and historians in the early twentieth century. These two buildings assumed special importance in the narrative that centered on the development of building technology as a metaphor for social progress. As one of the last tall buildings constructed with masonry load-bearing walls, but one of the first to display an aesthetic based on its materials rather than an applied historical style, the Monadnock is often considered a bridge between nineteenth- and twentieth-century modernism. In a similar way, with its unique façade, a thin veil of pale terra-cotta and glass undulating around two sides of its steel frame, the Reliance Building has been described as the most truly progressive building produced by the "first Chicago School," an early realization of the transparent glass tower.

THE MONADNOCK AND THE NEUE SACHLICHKEIT

In August of 1938, the German architect Ludwig Mies van der Rohe arrived in Chicago, reluctantly abandoning Berlin and his directorship of the Bauhaus for a new home in the United States. On his arrival a reporter for the *Chicago Daily News* asked the German master how he liked the architecture of the city. "I should not like to choose any one particular building in Chicago as an outstanding architectural example," Mies apparently replied, "although I think the Monadnock block is a true expression of such vigor and force that I am at once proud and happy to make my home here."[3] As his comments suggest, although he was seeing it for the first time, Mies was already familiar with the nearly fifty-year-old Monadnock.

America, and Chicago in particular, acted as a mythical site for early twentieth-century German architects.[4] As Arnold Lewis has shown, Germans were the first foreign critics to treat the tall office building as a serious architectural artifact rather than an aberration.[5] The terms of the critical praise afforded to the Monadnock by nineteenth-century critics tempted later writers to associate it with a protomodernism, in which ornament is discarded in favor of structural and functional expression. In 1894 the art critic Wilhelm Bode praised Chicago's tall office buildings as exhibiting, "above all, purposefulness [*Zweckmässigkeit*] itself," and American architecture in general as being conceived outward from interior functional requirements.[6] For many early twentieth-century Europeans, this attention to a building's real purpose instead of design for its own sake was inspiring. From the 1920s until the late 1930s, German and Austrian avant-garde architects and critics, including Ludwig Hilberseimer, Erich Mendelsohn, Bruno Taut, Walter Behrendt, and Richard Neutra, published books and articles based on their visits to America, showing the Chicago skyscraper as part of an anonymous and objective industrial vernacular landscape, the model for twentieth-century functionalism (figs. 7.01 and 7.02).[7]

In this criticism the heavy brick walls of the Monadnock were seen as superlative examples of the Neue Sachlichkeit, the "new objectivity."[8] They were celebrated for their derivation from pragmatic need rather than capricious and subjective design preferences. In 1922 Mies's Bauhaus colleague Ludwig Hilberseimer wrote, "this building shows that here the problem of all architecture, the question of line and mass, is once more recognized and adapted in a new way to meet new conditions. The false solution—unfortunately too common—of applying meaningless and misplaced adornment is here instinctively avoided. An innate feeling for proportion gives this great building inner consistency and logical purity."[9] Hilberseimer's use of the words *instinctively* and *innate* suggests that he believed the designers were naïve in their expression of the problems of the tall office building; that they solved them in an unconscious response to practical functions rather than with any specific aesthetic aim in mind. While earlier European critics had dismissed Chicago architects for their apparent lack of attention to architectural conventions, later critics were unwilling to give the Americans credit for the very goal they sought to achieve themselves: the aesthetic expression of modern industrial life. It was more convincing to argue that such a reconciliation between modern form and function arose autonomously and organically, within the unconscious, as the Swiss critic Siegfried Giedion would later argue.

Mies probably knew of the Monadnock through a book of expressionistic photographs of New York, Buffalo, Chicago, and Detroit produced by the German architect Erich Mendelsohn and entitled *Amerika: Bilderbuch eines Architekten* (1926). Though Mendelsohn included the Monadnock in his collection, he did not identify it by name (fig. 7.03). Instead, he described it as a "skyscraper of the second period."[10] For Mendelsohn, shocked by the scale and speed of the American metropolis, the skyscraper was the ultimate expression of capitalism. The will of the

individual architect involved in creating it seemed unimportant compared to the economic forces that called it into being. Ludwig Hilberseimer and Bruno Taut were more generous in their own books on American architecture published in the late 1920s. Both men named John Wellborn Root as the architect of the Monadnock and praised his design, arguing that it ushered in a new generation of American architecture.[11] While he reserved his greatest praise for the work of Louis Sullivan, Taut suggested the Monadnock was one of the few instances where an American tall office building could be seen as "the visible materialization of the architect's aim and object imbued through and through by his sentiments and ideas."[12]

Both the Austrian architect Richard Neutra and the German critic Walter Behrendt cited the Monadnock approvingly as an example of a building completely suited to its context and purpose. Although neither described it as anonymous, both left ambiguous the role of the architect in achieving this result. In *Amerika: Das Stilbildung des neuen Bauens in der Vereinigten Staaten* (1930), a book describing his experience working for Holabird and Roche and for Frank Lloyd Wright, Neutra described the Monadnock as a generic and faceless building, one that blended faultlessly with the passing double-decker buses. (Encouraging the European belief in the Monadnock's progressivism, he mistakenly claimed it had been completed in 1883.) While Neutra praised the "smooth clothing of the frame

7.01 *(left)* "Chicago Hinterstrasse"; from Erich Mendelsohn, *Amerika: Bilderbuch eines Architekten* (1926), 149. Mendelsohn's book was not a dry catalogue of North American urban typologies but a subjective representation of the psychological effect of the new American city. Used by permission from the Avery Architectural and Fine Arts Library, Columbia University.

7.02 *(right)* Grain elevators; from Mendelsohn, *Amerika*, 60. Mendelsohn saw little difference between skyscrapers and these industrial buildings, which he described as "childhood forms, clumsy, full of primeval power, dedicated to purely practical needs." For him they were "a preliminary stage in a future world that is just beginning to achieve order." Used by permission from the Avery Architectural and Fine Arts Library, Columbia University.

construction [*sic*]," he claimed that both the Monadnock and the nearby Tacoma Building were doomed to extinction, because they represented the mechanical perfection of the type, not individual artistic achievement.[13]

Behrendt admired the Monadnock for its "rigid functionalism," describing it as a triumph of social will over the individual caprice of the architect. Here the designer had removed his personal creativity in favor of the needs of the "actual social and economic world," he wrote.[14] He used the Monadnock to illustrate what he saw as the vital technological change responsible for the creation of modern architecture: the transformation of the wall from supporting to supported element. While he believed Walter Gropius's recently completed Bauhaus Building at Dessau represented this transformation most perfectly, he claimed it was first conceived in American high-rise buildings.[15] (In an earlier version of his book, published in Germany in 1927, Behrendt used Burnham and Root's Masonic Temple as his Chicago example. By the time the expanded version of his book appeared in English ten years later, he discarded the Masonic Temple in favor of the more aesthetically "modern" Monadnock, even though its use of steel framing was limited to the interior.)

But at the same time that European architects were praising it for its modernity, Chicagoans already thought the Monadnock was out-of-date. In 1938, the very year Mies arrived in town, Aldis and Co., the owners of the

7.03 "Chicago: Hochaus der Zweiten Periode" (Chicago: Skyscraper of the Second Period); from Mendelsohn, *Amerika*, 181. Mendelsohn did not identify the Monadnock or its architects by name. But he appreciated it as an attempt to "find expressive forms that correspond to our own era in terms of function and materials." Used by permission from the Avery Architectural and Fine Arts Library, Columbia University.

building, were seriously considering demolition. Dissuaded by the high cost of rebuilding rather than any sense of the building's historic value, they subjected it to a substantial "program of progressive styling" by Skidmore, Owings and Merrill.[16] The original interiors were completely removed in order to enlarge and renovate the offices in the fashionable new art-deco style. The mosaic floors installed by Italian workmen brought to America specifically for the job were replaced by terrazzo. Unfortunately, the very building celebrated for its purposefulness and exterior expression of interior function no longer suited the requirements of the twentieth-century business office.

As we have seen, John Wellborn Root's essays published in the *Inland Architect* between 1883 and 1891 complicate the insistence on the Monadnock's objectivity, and on its lack of design. This writing reveals his deliberate and polemical attitude toward the design of the tall office building. Root was no functionalist. In an 1888 essay he emphasized that the art of building lies not in the technically adept use of material but in the representation of larger ideals.[17] Art should not mimic the visible world, he believed, but express the invisible metaphysical truths behind it. Like his friend Sullivan, Root's definition of the function of the tall office building was not pragmatic or utilitarian but social and spiritual.

The Monadnock arose from a conjunction of practical and aesthetic considerations. From the point of view of the client, its design was to be simple and unornamented, befitting a commercial building in the less fashionable southern part of the Loop. The finished building is evidence that Burnham and Root used this opportunity to express modern business in an entirely new way. As Root and other writers noted, the interior functions of the tall office building were far too complex to be usefully represented on the exterior in the way that Beaux-Arts planning demanded. Instead, the three street façades were designed to lend gravity to the obscure world of business inside, and to act as an antidote to the highly volatile street life outside. In this context, even if it had been desired by the client, finely detailed ornament was all but irrelevant. It was not appreciated by busy city dwellers urgently pushing their way forward through the crowds, blinded by dust and smoke and deafened by noise. Consequently, Burnham and Root proposed a new aesthetic of simple massing and monochromatic surfaces using finished brick as the design generator.

The Monadnock should be interpreted, then, not as aesthetically invisible, as the modernist reading implies, but as quite the opposite. It is not an objective building. Its heavy brick walls do not purely transmit their interior function and construction. Rather, the Monadnock is an entirely subjective building. It is truly modern in quite a different way than modernist architects imagined. It does not represent a new model of perfection based in technology, or a new standard to replace classicism. Instead, it offers a way of thinking about form as something continuously reinvented according to the local situation.

SPACE-TIME AND THE RELIANCE BUILDING

The Reliance Building assumed special importance in modernist histories of architecture when early twentieth-century critics situated it as a naïve precursor to European experiments in glass architecture of the 1920s. The Swiss critic and art historian Sigfried Giedion co-opted it as the beginning of a "new tradition" in his polemical history, *Space, Time and Architecture*, published in 1941 after his emigration to the United States. Calling the Reliance "an architectonic anticipation of the future," he employed it as a symbolic watershed from one movement in American architecture to another, from historical eclecticism to experiments with what he called the "potentialities" of architectural technology.[18] He praised the way the large sheets of plate glass and the terra-cotta tile appeared to form a single undulating veil barely disguising the steel frame underneath. In this way it could be seen as a precursor to modernist transparency, with all the aesthetic and political significance that the term *transparency* entails.[19] The modernist reading of the terra-cotta-tiled building as a transparent glass building has dominated discussion of the Reliance ever since.

The origins of this view may be seen in reviews of Chicago architecture published following the 1893 World's Columbian Exhibition. In an 1896 essay on the work of Daniel Burnham, the American critic Montgomery Schuyler, otherwise a promoter of Chicago architecture, described the slender, cream terra-cotta and glass façade of the Reliance as the failure of the traditional load-bearing role of the wall.[20] Overtly industrial in its construction, more akin to a bridge than anything else, it seemed to Schuyler an abdication of authorial responsibility in favor of technological expediency. It appeared to break entirely with earlier traditions of construction, and to mark the terrible descent of building art into an industrial process. Both Schuyler and Giedion agreed that the Reliance represented an important and irreversible change from one concept of architecture to another, and both saw its curtain walls as a provisional solution. They were too fragile and thin for Schuyler and too solid and heavy for Giedion. In this way the Reliance is forever caught between being too transparent and too opaque; too industrial and too handmade; too plain and too eclectic; too new and too old.

Giedion's *Space, Time and Architecture* canonized the modernist view of Chicago architecture as a bridge to a new age. It combined German functionalist polemics of the 1920s with more specific historical data uncovered in the 1930s. Between 1931 and 1933, American authors added an element of self-consciousness to the German view, promoting H. H. Richardson, John Wellborn Root, and Louis Sullivan not as unwitting midwives but as conscious creators of a new modern style.[21] In *The Brown Decades: A Study of the Arts in America, 1865–1895* (1931), the New York critic Lewis Mumford described the appearance of indigenous expression in American art in the decades immediately following the Civil War, first in the literature of Walt Whitman, Ralph Waldo Emerson, Henry Thoreau, and Herman Melville, and then in the fine and applied arts. Between 1880 and 1895, he claimed, H. H. Richardson, Whitman's architectural counterpart, threw off "spurious romanticism" in favor of absolute originality. "Richardson was the real founder of the *Neue Sachlichkeit*," Mumford pronounced.[22] He went on to praise three Chicago architects, the familiar triumvirate of Sullivan, Root, and Wright, for carrying on Richardson's legacy.

In early 1933 the idea of American, more specifically Midwestern, architecture's claim to formal originality received institutional approbation when the Museum of Modern Art in New York hosted the exhibition "Early Modern Architecture, Chicago 1870–1910: The Beginnings of the Skyscraper and the Growth of a National American Architecture."[23] Curated by Henry-Russell Hitchcock and Philip Johnson, the exhibition was relatively modest in scope, consisting of only thirty-three photographs and three models (fig. 7.04). However, it helped popularize Mumford's audacious hypothesis that late nineteenth-century Chicago architecture, particularly the work of Richardson, Sullivan, and Wright, was the American precursor to the European avant-garde (which, of course, had been the subject of "The International Style" exhibition at MoMA the year before). Hitchcock and Johnson had little interest in the specifics of Chicago's architectural or urban history; instead, they promoted the Chicago skyscraper for its supposed structural rationalism.[24] They presented the thirty-three buildings as isolated moments within the linear progress of typological development. Their aim was to demonstrate a philosophy of structural determinism in which technical innovation generated aesthetic invention. Hitchcock and Johnson argued that with the transition from masonry construction to the steel frame, Chicagoans had pioneered modernism.

In the summer of 1933, the MoMA show was exhibited at the Marshall Field Department Store in Chicago, precisely at the time when many tall office build-

FROM MASONRY TO STEEL

7.04 Philip Johnson standing next to models demonstrating the stages in the structural evolution of the skyscraper commissioned for "Early Modern Architecture, Chicago 1870–1910," Museum of Modern Art. New York, January 18–February 23, 1933. The exhibition focused mainly on the tectonic transformation from load-bearing to curtain walls. Digital image © The Museum of Modern Art / Licensed by SCALA / Art Resource.

ings in the Loop were being demolished because they were no longer economically successful. Although some of the buildings in the show had already been destroyed, the myth of the "Chicago School" had begun. The show reinforced two ideas about Chicago architecture in particular: its technical and thus formal originality, and its isolation from outside influence. Hitchcock and Johnson cemented the view that William Le Baron Jenney's Home Insurance Building was the first steel-framed skyscraper. This claim had gained national attention in 1931, when the Marshall Field Estate commissioned a committee to investigate the structure of the building as it was being demolished. Thomas Tallmadge, the chairman of the committee, released a report claiming the Home Insurance Building as the first tall office building made up of an entirely steel frame.[25] The MoMA show also claimed that Chicago was able to develop a bold new style because it was removed from the "influence of traditional architecture on the Atlantic Seaboard."[26]

In his own history of modern architecture, Sigfried Giedion repeated Hitchcock and Johnson's claim that the Chicago skyscrapers of the 1880s and '90s were the immediate forerunners to a new generation of European architecture in the 1920s. He made this genealogy explicit by placing images of Chicago buildings next to avant-garde European projects from thirty years later. Jenney's Leiter Building (1889) was partnered with Le Corbusier's Maison Clarté (1930–32), Louis Sullivan's Schlesinger Mayer (now Carson Pirie Scott) Building (1899–1904) with Walter Gropius's project for the Tribune Tower competition (1923), and D. H. Burnham and Co.'s Reliance Building (1894) with Mies van der Rohe's "Project for a Glass Skyscraper" (1921) (fig. 7.05). Privileging Jenney as the father of the so-called Chicago School, Giedion granted authorship to individual architects, but described the buildings they designed largely in terms of technical innovation, emphasizing steel-frame construction and the elevator. While late nineteenth-century Chicago architects tried hard to establish their professional position as separate from contractors and engineers, by the mid-twentieth century they were being celebrated as technicians first, and designers second.

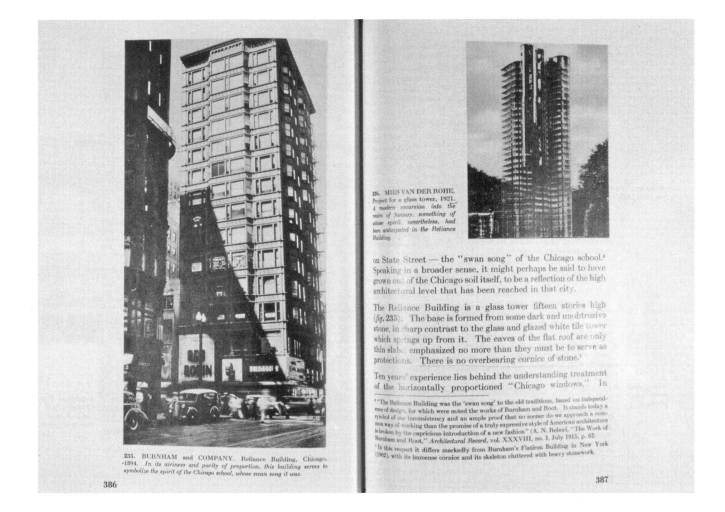

7.05 The Reliance Building paired with Mies van der Rohe's "Project for a Glass Skyscraper" of 1921; from Sigfried Giedion, *Space, Time and Architecture* (1941), 308–9. This pairing illustrates Giedion's contention that late nineteenth-century Chicago architecture was the unconscious forebear to early twentieth-century European modernism.

This pragmatic understanding of Chicago architecture purposefully overlooked the writing of the architects who built it. "The works concerned with the Chicago School in its development between 1883 and 1893 are for the most part anonymous," Giedion claimed. His chief source of information was the three-volume anthology *Industrial Chicago* (1891), which he described as the "Vasari of the Chicago School."[27] Although he also consulted the *Inland Architect*, Giedion cited only factual descriptions of buildings published in the magazine, not the more speculative essays. The voices of individual architects were of little interest to him, except in the case of Jenney, whom he was careful to describe as an engineer, not an architect. Giedion's aim was to construct a history of modern American building as an anonymous building tradition of farmhouses and commercial buildings extending back to the seventeenth century, suppressing questions of authorship and broader aesthetic influences. For modern architecture to be indisputably objective, there could be no ambiguity; only a battle between those who saw the way forward and those still stuck in the past.

Three books published after the Second World War confirmed Chicago's claim to technological originality and aesthetic autonomy. In 1949 Frank A. Randall, a structural engineer, published his *History of the Development of Building Construction in Chicago*, a detailed chronology of advances in building construction from the balloon frame to the caisson foundation.[28] In 1952 Carl Condit, a professor of architectural history at Northwestern University, published *The Rise of the Skyscraper*, and in 1964 *The Chicago School of Architecture: A History of Commercial and Public Buildings in the Chicago Area, 1875–1925*, which remains the authoritative and most-often-cited text on Chicago architecture.[29] Drawing on Randall's research, Condit compiled documentary evidence to support the functionalist argument. While he credited Mumford with "rediscovering" Chicago's late nineteenth-century architecture, Condit cited Behrendt and Giedion as his principal influences. For Condit and the postwar generation, the Chicago skyscraper was the building type that gave America a place in the history of modern architecture. "One sees here," he noted, "the genesis of the simple functionalism and structuralism of modern architecture, of Mies van der Rohe's theory of 'less through more.'"[30] In 1964 Condit echoed Giedion's claim about the Reliance. "If any work of structural art in the nineteenth century anticipated the future, it is this one," he declared. "Atwood succeeded in developing almost to its ultimate refinement the modern demater-ialized curtain wall, and this made the building a direct forerunner of the work of Le Corbusier and Mies in the twenties."[31]

The association between the Reliance and early twentieth-century visions of glass towers was encouraged by a particular way of reading its image. In photographs taken between the 1890s and the turn of the century, the Reliance is almost obscured by smoke, shadows, and fog. In later reproductions these same images are cropped and touched up so that the sky, reflections, painted advertising signs, curtains, and shades all disappear, and the building appears to float in space. For Giedion, the Reliance must be seen through half-closed eyes, its shadows and in-convenient details obliterated through graphic editing. Cleaned of smoke, shades, and commercial display, the thin curtain walls could be claimed as prophetic of Mies's 1921 "Project for a Glass Skyscraper," and the pale terra-cotta cladding a stand-in for the glass curtain wall, a placeholder for a material that was not yet technically feasible.

According to this genealogy, the Reliance was a short-lived step in the evolution of the curtain wall toward complete transparency. However, as we have seen, this transition was far from linear. In the 1890s, American architects and critics struggled to establish an autonomous aesthetic for terra-cotta-clad buildings as not merely a simulacrum of brick and stone or a precursor to glass but a material in its own right. If the solidity of masonry had become unsuitable because of the structural and programmatic constraints of the tall office building, this building type had other symbolic and functional requirements that also made transparency undesirable. The glazed-terra-cotta and glass surface was designed not only to let light in but also to protect the interior from the dangerous environment outside.

The Reliance did not exist in abstract ether, but in a very real environment with very real properties. The utopian ideal of unlimited sunlight and fresh air was far from a reality in Chicago, so the building was celebrated for its ability to resist rather than absorb the foul air around it. Because the climate of the city was so polluted, contemporary critics were interested in the Reliance less for its transpar-ency than for its opacity. Described as flimsy, dangerous, and ugly, the building was intriguing because it presented a new model of "washability," a utopian vision of hygienic design. Its gleaming white surface could repel dirt, soot, and germs. To more positive reviewers, the white terra-cotta skyscraper showed that the tall office building could be a solution to, rather than a cause of, problems of urban hygiene. But of course this solution was more symbolic than operative. Bright and clean, the Reliance stood for progressive design in a progressive city dedicated to health and beauty. In 1895 the glazed, white terra-cotta tower was a symbol of light and cleanliness in the heart of a dark city filled with disease and dirty black smoke.

In a 1956 article, "Chicago Frame," the English architectural historian Colin Rowe, inheritor of Giedion's mantle as European spokesman for architectural modernism in America, argued that late nineteenth-century Chicago architects used new materials for reasons of economy, not in an attempt to remake the social world.[32] For him the pragmatic "fact" of the frame in Chicago became an abstract "idea" only a generation later, when it was adopted by European architects of the modern movement. But the largely symbolic use of white terra-cotta cladding on the Reliance suggests that, contrary to Rowe's assertions, the Chicago skyscraper was not only a direct answer to technical and functional problems. Like Mies's glass-tower project, it lived simultaneously in the realms of rationality and fantasy, engaged with moral and aesthetic ideals, and pointed in its own way toward a future, transformed society.

NOTES

INTRODUCTION

1. The same basic story is repeated in Lewis Mumford, *The Brown Decades: A Study of the Arts in America, 1865–1895* (New York: Harcourt, Brace and Company, 1931); Henry Russell Hitchcock, *Modern Architecture: Romanticism and Reintegration* (orig. pub. 1929; reprint, New York: Arno, 1972); Lewis Mumford, *Sticks and Stones: A Study of American Architecture and Civilization* (New York: W. W. Norton and Company, 1934); and Henry Russell Hitchcock, *The Architecture of H. H. Richardson and His Times* (New York: MoMA, 1936).

2. Sarah Bradford Landau and Carl W. Condit, *Rise of the New York Skyscraper 1865–1912* (New Haven, CT: Yale University Press, 1996), xii.

3. Carl Condit, *The Chicago School of Architecture: A History of Commercial and Public Buildings in the Chicago Area, 1875–1925* (Chicago: University of Chicago Press, 1964).

4. Carol Willis, *Form Follows Finance: Skyscrapers and Skylines in New York and Chicago* (New York: Princeton Architectural Press, 1995).

5. Mario Manieri-Elia, "Introduction: The Laissez-Faire City" and "Chicago in the 1890s and the Idea of the Fair of 1893," in *The American City: From the Civil War to the New Deal*, ed. Giorgio Ciucci, Francesco Dal Co, Mario Manieri-Elia, and Manfredo Tafuri, trans. Barbara Luigia La Penta (Cambridge, MA: MIT Press, 1979), 1–20.

6. Daniel Bluestone, *Constructing Chicago* (New Haven, CT: Yale University Press, 1991). See also Roberta Moudry, ed., *The American Skyscraper: Cultural Histories* (Cambridge: Cambridge University Press, 2005); and Charles Waldheim and Katarina Ruedi-Ray, eds., *Chicago Architecture: Histories, Revisions, Alternatives* (Chicago: University of Chicago Press, 2005).

7. See in particular Robert Bruegmann, *Holabird and Roche, Holabird and Root: An Illustrated Catalogue of Works, 1880–1940*, vol. 1 (New York: Garland, 1991), and *The Architects and the City: Holabird and Roche of Chicago 1880–1918* (Chicago: University of Chicago Press, 1997); Donald Hoffman, *The Architecture of John Wellborn Root* (Chicago: University of Chicago Press, 1973); Narciso Menocal, *Architecture as Nature: The Transcendentalist Idea of Louis Sullivan* (Madison: University of Wisconsin Press, 1981); Joseph Siry, *Carson Pirie Scott: Louis Sullivan and the Chicago Department Store* (Chicago: University of Chicago Press, 1988), and *The Chicago Auditorium Building: Adler and Sullivan's Architecture and the City* (Chicago: University of Chicago Press, 2002); Theodore Turak, "William Le Baron Jenney, Teacher," *Threshold: Journal of the University of Illinois at Chicago School of Architecture* (Fall 1991): 61–82, and "The Ecole Centrale and Modern Architecture: The Education of William Le Baron Jenney," *Journal of the Society of Architectural Historians* 29, no. 1 (March 1970): 40–47; David Van Zanten, *Sullivan's City: The Meaning of Ornament for Louis Sullivan* (New York: W. W. Norton, 2000), and "Sullivan to 1890," in *Louis Sullivan: The Function of Ornament*, ed. Wim de Wit (New York: W. W. Norton, 1986), 13–64; and Lauren S. Weingarden, "The Colors of Nature: Louis Sullivan's Architectural Polychromy and Nineteenth-Century Color Theory," *Winterthur Portfolio* 20, no. 4 (Winter 1985): 243–60, and "Naturalized Nationalism: A Ruskinian Discourse on the Search for an American Style of Architecture," *Winterthur Portfolio* 24, no. 1 (Spring 1989): 43–68.

8. These relationships are explored in David Van Zanten, "The Nineteenth Century: The Projecting of Chicago as a Commercial City and the Rationalization of Design and Construction," in *Chicago and New York: Architectural Interactions* (Chicago: Art Institute of Chicago, 1984); and John Zukowsky, ed., *Chicago Architecture 1872–1922: Birth of a Metropolis* (New York: Prestel, 1987).

9. William Cronon, *Nature's Metropolis: Chicago and the Great West* (New York: W. W. Norton and Co., 1991). The metaphor of the machine and the garden comes from Leo Marx's *The Machine in the Garden: Technology and the Pastoral Ideal in America* (orig. pub. 1964; reprint, London: Oxford University Press, 1967).

10. Carl Smith, *Urban Disorder and the Shape of Belief: The Great Chicago Fire, the Haymarket Bomb and the Model Town of Pullman* (Chicago: University of Chicago Press, 1995). See also Eric L. Hirsch, *Urban Revolt: Ethnic Politics in the Nineteenth-Century Chicago Labor Movement* (Berkeley and Los Angeles: University of California Press, 1998).

11. Siry, *The Chicago Auditorium Building.*

12. Richard Schneirov describes this transformation in detail in *Labor and Urban Politics: Class Conflict and the Origins of Modern Liberalism in Chicago, 1864–97* (Urbana: University of Illinois Press, 1998).

13. Harold L. Platt, *Shock Cities: The Environmental Transformation and Reform of Manchester and Chicago* (Chicago: University of Chicago Press, 2005).

14. Robert Prestiano has written the only history of the magazine, *The Inland Architect: Chicago's Major Architectural Journal, 1883–1908* (Ann Arbor, MI: UMI Research Press, 1973).

15. On the impact of media on architectural practice in the modern era, see Beatriz Colomina, introduction to *Architecture Production* (Princeton Architectural Press, 1988).

16. Peter Bacon Hales discusses the way photography was employed to catalogue, describe, and advertise American cities and to promote American business in *Silver Cities: Photographing American Urbanization, 1839–1939*, rev. and expanded 2nd ed. (Albuquerque: University of New Mexico Press, 2005). For contemporary street scenes, see also Larry A. Viskochil, *Chicago at the Turn of the Century in Photographs: 122 Historic Views from the Collections of the Chicago Historical Society* (New York: Dover Publications Inc., 1984).

17. Sullivan's essays are anthologized in *"Kindergarten Chats" and Other Writings* (orig. pub. 1918; reprint, New York: Dover, 1979), and in *Louis Sullivan: The Public Papers*, ed. Robert Twombley (Chicago: University of Chicago Press, 1988).

18. See Hoffman, *The Architecture of John Wellborn Root*, and his anthology of Root's writing, *John Wellborn Root: The Meanings of Architecture; Buildings and Writings* (New York: Horizon Press, 1967).

19. See in particular Sigfried Giedion, "The Chicago School," in *Space Time and Architecture, the Growth of a New Tradition* (orig. pub. 1941; reprint, Cambridge, MA: Harvard University Press, 1974), 385–88.

20. T. J. Jackson Lears, *No Place of Grace: Antimodernism and the Transformation of American Culture 1880–1920* (New York: Pantheon Books, 1981), xix.

21. Rosemarie Haag Bletter, "The Invention of the Skyscraper: Notes on Its Diverse Histories," *Assemblage* no. 2 (1987): 110–17.

22. John J. Flinn, *Chicago: The Marvelous City of the West; A History, An Encyclopedia* (Chicago: Standard Guide Co., 1892), 128. By 1896 the term was common enough to be used in a newspaper headline without quotation marks: "Tale of a Skyscraper. Curious Statistics about the Monadnock Building," *Chicago Daily Tribune*, February 24, 1896, p. 3.

23. "High Buildings," *California Architect and Building News* 14, no 10 (October 20, 1895): 110.

CHAPTER ONE

1. *Inland Architect and Builder* (1883–87). The magazine changed its name to the *Inland Architect and News Record* in 1887 and ceased publication in 1908. Robert Prestiano has written the only comprehensive study of the journal, *The Inland Architect: Chicago's Major Architectural Journal 1883–1908* (Ann Arbor, MI: UMI Research Press, 1973). Mary Woods describes the first architectural journals published in the United States in "The First American Architectural Journals: The Profession's Voice," *Journal of the Society of Architectural Historians* 48 (June 1989): 117–38.

2. The canonical works on the mythical idea of the West in American culture are Henry Nash Smith, *Virgin Land: The American West as Symbol and Myth* (orig. pub. 1950; reprint, Cambridge, MA: Harvard University Press, 1978); Marx, *The Machine in the Garden*; and Roderick

Nash, *Wilderness and the American Mind* (orig. pub. 1967; reprint, New Haven, CT: Yale University Press, 1982).

3. George W. Maher, "Originality in American Architecture," *Inland Architect* 10, no. 4 (October 1887): 34–35.

4. On early architectural education in the Midwest, see Anthony Alofsin, "Tempering the Ecole: Nathan Ricker at the University of Illinois, Langford Warren at Harvard," in *The History of History in American Schools of Architecture, 1865–1975*, ed. Gwendolyn Wright and Janet Parks (New York: Princeton Architectural Press, 1990), 73–88. Nathan Ricker's influence in architectural education is described in Mark L. Peish, "Nathan Clifford Ricker and the Beginnings of Midwestern Education," in *The Chicago School of Architecture: Early Followers of Sullivan and Wright* (New York: Random House, 1965), 7–15; Alan K. Laing, *Nathan Clifford Ricker, 1843–1924: Pioneer in American Architectural Education* (Urbana: University of Illinois Press, 1973); and Paul Kruty, "Nathan Clifford Ricker: Establishing Architecture at the University of Illinois," in *No Boundaries: University of Illinois Vignettes* (Urbana: University of Illinois Press, 2004), 3–14.

5. Arnold Lewis has described the European reaction to Chicago architecture in *An Early Encounter with Tomorrow: Europeans, Chicago's Loop, and the World's Columbian Exposition* (Urbana: University of Illinois Press, 1997).

6. "New Business Buildings of Chicago," *Builder* (Great Britain) 63, no. 2579 (July 9, 1892): 23–25. An American critic made a similar critique four years earlier: "Chicago: The Effect on the Profession of the Commercial Atmosphere of the City," *American Architect and Building News* 23 (February 18, 1888): 76.

7. Articles on this topic published in the *Inland Architect* include R. H. Vickers, "Development of American Architecture," vol. 3, no. 4 (May 1884): 50; Peter B. Wight, "The Development of New Phases of the Fine Arts in America," vol. 4, no. 4 (November 1884): 51–53 and vol. 4, no. 5 (December 1884): 63–65; Louis Sullivan, "Characteristics and Tendencies of American Architecture," vol. 6 (November 1885): 58–59; Isaac Hodgson, "Hints on a National Style of Architecture," vol. 8, no. 8 (December 1886): 71–72; "What Are the Present Tendencies of American Architecture?" vol. 9, no. 3 (March 1887): 23–26; S. Rowe, "American Architecture of the Nineteenth Century," vol. 10, no. 4 (October 1887): 33–34; Maher, "Originality in American Architecture"; W. W. Boyington, "Architecture at the Present Time as Compared with That of Fifty Years Ago," vol. 10, no. 5 (October 1887): 51; Henry Van Brunt, "Architecture in the West," vol. 14, no. 7 (December 1889): 78–80; Allen B. Pond, "The Evolution of an American Style," vol. 10, no. 9 (January 1888): 98; and Barr Ferree, "Architecture and Environment," vol. 15, no. 7 (December 1890): 72–74.

8. Louis Sullivan, *Autobiography of an Idea* (orig. pub. 1924; reprint, New York: Peter Smith, 1949), 200.

9. William Cronon's masterly book describes how Chicago was created out of the mythical idea of western expansion: *Nature's Metropolis*, 23–38, 46–54, 90–93. Harold L. Platt expands on Cronon's thesis to describe how patterns of land and energy use created a unique social geography in Chicago in *Shock Cities*, 78–134, 135–195. Both authors build on the scholarship of Leo Marx and Alan Trachtenberg, who described the mechanization and incorporation of the American West in a broader context: Marx, *The Machine in the Garden*, and Trachtenberg, *The Incorporation of America: Culture and Society in the Gilded Age* (New York: Hill and Wang, 1982). Janet L. Abu-Lughod provides a summary of these arguments in "Chicago Becomes Fordist," in *New York, Chicago, Los Angeles: America's Global Cities* (Minneapolis: University of Minnesota Press, 1991), 100–132.

10. On the process through which whites first shared, then took control of, the land around the Great Lakes, see Richard White, *The Middle Ground: Indians, Empires, and Republics in the Great Lakes Region, 1650–1815* (Cambridge: Cambridge University Press, 1991), 469–517; and Robert M. Owens, "Jeffersonian Benevolence on the Ground: The Indian Land Cession Treaties of William Henry Harrison," *Journal of the Early Republic* 22, no. 3 (Autumn 2002): 405–35.

11. John Reps describes the planning of these frontier towns in "Urban Planning on the Great Lakes Frontier," in *Town Planning in Frontier America* (Princeton, NJ: Princeton University Press, 1969), 344–81.

12. On the early planning of the city, see Alfred T. Andreas, *History of Chicago: From the Earliest Period to the Present Time*, 3 vols. (Chicago, 1884–88); Harold M. Mayer and Richard C. Wade,

Chicago: Growth of a Metropolis (Chicago: University of Chicago Press, 1969), 3–192; Reps, *Town Planning in Frontier America*, 376–81; and Robert A. Holland, *Chicago in Maps 1612–2002* (New York: Rizzoli, 2005), 38–129.

13. Karen Sawislak has described the postfire building regulations that hastened the physical segregation of Chicago into downtown business district and outlying suburbs in *Smoldering City: Chicagoans and the Great Fire, 1871–74* (Chicago: University of Chicago Press, 1995). See also Homer Hoyt, *One Hundred Years of Land Values in Chicago* (Chicago: University of Chicago Press, 1933), 101–4; and Carlos Eduardo Martin, "Constructing City," in "Riveting: Steel Technology, Building Codes and the Production of Modern Places" (Ph.D. diss., Stanford University, 1999), 223–30. Robert Fogelson discusses the rise of the downtown business district in America in "The Business District: Downtown in the Nineteenth Century," in *Downtown: Its Rise and Fall, 1880–1950* (New Haven, CT: Yale University Press, 2001), 9–43.

14. Homer Hoyt describes the rise of this type of building in Chicago in *One Hundred Years of Land Values in Chicago*, 128–95. See also Van Zanten, "The Nineteenth Century"; Bluestone, "A City under One Roof: Skyscrapers 1880–95," in *Constructing Chicago*, 104–51; and Bruegmann, *The Architects and the City*, 65–68.

15. Willis, *Form Follows Finance*, 19–34, 49–77.

16. "Building in Chicago," *Manufacturer and Builder* 9, no. 11 (November 1877): 250. The Montauk was described as the first skyscraper by the Chicago fireproofing expert Peter B. Wight in "The Fire-Proofing of High Office Buildings," *Brickbuilder* 2, no. 7 (July 1902): 145; by Theodore Starrett, a former employee of Burnham and Root, in "Daniel Hudson Burnham," *Architecture and Building* 44, no. 7 (July 1912): 281; and by the contractor Henry Ericsson in *Sixty Years A Builder: The Autobiography of Henry Ericsson* (Chicago: A. Kroch and Sons, 1942), 216. See also Frank A. Randall, *History of the Development of Building Construction in Chicago* (Urbana: University of Illinois Press, 1949), 5; and Condit, *The Chicago School of Architecture*, 68.

17. Condit, *The Chicago School of Architecture*, 51; Bruegmann, *The Architects and the City*, 68. In 1896 the *Chicago Tribune* described the Montauk as the first commercial building to be designed differently from its predecessors: "Old and New Chicago. Vast Changes That Have Taken Place in Architecture," *Chicago Daily Tribune*, May 24, 1896, p. 43.

18. On the urban impact of the Board of Trade, see H. T. Sudduth, "LaSalle St. Chicago," *Harper's Weekly* 34 (May 31, 1890), 346–47; Hoyt, *One Hundred Years of Land Values in Chicago*, 149–53; Randall, *History of the Development of Building Construction in Chicago*, 93–150; and Siry, *The Chicago Auditorium Building*, 82–87.

19. On the aesthetic and technical innovations of these buildings, see Randall, *History of the Development of Building Construction in Chicago*, 93–150; and Condit, *The Chicago School of Architecture*, 26–94. On their cultural symbolism, see Bluestone, *Constructing Chicago*, 104–51.

20. McLean wrote these words in anticipation of the demolition of the Woman's Temple on LaSalle and Monroe streets. Robert Craik McLean, "The Passing of the Woman's Temple," *Western Architect* 31, no. 1 (January 1922): 13–14.

21. Van Brunt, "Architecture in the West," 80. Van Brunt was born and educated in Boston, where he formed a partnership with William Ware in 1860. By the 1880s he was a respected practitioner and critic. After moving to Kansas City in 1887, where he designed railway stations for the Union Pacific Railroad Company, Van Brunt became an advocate for the strength, simplicity, and independence of western architecture.

22. Alan Colquhoun discusses the nineteenth-century origins of architectural regionalism in "The Concept of Regionalism," in *Postcolonial Space(s)*, ed. G. B. Nalbantoglu and C. T. Wong (New York: Princeton Architectural Press, 1997), 13–23.

23. The Western Association of Architects was formed as a subsidiary of the *Inland Architect* magazine in November 1884. In 1885 many of the same members formed the Illinois State Association of Architects. The WAA merged with the American Institute of Architects in 1889. See *Inland Architect and News Record* 14, no. 7 (December 1889): 71; Prestiano, *The Inland Architect*, 8–12.

24. On Daniel Burnham's life, see Peter. B. Wight, ed., *Daniel Hudson Burnham and His Associates* (New York, 1915); Charles Moore, *Daniel H. Burnham: Architect, Planner of Cities* (orig. pub. 1921; reprint, New York: Da Capo Press, 1968); and Thomas S. Hines, *Burnham of Chicago, Architect and Planner* (Chicago: University of Chicago Press, 1979).

25. Daniel Burnham, "Address on the Founding of the WAA," *Inland Architect and Builder* 4, extra number (November 1884): 10.

26. Robert Craik McLean, speech at banquet celebrating founding of the WAA, published in *Inland Architect and Builder* 4 (November 1884): 13.

27. On the influence of Spencer's ideas in America, see Richard Hofstadter, "The Vogue of Spencer," in *Social Darwinism in American Thought* (New York: George Braziller Inc., 1944), 31–50; and Robert M. Young, "Victorian Values: Herbert Spencer and 'Inevitable Progress,'" *History Today* 37 (August 1987): 18–22. Essays and articles on Spencer's philosophy were widely published in Chicago in the 1880s, especially in the *Dial, A Monthly Review and Index of Current Literature* (Chicago, 1880–93). See for example Kate Byam Martin, "A Text from Herbert Spencer," 3 (1882–83): 205; and W. H. Hudson, "Introduction to the Philosophy of Herbert Spencer," 17 (1894): 158.

28. Burnham, "Address on the Founding of the WAA," 11.

29. Sullivan, *Autobiography of an Idea*, 254–55. Barry Byrne, a member of Frank Lloyd Wright's studio from 1902 until 1908, remembered that "Herbert Spencer was read by all." H. Allen Brooks, *The Prairie School: Frank Lloyd Wright and His Midwest Contemporaries* (Toronto: University of Toronto Press, 1972), 79.

30. Herbert Spencer, "Use and Beauty" and "The Sources of Architectural Types" (1852), in *Essays: Scientific, Political and Speculative* (New York: D. Appleton and Co., 1910), 2:371–80.

31. On this wider movement, see Donald Drew Egbert, "The Idea of Organic Expression and American Architecture," in *Evolutionary Thought in America*, ed. Stow Persons (New Haven, CT: Yale University Press, 1950), 336–96; Philip Steadman, *The Evolution of Designs: Biological Analogy in Architecture and the Applied Arts* (New York: Cambridge University Press, 1979); and Caroline Van Eck, *Organicism in Nineteenth-Century Architecture: An Inquiry into Its Theoretical and Philosophical Roots* (Amsterdam: Architectura and Natura Press, 1994).

32. On Emerson and Thoreau and their influence on art and architecture, see F. O. Matthiessen, *American Renaissance: Art and Expression in the Age of Emerson and Whitman* (London: Oxford University Press, 1941); Vivian Hopkins, *Spires of Form: A Study of Emerson's Aesthetic Theory* (Cambridge, MA: Harvard University Press, 1951); and Charles Reid Metzger, *Emerson and Greenough: Transcendental Pioneers of an American Aesthetic* (Berkeley and Los Angeles: University of California Press, 1954).

33. Horatio Greenough, "American Architecture (1843–52)," in Greenough, *Form and Function: Remarks on Art, Design, and Architecture*, ed. Harold Small (Berkeley and Los Angeles: University of California Press, 1947), 51–68.

34. As part of an investigation into American architectural history for signs of incipient modernist, or "functionalist," tendencies, Edward De Zurko catalogued the more practical expressions of the organic philosophy in architecture, dating back to the late eighteenth century, in *Origins of Functionalist Theory* (New York: Columbia University Press, 1957). De Zurko especially notes the influence in America of the English architect Edward Lacey Garbett's *Rudimentary Treatise on the Principles of Design in Architecture* (London, 1850). See also Robert R. Winter, "Fergusson and Garbett in American Architectural Theory," *Journal of the Society of Architectural Historians* 17, no. 4 (1958): 25–31; Donald A. Ringe, "Horatio Greenough, Archibald Allison and the Functionalist Theory of Art," *College Art Journal* 19 (Summer 1960): 314–21; and Nikolaus Pevsner, "Bartholomew and Garbett," *Architectural Review* 152 (October 1972): 239–41.

35. William Le Baron Jenney, "Architecture," *Inland Architect and Builder* 1 (June 1883): 63.

36. On Jenney's role as a mentor, see Turak, "William Le Baron Jenney, Teacher."

37. Louis Sullivan, "What Is the Just Subordination, in Architectural Design, of Details to Mass?" *Inland Architect and Builder* 9, no. 5 (April 1887): 51–54.

38. On Ruskin's influence on American architecture, see Roger B. Stein, *John Ruskin and Aesthetic Thought in America, 1840–1900* (Cambridge, MA: Harvard University Press, 1967); Henry Russell Hitchcock, "Ruskin and American Architecture, or Regeneration Long Delayed," in *Concerning Architecture: Essays on Architectural Writers and Writing Presented to Nikolaus Pevsner*, ed. John Summerson (London: Penguin Press, 1968), 166–206; Michael W. Brooks, "Ruskin's Influence in America," in *John Ruskin and Victorian Architecture* (New Brunswick, NJ: Rutgers University Press, 1987), 277–97; and Weingarden, "Naturalized Nationalism."

39. John Ruskin, *The Stones of Venice*, vol. 1 (orig. pub. 1851; reprint, New York: Garland Publishing Inc., 1979), 58.

40. The *New Path* was modeled on the English journal the *Germ*, published by members of the Pre-Raphaelite Brotherhood. On the *New Path*, see Lawrence Wodehouse, "'New Path' and the American Pre-Raphaelite Brotherhood," *Art Journal* 25, no. 4 (Summer 1966): 351–54.

41. Leopold Eidlitz, "On Style," *Crayon* 5 (1858): 140.

42. On Downing's advocacy of the picturesque neo-Gothic style, see David Schuyler, *Apostle of Taste: Andrew Jackson Downing, 1815–1852* (Baltimore: Johns Hopkins University Press, 1996); and Judith K. Major, *To Live in the New World: A.J. Downing and American Landscape Gardening* (Cambridge, MA: MIT Press, 1997). On Downing's influence on the design of the American house and suburban landscape, see Vincent Scully, *The Shingle Style and the Stick Style* (orig. pub. 1955; reprint, New Haven, CT: Yale University Press, 1971), xxiii–lix; and Kenneth T. Jackson, *Crabgrass Frontier: The Suburbanization of the United States* (New York: Oxford University Press, 1985), 63–65.

43. On Wight, see Michael Thomas Klare, "Life and Architecture of P. B. Wight," (MA thesis, Columbia University, 1968); and Sarah Bradford Landau, *P. B. Wight, Architect, Contractor, and Critic, 1838–1925* (Chicago: Art Institute of Chicago, 1981).

44. Wight, "The Development of New Phases of the Fine Arts in America."

45. "What Are the Present Tendencies of American Architecture?"

46. Peter B. Wight, "Modern Architecture in Chicago," *Pall Mall* 18 (July 1899): 299.

47. John Wellborn Root, "A Few Practical Hints on Design," quoted in Harriet Monroe, *John Wellborn Root, A Study of His Life and Art* (orig. pub. Boston: Houghton, Mifflin and Co., 1896; reprint, Park Forest, IL: The Prairie School Press, 1966), 69.

48. Georges Teyssot discusses the racial ideology behind discussions of architectural "type" in the nineteenth century in "Norm and Type: Variations on a Theme," in *Architecture and the Sciences: Exchanging Metaphors*, ed. Antoine Picon and Alessandra Ponte (New York: Princeton Architectural Press, 2002), 140–73.

49. Translated extracts by Benjamin Bucknell were published in *American Architect and Building News* 1 (February 26, 1876). A book-form translation was published as *Habitations of Man in All Ages* in the same year.

50. "The History of Habitations," *Building Budget* (Chicago) 4, no. 12 (December 1888). The editors of the *Inland Architect* called for such an exhibition to be included in the World's Columbian Exposition. Editorial, *Inland Architect* 16, no. 5 (November 1890): 56. On Viollet-le-Duc's ideas of the racial bias of human progress, see Martin Bressani, "Notes on Violet-le-Duc's Philosophy of History: Dialectics and Technology," *Journal of the Society of Architectural Historians* 48 (December 1989): 327–50.

51. William Le Baron Jenney, "Architecture," *Inland Architect* 1 (March 1883): 18–20; (April 1883): 33–34; (May 1883): 48–50; (June 1883): 63; (July 1883): 76–78; vol. 2 (September 1883): 105–6; (October 1883): 117; (November 1883): 130–32; (December 1883): 144–46; (January 1884): 158; and vol. 3 (February 1884): 3. On Jenney's Parisian education, see Turak, "The Ecole Centrale and Modern Architecture."

52. Jenney, "Architecture," *Inland Architect* 3 (February 1884): 49.

53. Ibid., *Inland Architect* 1 (March 1883): 20.

54. Ibid., *Inland Architect* 1 (April 1883): 34.

55. On the sources of Semper's own ethnographic knowledge, see Harry Francis Mallgrave, "Semper, Klemm and Ethnography," *Lotus International* 109 (2001): 118–31. Recent scholars have speculated about the possible influence of Semper's theory of cladding on the design of terra-cotta-clad, steel-framed buildings in Chicago. However, on the evidence of the *Inland Architect*, it seems that his claim that textiles were the first architectural element was not widely known. The only reference to this idea is a brief comment by Root to the effect that the origins of architecture lay in "the shelter afforded by a bearskin . . . grandfather to a fig leaf." John Root, "Art of Pure Color," *Inland Architect* 1, no. 5 (June 1883): 66. On discussion of the Chicago curtain wall in relation to Semper, see Kenneth Frampton, "Frank Lloyd Wright and the Text-Tile Tectonic," in *Studies in Tectonic Culture: The Poetics of Construction in the Nineteenth and Twentieth Century Architecture* (Cambridge, MA: MIT Press, 1995), 93–120; Joseph Rykwert,

"Architecture Is All on the Surface: Semper and Bekleidung," *Rassegna* 20, no. 73 (1998): 20–29; and Richard Pommer and Barry Bergdoll, "American Architecture and the German Connection," *Kunstchronik* 42, no. 10 (October 1989): 570–74.

56. Frederick Baumann immigrated to Chicago from Germany in 1851 and was well established in practice by the 1870s. While his writing on the design of a system of isolated pier foundations is well known, his intellectual contribution has been only recently rediscovered. On Baumann's life and influence, see Roula Geraniotis, "German Architectural Theory and Practice in Chicago, 1850–1900," *Winterthur Portfolio* 21 (Winter 1986): 293–306. On Baumann's structural writings, see Roula Geraniotis and Gerald R. Larson, "Toward a Better Understanding of the Iron Skeleton Frame in Chicago," *Journal of the Society of Architectural Historians* 46, no. 1 (March 1987): 39–48.

57. Gottfried Semper, "Development of Architectural Style," trans. John W. Root and Fritz Wagner, part 1, *Inland Architect* 14, no. 7 (December 1889): 76, 78; part 2, vol. 12, no. 8 (January 1890): 92–94; part 3, vol. 15, no. 1 (February 1890): 5–6; part 4, vol. 15, no. 2 (March 1890): 32–33. Semper's ideas were also described in a series of essays published in Chicago by his former pupil, the English architect Lawrence Harvey. See Lawrence Harvey, "Style and Styles in Building," part 1, *Building Budget* (Chicago) 3, no. 9 (September 1887): 110–11; part 2, vol. 3, no. 10 (October 1887): 119–21; part 3, vol. 3, no. 11 (November 1887): 143–45; part 4, vol. 3, no. 12 (December 1887): 165–67; part 5, vol. 4, no. 1 (January 1888): 3–6. James Duncan Barry describes Harvey's dissemination of Semper's ideas in Britain in "The Legacy of Gottfried Semper: Studies in 'Späthistorimus'" (Ph.D. diss., Brown University, 1989), 191–213.

58. Semper, "Development of Architectural Style," part 1, 76.

59. Sidney Smith, toast at the WAA banquet, *Inland Architect*, vol. 4, extra no. (November 1884): 14.

60. On the centrality of the Aryan myth for some nineteenth-century advocates of western expansion, see Reginald Horsman, *Race and Manifest Destiny: The Origins of American Racial Anglo-Saxonism* (Cambridge, MA: Harvard University Press, 1981); Richard Slotkin, *The Fatal Environment: The Myth of the Frontier in the Age of Industrialization 1800–1890* (New York: Atheneum, 1985); and Andrew R. L. Cayton and Susan Gray, eds., *The American Midwest: Essays on Regional History* (Bloomington: Indiana University Press, 2001).

61. Theories of "Aryanism" abounded in the United States in this period. See for example W. M. Blackburn, "Aryan Literatures," *Dial* 1 (1880–81): 261; Isaac Taylor, *The Origin of the Aryans* (New York, 1890); Samuel Ball Plather, "The Aryan Question as It Stands Today: May Not the Original Home of the Indo-Germanic Peoples Have Been in Europe?" *New Englander and Yale Review*, no. 52 (March 1891): 205–35; Daniel G. Brinton, "The American Race," *Dial* 12 (1891–92), 27; Julius E. Olsen, "The Early Home of the Aryans," *Dial* 16 (1894): 235; and John Berry Haycroft, "Darwinism and Race Progress," *Dial* 19 (1895): 89.

62. Thomas G. Dyer, *Theodore Roosevelt and the Idea of Race* (Baton Rouge: Louisiana State University Press, 1980), 24–25.

63. Theodore Roosevelt, *The Winning of the West*, in *The Works of Theodore Roosevelt* (New York: C. Scribner Sons, 1926), 2:421.

64. Frederick Jackson Turner, "The Significance of the Frontier in American History. A Paper Read at the Meeting of the American Historical Association in Chicago, July 12, 1893" (1893). This essay is included in Frederick Jackson Turner, *The Significance of the Frontier in American History* (orig. pub. 1893; reprint, New York: Henry Holt and Co., 1920). On Turner's importance to the creation of the "frontier mythology," see Slotkin, *The Fatal Environment*, 41–43.

65. Strangely, Pond is here referring to the kind of open-plan residential dwelling that Frank Lloyd Wright would later make famous. Pond, "The Evolution of an American Style," 98.

66. Irving Pond, "Architectural Kinships," *Inland Architect* 17, no. 2 (March 1891): 22–23. This and other essays reflect the widespread popularity of physiognomic and phrenological studies in establishing the superiority of the white race in the mid- to late nineteenth century. On the nineteenth-century popularity of phrenology, see Horsman, "Superior and Inferior Races," in *Race and Manifest Destiny*, 116–38.

67. See for example Peter B. Wight, "H. H. Richardson," *Inland Architect* 7, no. 7 (May 1886): 59–61; A. J. Bloor, "Some Considerations on the Relations of H. H. Richardson to American

Architecture and Its Practice," *Building Budget* 2, no. 7 (July 1886): 80; Mariana Griswold Van Rensselaer, *H. H. Richardson and His Work* (orig. pub. 1888; reprint, New York: Dover, 1969); and A. O. Elzner, "A Reminiscence of Richardson," *Inland Architect* 20, no. 2 (September 1892): 15. On the eulogizing of Richardson in nineteenth-century American architecture journals, see Woods, "The First American Architectural Journals," 117–38. On Richardson's influence, see James F. O'Gorman, "America and H. H. Richardson," in *American Architecture: Innovation and Tradition*, ed. David G. DeLong, Helen Searing, and Robert A. M. Stern (New York: Rizzoli, 1986), 93–111; and Thomas J. Schlereth, "H. H. Richardson's Influence in Chicago's Midwest, 1872–1914," in *The Spirit of H. H. Richardson on the Midland Prairies*, ed. Paul Clifford Larson and Susan M. Brown (Ames: Iowa State University Press, 1988), 45–64. This idea of architectural genealogy lived on in twentieth-century architectural histories, where authors traced a heroic lineage from Richardson, through Root and Sullivan, to Frank Lloyd Wright. See for example Hitchcock, *Modern Architecture*; Mumford, *The Brown Decades*; Mumford, *Sticks and Stones*; Hitchcock, *The Architecture of H. H. Richardson and His Times*; and James F. O'Gorman, *Three American Architects: Richardson, Sullivan, and Wright, 1865–1915* (Chicago: University of Chicago Press, 1991).

68. John Wellborn Root, "The City House in the West," *Scribner's Magazine* 8, no. 4 (October 1890): 416–34.

69. Louis Sullivan, "Oasis," in *"Kindergarten Chats" and Other Writings*, 29.

70. On the specific connections between the architecture profession and the labor movement in Chicago, see Robert Twombly, "Cuds and Snipes: Labor at Chicago's Auditorium Building, 1887–89," *Journal of American Studies* 31 (1997): 79–101; and Siry, "Anarchist Counterculture, the Board of Trade Building, and Haymarket, 1885–86," in *The Chicago Auditorium Building*, 114–65. Sarah Watts describes the rhetoric surrounding the skyscraper in the labor movement in "Built Languages of Class: Skyscrapers and Labor Protest in Victorian Public Space," in Moudry, *The American Skyscraper*, 185–200. The literature on the American labor movement in the 1880s is extensive. Schneirov's *Labor and Urban Politics* and Hirsch's *Urban Revolt* deal with Chicago specifically. Other useful texts are Leon Fink, *Workingmen's Democracy: The Knights of Labor and American Politics* (Urbana: University of Illinois Press, 1983); and David R. Roediger and Philip S. Foner, *Our Own Time: A History of American Labor and the Working Day* (New York: Greenwood Press, 1989).

71. The most detailed ethnic maps were those made as a neighborhood survey of the Near West Side under the direction of Jane Addams and published as *Hull House Maps and Papers* (Chicago, 1895).

72. On the idea of "race" in American history, see Thomas F. Gossett, *Race: The History of an Idea in America* (Dallas: Southern Methodist University Press, 1963); Alexander Saxton, *The Rise and Fall of the White Republic: Class Politics and Mass Culture in Nineteenth-Century America* (London: Verso, 1990); David R. Roediger, *The Wages of Whiteness: Race and the Making of the American Working Class* (London: Verso, 1991); Theodore W. Allen, *The Invention of the White Race*, 2 vols. (London: Verso, 1994–97); Matthew Jacobsen, *Whiteness of a Different Color: European Immigrants and the Alchemy of Race* (Cambridge, MA: Harvard University Press, 1998); and Bruce Baum, "Racialized Nationalism and the Partial Eclipse of the 'Caucasian Race,' c.1840–1935," in *The Rise and Fall of the Caucasian Race: A Political History of Racial Identity* (New York: New York University Press, 2006), 118–61. David R. Roediger discusses the central role played by race in American labor history in a number of books. See in particular "In-Between Peoples: Race, Nationality, and the 'New Immigrant' Working Class," in *Colored White: Transcending the Racial Past* (Berkeley and Los Angeles: University of California Press, 2002). Herbert Gutman has discussed the importance of eastern European workers in the formation of working-class power in America during the nineteenth century in, "Class Composition and the Development of the American Working Class, 1840–90," in *Power and Culture: Essays on the American Working Class*, by Herbert Gutman and Ira Berlin (New York: Pantheon, 1987), 380–94. On the role of immigrants in Chicago, see Thomas Lee Philpott, *The Slum and the Ghetto: Immigrants, Blacks and Reformers in Chicago, 1880–1930* (orig. pub. 1978; reprint, Belmont, CA: Wadsworth, 1991). On the role of immigrants in American urban life in general, see David Ward, *Cities and Immigrants: A Geography of Change in Nineteenth-Century America* (New York: Oxford University

Press, 1971), and *Poverty, Ethnicity and the American City 1840–1925* (New York: Cambridge University Press, 1989).

73. See Noel Ignatiev, *How the Irish Became White* (New York: Routledge, 1995).

74. On the role played by German immigrants in the Chicago labor movement, see George A. Schilling, "A History of the Labor Movement in Chicago," in *The Life of Albert R. Parsons with Brief History of the Labor Movement in America*, ed. Lucy Parsons (Chicago: Lucy E. Parsons, 1903); Hartmut Keil and John B. Jentz, eds., *German Workers in Industrial Chicago, 1850–1910: A Comparative Portrait* (DeKalb: Northern Illinois University Press, 1983); and Hartmut Keil, ed., *German Workers' Culture in the United States, 1850 to 1920* (Washington, DC: Smithsonian Institution Press, 1988).

75. Schneirov, *Labor and Urban Politics*, 173–75.

76. James F. O'Gorman, "The Marshall Field Wholesale Store: Materials toward a Monograph," *Journal of the Society of Architectural Historians* (October 1978): 175–94. Joseph Siry describes the effects of labor actions on the construction of the Auditorium in *The Chicago Auditorium Building*. On the Chicago building trades disputes from 1883 to 1902, see James Beeks, *30,000 Locked Out! The Great Strike of the Building Trades in Chicago* (Chicago, 1887); Royal E. Montgomery, *Industrial Relations in the Chicago Building Trades* (Chicago: University of Chicago Press, 1927); Earl McMahon, *The Chicago Building Trades Council: Yesterday and Today* (Chicago: Chicago Building Trades Council, 1947); Schneirov, *Labor and Urban Politics*, 169–171; and Siry, *The Chicago Auditorium Building*, 85–89.

77. Editorial, *Inland Architect* 9, no. 8 (June 1887): 73–74; editorial, *Inland Architect* 10, no. 6 (November 1887): 62.

78. See Elliott Shore, Ken Fones, and James P. Darby, *The German-American Radical Press: The Shaping of a Left Political Culture, 1850–1940* (Chicago: University of Illinois Press, 1992). On the Parsonses' involvement with the *Alarm* and Spies's involvement with the *Arbeiter-Zeitung*, see James Green, *Death in the Haymarket: A Story of Chicago, the First Labor Movement, and the Bombing That Divided America* (New York: Pantheon, 2006), 91–92, 127, 134–37.

79. "To the Workingmen of America," *Alarm: A Socialist Weekly* 1, no. 5, November 1, 1884, p. 1. The IWPA was a precursor to the Industrial Workers of the World (IWW) founded in 1905, also known as the Wobblies. On the principles of the IWPA, see Schneirov, *Labor and Urban Politics*, 173.

80. Editorial, *Alarm: A Socialist Weekly*, special edition, October 8, 1886, p. 1.

81. The black flag was reportedly first flown in Chicago on November 27, 1884, at an anarchist demonstration. See Paul Avrich, *The Haymarket Tragedy* (Princeton, NJ: Princeton University Press, 1984), 144–45. Lucy Parsons carried the black flag at the front of the march on the Board of Trade, at its opening on April 28, 1885.

82. Editorial, *Alarm: A Socialist Weekly* 2, no. 7, November 14, 1885, p. 2. See also "Anarchism," *Alarm: A Socialist Weekly* 1, no. 5, November 1, 1884, p. 1.

83. "Anarchy vs. Government," *Alarm: A Socialist Weekly* 2, no. 4, August 22, 1885, p. 1.

84. Henry George, *Progress and Poverty: An Inquiry into the Cause of Industrial Depressions and of Increase of Want with Increase of Wealth; The Remedy* (New York: D. Appleton and Company, 1881).

85. "To the Workingmen of America," 1.

86. On the lives of Lucy and Albert Parsons, see Lucy Parsons, ed., *The Life of Albert R. Parsons* (Chicago, 1889); Philip S. Foner, ed., *The Autobiographies of the Haymarket Martyrs* (New York: Humanities Press, 1969); and Carolyn Ashbaugh, *Lucy Parsons: American Revolutionary* (Chicago: Charles H. Kerr, 1976).

87. Lucy Parsons, "Our Civilization. Is it Worth Saving?" *Alarm: A Socialist Weekly* 1, no. 28, August 8, 1885, p. 3.

88. Editorial, *Alarm: A Socialist Weekly* 1, no. 5, November 1, 1884, p. 1.

89. The *Alarm* quoted Proudhon's famous maxim, "property is theft" (vol. 1, no. 10, December 6, 1884, p. 1).

90. "Explosives: A Practical Lesson in Popular Chemistry; The Manufacture of Dynamite Made Easy," *Alarm: A Socialist Weekly* 1, no. 20, April 4, 1885, p. 1. See also "Dynamite: The Protection of the Poor against the Armies of the Rich," *Alarm: A Socialist Weekly* 1, no. 10, December 6, 1884; "Dynamite," *Alarm: A Socialist Weekly*, February 21, 1885; "How to Make Dynamite," *Alarm: A Socialist Weekly*, March 21, 1885; "Dynamite: Instructions Regarding Its Use and Operations," *Alarm:*

A Socialist Weekly, June 27, 1885; and "Voice from the People: Nitro-glycerine," *Arbeiter-Zeitung*, January 4, 1885.

91. The *Alarm* quoted from Sheridan's report of November 10, 1884, in which he warned of the dangers of dynamite. *Alarm: A Socialist Weekly* 1, no. 10, December 6, 1884, p. 1.

92. Chicago anarchists disowned this bomb. Instead, they blamed local Pinkerton agents, accusing them of planting a fake bomb to precipitate a violent showdown between the two sides. "Another Infernal Machine. A Curious Package Which Frightened Several Chicago People," *New York Times*, January 2, 1886, p. 1; "The Chicago Socialists. How They Have Prepared for a Threatened 'Revolution.' Bombs and Infernal Machines for Future Use—Plans for Fighting in the Streets and from the Housetops," *New York Times*, January 15, 1886, p. 1.

93. Lucy Parsons, "Word to Tramps," *Alarm: A Socialist Weekly* 1, no. 1, October 4, 1884, p. 1.

94. Thomas C. Hubka refers to the possible relationship between Richardson's defensive design and the unstable political climate of Chicago in "H. H. Richardson's Glessner House: A Garden in the Machine," *Winterthur Portfolio* 24, no. 4 (Winter 1989): 209–30.

95. Richard Sennett has explored the middle-class reaction to these events in "Middle-Class Families and Urban Violence: The Experience of a Chicago Community in the Nineteenth Century," in *Nineteenth-Century Cities: Essays in the New Urban History*, ed. Stephan Thernstrom and Richard Sennett (New Haven, CT: Yale University Press, 1969), 386–420.

96. On the Haymarket incident, see Michael J. Schaack, *Anarchy and Anarchists: A History of the Red Terror and the Social Revolution in America and Europe; Communism, Socialism and Nihilism in Doctrine and Deed; The Chicago Haymarket Conspiracy and the Detection and Trial of the Conspirators* (Chicago: F. J. Schulte and Co., 1889); Henry David, *The History of the Haymarket Affair: A Study in American Social-Revolutionary and Labor Movements* (New York: Russell and Russell, 1936); Avrich, *The Haymarket Tragedy*; C. Smith, *Urban Disorder and the Shape of Belief*, 101–46; and Green, *Death in the Haymarket*.

97. One of the accused, Louis Ling, committed suicide in prison before he could be hanged. Ling, Parsons, Spies, and the five others were not accused of perpetrating the actual bombing, merely of spreading radical language that may have prompted it. The bomb thrower was never identified.

98. Schaack, *Anarchy and Anarchists*, 25.

99. Sullivan's friend and mentor John Edelmann is the exception to the general disdain for socialist and anarchist politics among Chicago architects. Edelmann became interested in anarchist philosophy in Chicago in the 1880s. After a peripatetic career in the Midwest, he moved to New York in 1888, possibly to participate in Henry George's campaign for mayor. In 1892 he founded the Socialist League in New York, inspired by an English organization of the same name founded by William Morris in 1884. In 1893 he took over the editorship of *Solidarity*, an anarchist periodical. Donald Drew Egbert and Paul Sprague, "In Search of John Edelmann," *AIA Journal* 45 (February 1966): 35–41.

100. Editorial, *Inland Architect* 1, no. 4 (May 1883): 48. See also editorial, *Inland Architect* 5, no. 5 (June 1885).

101. Editorial, *Inland Architect* 7, no. 10 (June 1886). See also editorial, *Inland Architect* 9, no. 5 (April 1887).

102. Editorial, *Building Budget* 2, no. 8 (August 1886): 90.

103. Editorial, *Inland Architect* 7, no. 8 (May 1886).

CHAPTER TWO

1. Louis Sullivan, "The Tall Office Building Artistically Considered," *Inland Architect and News Record* 27 (February 1896): 32.

2. Sullivan's first biographer, Hugh Morrison, connected Sullivan's claim that he had "discovered" the true form of the skyscraper in 1890 to the Wainwright Building, and this association has stuck ever since. Hugh Morrison, *Louis Sullivan: Prophet of Modern Architecture* (orig. pub. 1935; reprint, New York: W.W. Norton, 1998), 115. The term "revolutionary architectural mode" comes from Sullivan, *Autobiography of an Idea*, 298. On Sullivan's life and early work on the

tall office building, see Robert Twombly, *Louis Sullivan: His Life and Work* (New York: Viking Penguin, 1986); William Jordy, "The Tall Buildings" and David Van Zanten, "Sullivan to 1890" in *Louis Sullivan: The Function of Ornament*, ed. Wim De Wit (New York: W. W. Norton, 1986), 13–64 and 65–156; Van Zanten, *Sullivan's City*; and Siry, *The Chicago Auditorium Building*.

3. Sullivan, "The Tall Office Building Artistically Considered," 32.

4. Editorial, *Building Budget* 2, no. 8 (August 1886): 90.

5. Howard Davis, *The Culture of Building* (New York: Oxford University Press, 1999). Davis describes architecture as the result of a complex set of social factors involving many different actors, not just architects and contractors.

6. The Chicago builder Henry Ericsson describes this process firsthand in *Sixty Years A Builder*. Richard Schneirov provides a detailed history of the changes to labor practice in late nineteenth-century Chicago in *Labor and Urban Politics*.

7. Schneirov, *Labor and Urban Politics*, 196.

8. In the 1880s a distinct category of ironworkers appeared, men who worked solely on building construction rather than bridges and railways. In Chicago three separate ironworkers' groups, each representing a different ethnicity (English-speaking, German, and Bohemian), merged in 1891 to form the Bridge and Construction Men's Union, the first structural ironworker's union. In 1892 the group merged with the ornamental ironworkers to form the Bridge and Structural Iron Workers. This group negotiated not only with the building contractors who employed them but also with unions representing the more traditional building trades. See Earl McMahon, *The Chicago Building Trades Council: Yesterday and Today* (Chicago: Chicago Building Trades Council, 1947).

9. On the reaction of Americans to the growing mechanization of labor in the second half of the nineteenth century, see Daniel T. Rodgers, "'Mechanicalized' Men," in *The Work Ethic in Industrial America, 1850–1920* (Chicago: University of Chicago Press, 1974), 65–93.

10. On the Chicago building trades disputes from 1883 to 1902, see Beeks, *30,000 Locked Out!*; Montgomery, *Industrial Relations in the Chicago Building Trades*; McMahon, *The Chicago Building Trades Council*; Schneirov, *Labor and Urban Politics*, 169–71; and Siry, *The Chicago Auditorium*, 85–89.

11. On the eight-hour movement, see David R. Roediger and Philip S. Foner, *Our Own Time: A History of American Labor and the Working Day* (New York: Greenwood Press, 1989).

12. Montgomery Schuyler, "Glimpses of Western Architecture: Chicago," *Harper's New Monthly Magazine* 83, no. 495 (August 1891): 395–406.

13. See for example editorial, *Inland Architect and Builder* 7, no. 8 (May 1886).

14. Editorial, *Inland Architect and Builder* 7, no. 10 (June 1886); "The Building Situation," *Inland Architect and Builder*, 7, no. 11 (July 1886): 101; and editorial, *Inland Architect and Builder* 9, no. 5 (April 1887).

15. Editorial, *Inland Architect and Builder* 9, no. 8 (June 1887): 73–74.

16. Editorial, *Inland Architect and Builder* 7, no. 5 (April 1886): 40.

17. The Building Contractors' Council passed a resolution that directly challenged the control of the Building Trades Council over the building industry, stating that they would no longer recognize many union rules, including the eight-hour day, and restrictions on the use of machinery or materials by specific trades. They also called for individual trade unions to withdraw their support for the BTC. As a result of this resolution, the Carpenters, Hod-Carriers and Building Laborers Unions struck in February of 1899. This strike snowballed until fifty thousand men walked off the job, causing huge disruptions to building in Chicago into 1900. Both sides attempted to win over public opinion and force their opponent to surrender. Starting in June the solidarity of the building trades unions started to break down, and the BCC was ultimately successful. See S. V. Lindholm, "Analysis of the Building-Trades Conflict in Chicago, from the Trades-Union Stand-Point," *Journal of Political Economy* 8, no. 3 (June 1900): 327–46; Ernest L. Bogart, "The Chicago Building Trades Dispute I," *Political Science Quarterly* 16, no. 1 (March 1901): 114–41; and Ernest L. Bogart, "The Chicago Building Trades Dispute II," *Political Science Quarterly* 16, no. 2 (June 1901): 222–47.

18. Robert Twombly has described Sullivan's involvement with the Western Association of Architects, beginning in 1885. He served on the executive committee from 1885 to 1891, and was secretary in 1886 and 1888. He was also a frequent member of committees on technical matters. Twombly, *Louis Sullivan*, 218–24.

19. Robert Twombly has pointed out the conflict between the social goals of the building's clients, the Auditorium Association, and those of the workmen responsible for building it in "Cuds and Snipes." On Sullivan's state of mind following the completion of the building, see Twombly, *Louis Sullivan*, 197. Joseph Siry documents the design and construction of the Auditorium in its social and urban context in *The Chicago Auditorium*.

20. On the development of the Chicago construction, see William Le Baron Jenney, "The Chicago Construction, or Tall Buildings on a Compressible Soil," *Inland Architect and News Record* 18 (November 1891): 41; Joseph Kendall Freitag, *Architectural Engineering with Special Reference to High Building Construction including Many Examples of Chicago Office Buildings* (New York: J. Wiley and Sons, 1906); W. A. Starrett, "Brick, Terracotta and the Ceramics—The Tectonic of Ceramic Masonry," in *Skyscrapers and the Men Who Built Them* (New York: Charles Scribner and Sons, 1928); Randall, *History of the Development of Building Construction in Chicago*, 11–19; Gerald R. Larson, "The Iron Skeleton Frame: Interactions Between Europe and the United States," in Zukowsky, ed., *Chicago Architecture 1872–192*, 39–56; Larson and Geraniotis, "Toward a Better Understanding of the Iron Skeleton Frame in Chicago," 39–47; Donald Friedman, "The Emergence of the Steel Skeleton Frame 1870–1904," in *Historical Building Construction, Design and Materials* (New York: W.W. Norton, 1995); and Sara E. Wermiel, *The Fireproof Building: Technology and Public Safety in the Nineteenth-Century American City* (Baltimore: Johns Hopkins University Press, 2000). On the value of the "Chicago construction" from a business perspective, see "Chicago's Big Buildings," *Chicago Sunday Tribune*, September 13, 1891, p. 25.

21. Ericsson's autobiography provides a firsthand account of this dramatic change in building practice. Ericsson, *Sixty Years a Builder*, 71.

22. Leopold Eidlitz, "Cast Iron and Architecture," *Crayon* vol. 6 (1859), 22.

23. Henry Van Brunt, "Cast Iron in Decorative Architecture," *Crayon* vol. 6 (1859), 15–20.

24. Ibid., 17.

25. On changes to the building trades in the United States in the second half of the nineteenth-century, see Martin, "Riveting"; and Grace Palladino, "Skyscrapers, Building Trades Councils, and the Rise of the Structural Building Trades Alliance," in *Skilled Hands, Strong Spirits: A Century of Building Trades History* (Ithaca, NY: Cornell University Press, 2005), 13–26.

26. William Le Baron Jenney, letter to the Regents of the University of Michigan, December 19, 1878; Chicago Historical Project, Microfilm Reel 11A, Scrapbook 2, Ryerson and Burnham Library, Art Institute of Chicago.

27. Jacques Hermant, "L'architecture aux Etats-Unis et a l'exposition universelle de Chicago," *L'Architecture* 7 (October 20, 1894): 341–46.

28. "New Business Buildings of Chicago."

29. Eidlitz, "Cast Iron and Architecture," 21.

30. On Johnson's iron storefronts in Chicago, see Ericsson, *Sixty Years A Builder*, 227; and Margot Gayle and Edmund Gillon Jr., "A Heritage Forgotten: Chicago's First Cast Iron Buildings," *Chicago History* 7, no. 1 (Summer 1978): 98–108. On early American cast-iron buildings, see William Fairburn, *On the Application of Cast and Wrought Iron to Building Purposes* (New York, 1854); James Bogardus (John W. Thomson), *Cast Iron Buildings: Their Construction and Advantages* (New York: J. W. Harrison, 1856); and William Fryer, "Iron Store Fronts," *Architectural Review* 1 (April 1869).

31. Clarence H. Blackall, "The Legitimate Design of the Architectural Casing for Steel Skeleton Structures," *American Architect and Building News* 66, no. 1249 (December 2, 1899): 78–80.

32. "Chicago's Great Masonic Temple—The Structure Will Be the Highest Building in the World," *Chicago Daily Tribune*, June 18, 1890, p. 5.

33. On the early use of aluminum in architecture, see Robert Friedel, "A New Metal! Aluminum in its Nineteenth-Century Context," and Denis P. Doorden, "From Precious to Pervasive: Aluminum and Architecture," in *Aluminum By Design*, ed. Sarah Nichol (New York: Harry N. Abrams, 2000), 58–83, 85–111. See also Margot Gayle, David W. Look, and John G. Waite, eds., *Metals in America's Historic Buildings* (Washington, DC: U.S. Department of the Interior, National Park Service, 1992), 84–86.

34. Nathan Clifford Ricker, "Possibilities for American Architecture," *Inland Architect and Builder* 6, no. 5 (November 1885): 62–63.

35. "The Chicago Architectural Sketch Club," *Inland Architect and News Record* 20, no. 5 (December 1892): 55. On the properties of aluminum, see also Professor Kedzie, "Alumina," *Inland Architect and News Record* 10, no. 3 (September 1887): 26. While Ricker and others enjoyed musing on the entirely hypothetical possibility of an aluminum-clad building, two Chicago architects and their clients were ready to act on it. As the Chicago *Economist* reported in 1892, Holabird and Roche's first proposal for the Champlain Building included drawings for an entirely aluminum-clad façade. *Economist*, September 10, 1892; reprinted in *Architecture and Building* (September 10, 1892): 128–29. A report on the Champlain by the New York critic Barr Ferree in *Engineering* magazine drew criticism from as far away as England, where the *Builder* condemned the design. Holabird and Roche abandoned the idea of aluminum cladding, and the Champlain was built with white terra-cotta walls. Aluminum was not used extensively until the 1930s, when it finally received its confirmation as the metal of the future in two New York buildings: William Van Alen's Chrysler Building (1928–30) and Shreve, Lamb and Harmon's Empire State Building (1931). On the early aluminum designs for the Champlain, see Bruegmann, *The Architects and the City*, 195–97.

36. In 1897 the Chicago-based Luxfer Prism Company arranged an architectural competition to promote the use of its horizontally ribbed prismatic glass tiles. The three prizewinning entries illustrating different aesthetic possibilities of the company's product were published in the *Inland Architect and News Record* in 1898. "Architectural Possibilities of the Luxfer Prism," *Inland Architect and News Record* 29 (July 1897): 18; "Awards in Luxfer Prism Competition," *Inland Architect and News Record* 32, no. 2 (September 1898): 15–16. As Dietrich Neumann has shown, the competition was an attempt on the part of the manufacturers to stress the decorative nature of the prismatic tiles, countering criticism that glass was an ugly, utilitarian product, only to be used when lighting could be achieved in no other way. Dietrich Neumann, "The Century's Triumph in Lighting: The Luxfer Prism Companies and Their Contribution to Early Modern Architecture," *Journal of the Society of Architectural Historians* 54, no. 1 (March 1995): 24–53. Thomas Leslie has argued that Chicago's early experiments with glass architecture coincided with a period in which plate glass was relatively inexpensive. After 1900 the material became more expensive, and better-quality electric light was available, negating the need for large plate-glass windows. Thomas Leslie, "Glass and Light: The Influence of Interior Illumination on the Chicago School," *Journal of Architectural Education* 58, no. 1 (September 2004): 13–23.

37. Freitag particularly notes terra-cotta's fireproof characteristics in *Architectural Engineering*.

38. On the use of terra-cotta cladding in American architecture, see Sharon S. Darling, "Architectural Terra-Cotta," in *Chicago Ceramics and Glass: An Illustrated History from 1871 to 1933* (Chicago: Chicago Historical Society, 1979), 161–98; Robert C. Mack, "The Manufacture and Use of Architectural Terra-Cotta in the United States," in *The Technology of Historic American Buildings*, ed. H. Ward Jandel (Washington, DC: Foundation for Preservation Technology, 1983), 117–50; Michael Stratton, "The Adoption of Terra-Cotta in North America," in *The Terra-Cotta Revival: Building Innovation and the Industrial City in Britain and North America* (London: Victor Gollancz, 1993), 142–63; and Susan Tunnick, *Terra-Cotta Skyline: New York's Architectural Ornament* (New York: Princeton Architectural Press, 1997).

39. "Review of Chicago Building for 1883," *Inland Architect and Builder* 2, no. 6 (January 1884): 155.

40. On the assembly of terra-cotta façades, see National Terra Cotta Society, *Architectural Terra Cotta: Standard Construction* (New York: National Terra Cotta Society, 1914); and Donald Friedman, "Anchoring Systems for Architectural Terra Cotta in Curtain-Wall Construction," *APT Bulletin* 32, no. 4 (2001): 17–21.

41. Clarence H. Blackall, "On the Use of Colored Terracotta," *Brickbuilder* 1 (1892): 12.

42. George M. R. Twose, "Steel and Terra Cotta Buildings in Chicago," *Brickbuilder* 3 (1894): 2.

43. George M. R. Twose, "The Use of Terra-Cotta in Modern Buildings," *Engineering*, no. 8 (October 1894–March 1895): 203–19.

44. William Le Baron Jenney wondered if the architect would lose control of the exterior design of his buildings if he let the stock designs of the tile and brick manufacturers take too large a role. William Le Baron Jenney, "A Few Practical Hints," address delivered to the Chicago Architectural Sketch Club, January 1889, excerpted in *Industrial Chicago*, vol. 2, *The Building Interests* (Chicago: Goodspeed Publishing Co., 1891), 609–21.

45. On the Tacoma, see Bruegmann, *Holabird and Roche, Holabird and Root*, 1:11–21.

46. Edward A. Renwick, a Holabird and Roche employee, made this claim in a 1932 manuscript. See Thomas Tallmadge, *Architecture in Old Chicago* (Chicago: University of Chicago Press, 1941); and Bruegmann, *Holabird and Roche*, 12, 20.

47. *Chicago Daily Tribune*, January 13, 1899, p. 2.

48. John Root had described much the same idea in "Architectural Ornamentation," *Inland Architect and Builder* 5 (April 1885): 54–55.

49. Mary N. Woods has described this rhetorical opposition in *From Craft to Profession: The Practice of Architecture in the Nineteenth Century* (Berkeley and Los Angeles: University of California Press, 1999).

50. On the modeling of terra-cotta ornament in this period, see Ronald E. Schmitt, *Sullivanesque: Urban Architecture and Ornamentation* (Urbana: University of Illinois Press, 2002), especially chapters 5 and 6; and George A. Berry and Sharon Darling, *Common Clay: A History of the American Terra Cotta Corporation, 1881–1966* (Chicago: TCR Corporation, 2004).

51. Frank Lloyd Wright, "The Art and Craft of the Machine" (1901) in *Frank Lloyd Wright Collected Writings*, vol. 1, *1894–1930*, ed. Bruce Brooks Pfeiffer (New York: Rizzoli, 1992), 65.

52. The issues of architecture and design in the industrial era were addressed more directly by the Chicago Arts and Crafts Society, founded in 1897, and the Industrial Art League, founded in 1899. Sullivan was one of the trustees of the league, but apparently not an active participant. On the Arts and Crafts movement in Chicago, see H. Allen Brooks, "Chicago Architecture: Its Debt to the Arts and Crafts," *Journal of the Society of Architectural Historians* 30 (December 1971): 312–16; Bruce R. Kahler, "Joseph Twyman and the Arts and Crafts Movement in Chicago," in *Selected Papers in Illinois History, 1981*, ed. Bruce D. Cody (Springfield: Illinois State Historical Society, 1982), 60–69; and Eileen Boris, *Art and Labor: Ruskin, Morris, and the Craftsman Ideal in America* (Philadelphia: Temple University Press, 1986), 45–52. Frank Lloyd Wright, in particular, took Sullivan's ideas and gave them a social reality, fulfilling the same role in relation to Sullivan as Morris did to Ruskin. As Lauren Weingarden has noted, Morris bought Ruskin's craft values out of the realm of the spiritual and transcendental and into the realm of everyday human experience. Lauren Weingarden, "Aesthetics Politicized: William Morris to the Bauhaus," *Journal of Architectural Education* 38, no. 3 (Spring 1985): 8–13.

53. Walt Whitman, *Democratic Vistas* (Washington, 1871).

54. Sullivan, *"Kindergarten Chats" and Other Writings*, 97.

55. Louis Sullivan, *Democracy: A Man Search* [1905–8], with an introduction by Elaine Hedges (Detroit: Wayne State University Press, 1961), 311.

56. Ibid., 106.

57. Louis Sullivan, "Remarks on an Architect's Code of Ethics" (1888), in *Louis Sullivan: The Public Papers*, ed. Robert Twombly (Chicago: University of Chicago Press, 1988), 37–38.

58. Louis Sullivan, "Sub-Contracting" (1890), in *Louis Sullivan: The Public Papers*, 67–72.

59. Sullivan criticized business as "undermin[ing] the vital constitution of the multitudes," and the labor leader for being a money-grubbing tyrant whose "prime thought centers on wages, that is, money; his second thought upon how little he can give in return, that is, how much money he can steal" (Sullivan, *Democracy: A Man Search*, pp. 244–47, 315).

60. This idea appeared as early as his 1894 essay "Emotional Architecture as Compared with Intellectual: A Study in the Subjective and Objective," an address to the American Institute of Architects, and then reappeared in all his subsequent writing. *Inland Architect and News Record* 24 (November, 1894): 32–34.

61. "Plans for the Odd Fellows Temple," *Chicago Daily Tribune*, September 6, 1891, p. 29; "Chicago—Proposed Odd Fellows Temple," *Graphic* vol. 5 (December 19 1891), 404; Donald Hoffmann, "The Setback Skyscraper City of 1891: An Unknown Essay by Louis H. Sullivan," *Journal of the Society of Architectural Historians* 29, no. 2 (May 1970): 181–87.

62. Louis Sullivan, "The High Building Question," *Graphic* 5 (December 19, 1891): 405.

63. Daniel Bluestone discussed this transition in "Sullivan's Chicago: From 'Shirt-Front' to Alley to All-Round Structures," paper delivered at "Sullivan at 150 Symposium," Chicago History Museum, October 13–15, 2006.

64. On Sullivan's involvement with the Municipal Art League, see Twombly, *Louis Sullivan*, 363. Late in his life, Sullivan's disdain for the goals of social reformers became clear in his dismissal of his former client Ferdinand Peck, chief patron of the Auditorium Building, for his belief that it was the role of the educated middle classes to take care of the "peepul." Sullivan, *Autobiography of an Idea*, 299.

65. Sullivan, *Autobiography of an Idea*, 288–92.

66. Van Zanten, *Sullivan's City*, 133–53.

67. The *Alarm* often quoted Ruskin and Morris with approval.

68. Sullivan, "An Oasis," in *Kindergarten Chats*, 29. As Alan Trachtenberg has pointed out, Sullivan's understanding of the way in which business operated was naïve—he did not see that the economic success of the city was due to the corporation, not the actions of individuals. Trachtenberg, *The Incorporation of America*, 81.

69. Andrew Carnegie, "Wealth," *North American Review* 148 (June 1889): 653–64.

70. However, the unique aesthetic expression of that potential was obviously more important to Sullivan than it was to Carnegie, who employed conformist historical styles in his philanthropic project, the Carnegie Library buildings. See Abigail A. Van Slyck, *Free to All: Carnegie Libraries and American Culture 1890–1920* (Chicago: University of Chicago Press, 1995).

CHAPTER THREE

1. Root, "Architectural Ornamentation," 54.

2. "Commercial Architecture," *Industrial Chicago*, 1:183.

3. James F. O'Gorman has noted that Richardson may have been influenced in his design for the Marshall Field Wholesale Store by buildings Burnham and Root were erecting nearby, the McCormick Warehouse in particular. Situated away from the main business district, west of downtown and adjacent to the Chicago River, the McCormick Warehouse was simple in form. Its chief decoration was a series of large arches organizing groups of three windows, with no ornament on the roofline except for a simple cornice. O'Gorman discusses conversations Richardson had with Root when he visited Chicago in 1885. O'Gorman, "The Marshall Field Wholesale Store," 188.

4. The Rookery received particular praise from the Boston-based architect and critic Clarence H. Blackall. Blackall was less biased toward Chicago architecture than other easterners, since he had studied at University of Illinois under Nathan Clifford Ricker before attending the Ecole des Beaux-Arts in Paris. Clarence H. Blackall, "Notes on Travel—Chicago," *American Architect and Building News* 22, no. 626 (December 24 and 31, 1887): 299–300, 313–14. On the rise of the "commercial style" in Chicago, see also Van Zanten, "The Nineteenth Century," 34–38.

5. Daniel Bluestone discussed the desire to avoid party walls in "Sullivan's Chicago," a talk given in 2006 at the Chicago History Museum.

6. On the real estate developer Peter C. Brooks and his Chicago agent, Owen F. Aldis, see Miles L. Berger, *They Built Chicago: Entrepreneurs Who Shaped a Great City's Architecture* (Chicago: Bonus Books, 1992), 29–48. See also Owen F. Aldis and Peter C. Brooks, "Narrative Summary of Correspondence, 1879–1920," Archives and Manuscript Department, Chicago History Museum.

7. Hoffman, *The Architecture of John Wellborn Root*, 156.

8. On the design and construction of the building, see "Notes on the Monadnock" made by Aldis and Co., managers of the building (October 1957), and "Monadnock Building, Miscellaneous Pamphlets—Summary of Information on the Monadnock Building, 53 West Jackson Boulevard, Chicago Illinois" (April 30 1970), both in the Archives and Manuscript Department of the Chicago History Museum; and Hoffman, *The Architecture of John Wellborn Root*, 155–76.

9. *Building Budget* 1, no. 8 (October 1885): 75.

10. *Inland Architect and News Record* 14, no. 5 (November 1889), unpaginated plate.

11. The reason the Monadnock had at first two, then four names is that it really was four separate buildings on four separate titles: the Monadnock, Kearsage, Katahdin, and Wachusett. The

four buildings were owned by different branches of the Brooks family, each of whom could sell their portion at any time without consulting the others. All but one of the names was abandoned in the late 1890s, and the four-way split was discontinued in the early 1920s when no family member had sold his property. The only architectural traces of this division are the separate entrances to each building on Dearborn Street, and the letters *M*, *K*, and *W*, which can still be found on some doorknobs, indicating the part of the building the offices were in.

12. Bluestone, "Sullivan's Chicago."

13. Hoyt, *One Hundred Years of Land Values in Chicago*, 153.

14. This effect can be seen by current visitors. The original interior partitions were recreated during the Monadnock's 1979–89 renovation.

15. Aldis and Co., "Notes on the Monadnock." On Holabird and Roche's addition see "New Addition to the Monadnock Building," *Architectural Record* 5 (July–September 1895): 76; Bruegmann, *Holabird and Roche, Holabird and Root*, 93–95; and Bruegmann, *The Architects and the City*, 118–20.

16. "The new building is to be much more ornate," noted the *Chicago Daily Times* as the foundation was being laid. "Among Architects and Builders. What the Addition to the Monadnock Will Look Like," *Chicago Daily Times*, September 15, 1892, p. 30.

17. "Chicago Architectural Styles,"*Industrial Chicago*, 1:70.

18. "Commercial Architecture," 1:170.

19. Ibid., 1:215.

20. Hoffman, *The Architecture of John Wellborn Root*, 166–67.

21. Joseph Kirkland compared Chicago to Cairo in *The Story of Chicago* (Chicago: Dibble Publishing Co., 1892), 227.

22. Semper, "Development of Architectural Style," trans. Root and Wagner, part 4, pp. 32–33.

23. M. A. Lane, "High Buildings of Chicago," *Harper's Weekly* 35 (October 31, 1891), 854.

24. Lewis, *An Early Encounter with Tomorrow*, 195.

25. "Chicago," *American Architecture*, vol. 36 (May, 1892), 134.

26. Barr Ferree, "Chicago—The Buildings," part 2, *Architecture and Building* (January 9, 1892): 17.

27. "New Business Buildings of Chicago."

28. Robert D. Andrews, "The Broadest Use of Precedent," *Architectural Review* 2, no. 4 (May 15, 1893): 34–35.

29. Montgomery Schuyler, "D. H. Burnham and Co." (1896), in *"American Architecture," and Other Writings*, ed. William H. Jordy and Ralph Coe (Cambridge, MA: Harvard University Press, Belknap Press, 1961), 2:411. This essay was originally published as "Architecture in Chicago: D. H. Burnham and Co.," no. 2, part 2 of the Great American Architects series, *Architectural Record* (February 1896): 49–72.

30. Monroe, *John Wellborn Root*, 141.

31. Schuyler, "D. H. Burnham and Co.," 410. Moore, *Daniel H. Burnham*, 1:30; A. N. Rebori, "The Work of Burnham and Root, D. H. Burnham and Co., and Graham, Burnham and Co.," *Architectural Record* 38, no. 1 (July 1915): 32–168.

32. Edward S. Hammett, "The Building and the Designing of the 'Skyscraper,'" *American Architect and Building News* (November 1905): 158–60.

33. Berger, *They Built Chicago*, 29–46.

34. Although Jenney had business partners at various times, including Sanford Loring and William Mundie, his work is not usually described as the product of a partnership.

35. "Tale of a Skyscraper." "Most Remarkable Postal District in the World: Four Carriers Who Never Get Out of One Chicago Building," *Chicago Daily Tribune*, July 8, 1900, p. 49.

36. Lawrence Harvey, "Style and Styles in Building: First Lecture," part 3, *Building Budget* 3, no. 11 (November 1887): 143–45.

37. Ibid., 144.

38. Barr Ferree, "Chicago," part 1, *Architecture and Building* (January 2, 1892): 11.

39. Root, "Architectural Ornamentation," 54.

40. William Le Baron Jenney, "French Architecture in America," *Inland Architect and Builder* 3, no. 3 (April 1884): 38.

41. Jenney, "A Few Practical Hints," 2:618–19.

42. "New Business Buildings of Chicago."

43. Henry Van Brunt, "John Wellborn Root," *Inland Architect and News Record* 16, no. 8 (January 1891): 87.

44. Leopold Eidlitz (1823–1908) was educated in Vienna and Berlin. He came to New York in 1843, where he worked for Richard Upjohn and later collaborated with H. H. Richardson. See Montgomery Schuyler, "Leopold Eidlitz," part 1, *Architectural Record*, vol. 24 (September 1908): 164–79; part 2, vol. 24 (October 1908): 277–92; and part 3, vol. 24 (November 1908): 365–78; the introduction to Schuyler, *"American Architecture," and Other Writings*, 1:7–22; and Kathryn E. Holliday, *Leopold Eidlitz: Architecture and Idealism in the Gilded Age* (New York: W. W. Norton, 2008).

45. Leopold Eidlitz, *The Nature and Function of Art, More Especially of Architecture* (New York: A. C. Armstrong and Son, 1881), 113–14. Adrian Forty discusses Eidlitz's writing in relation to European theories of empathy in *Words and Buildings: A Vocabulary of Modern Architecture* (London: Thames and Hudson, 2000), 278.

46. John Wellborn Root, "Broad Art Criticism," *Inland Architect and News Record* 11 (February 1888): 3–5.

47. Heinrich Wölfflin, "Prologomena to the Psychology of Architecture" (1886), in *Empathy, Form and Space: Problems in German Aesthetics 1873–93*, ed. Harry Francis Mallgrave and E. Ikonomou (Santa Monica, CA: Getty Center, 1994), 149–90; and Heinrich Wölfflin, *Renaissance and Baroque* (1888), trans. K. Simon (London: Collins, 1984).

48. The *Open Court* was founded in Chicago in 1886 by the German-American Edward Carl Hegeler with a view to reconciling philosophy and religion. Under the editorship of Paul Carus, the magazine contained articles on religion, philosophy, and social issues. Produced by the same publishers starting in 1890, the *Monist* focused on more technical literature.

49. Review of Theodor Lipps, *Raumästhetik und geometrisch-optische täuschungen* (Leipzig, 1897), the *Monist* (Chicago) 8 (1897–98): 298–300.

50. Marshall lectured on aesthetics at Columbia and Princeton universities, as well as at conferences of the American Institute of Architects. Henry Rutgers Marshall, "The Science of Aesthetics," *Inland Architect and News Record* 16, no. 4 (October 1890): 38–40; Henry Rutgers Marshall, "The Science of Aesthetics (a paper read before the convention of the American Institute of Architects, Washington, October 31, 1890)," *Building Budget* (Chicago) 6, no. 10 (October 1890): 124–27. See also Henry Rutgers Marshall, "The Education of an Architect," *Architectural Record* 5 (July–September 1895): 82–92; *Aesthetic Principles* (New York: Macmillan and Co., 1895); and "Expression in Architecture," *Architectural Record* 9 (January 1900): 254–67.

51. Georg Simmel, "Die Grossstadt und das Geistesleben" (1903). Translated by Kurt Wolff as "The Metropolis and Mental Life," in *The Sociology of Georg Simmel* (New York: Free Press, 1950), 409–24. On Simmel's reading of city life in relation to contemporary theories of architecture and urbanism, see Anthony Vidler, "Agoraphobia: Psychopathologies of Urban Space," and "Spaces of Passage: The Architecture of Estrangement: Simmel, Kracauer and Benjamin," in *Warped Space: Art, Architecture, and Anxiety in Modern Culture* (Cambridge, MA: MIT Press, 2000), 25–50, 65–80.

52. Mario Manieri-Elia has suggested something similar in Ciucci et al., *The American City*, 6.

53. On the relationship between art nouveau and Jugendstil and contemporary urban life, see Siegfried Wichmann, *Jugendstil Art Nouveau: Floral and Functional Forms* (Boston: Little, Brown, 1984); and Debora L. Silverman, *Art Nouveau in Fin-De-Siecle France: Politics, Psychology, and Style* (Berkeley and Los Angeles: University of California Press, 1992).

54. Theodore Starrett, "John Wellborn Root," *Architecture and Building* 44, no. 11 (November 1912): 431.

55. *Economist* 2 (August 17, 1889): 717.

56. Monroe, *John Wellborn Root*, 141.

57. *Building Budget* 1, no. 4 (June 1885): 35. Root had also originally intended the Montauk Block to have colored glass windows. The building's developer, Peter C. Brooks, objected: "colored glass is mere nonsense—a passing fashion, inappropriate in a mercantile building and worse than all, it obstructs light. Strike it all out." Owen Aldis and Peter Brooks, correspondence, Chicago History Museum; Quoted in Berger, *They Built Chicago*, 33.

58. John Root, "Art of Pure Color," *Inland Architect and Builder* 1, no. 5 (June 1883): 66–67; 1, no. 6 (July 1883): 80, 82; 2, no. 1 (August 1883): 89; 2, no. 2 (September 1883): 106. On Root's essay, see Weingarden, "The Colors of Nature," 247–49.

59. "Chicago Art Guild," *Inland Architect and Builder* 1, no. 3 (April 1883): 36–37.

60. Gustave Kahn, "The Aesthetic of Polychrome Glass" (1886), reprinted in *Art in Theory 1815–1900*, ed. Charles Harrison, Paul Wood, and Jason Gaiger (London: Blackwell, 1998), 1011–14.

61. Root, "Art of Pure Color," 66.

62. Jones, *The Grammar of Ornament*, 7.

63. George Field, *Rudiments of the Painter's Art; or, A Grammar of Colouring* (London: John Weale, 1858), 36.

64. Max Nordau, *Degeneration* (orig. pub. 1895; reprint, Lincoln: University of Nebraska Press, 1968), 15–30. On Max Nordau and pathologies of perception as a symptom of cultural degeneration, see Jonathan Crary, *Suspensions of Perception: Attention, Spectacle and Modern Culture* (Cambridge, MA: MIT Press, 1999), 16–17. Nineteenth-century psychologists like Francis Galton, Alfred Binet, and Jean-Martin Charcot were especially interested in an abnormality called "color association," "color hearing," or "pseudochromoaesthesia," where people associate numbers, sounds, or shapes with particular colors. Binet and Charcot defined synaesthesia and other color pathologies as symptoms of hysteria and insanity. Francis Galton, *Inquiries into the Human Faculty and Its Development* (London: Macmillan, 1883), 105–14. On "color hearing" in nineteenth-century psychology, see John Gage, *Color and Culture: Practice and Meaning from Antiquity to Abstraction* (Boston: Little, Brown and Co., 1993), 209; and Michael Hauskeller, "Color as a Subject of Psychology," *Daidalos* 51 (March 15, 1994): 102–9. This concept was reported in the American press in articles such as Harold Wilson, MD, "The Relation of Color to the Emotions," *The Arena* (Boston) 19 (January–June 1898): 810–27.

65. The mystical strain of late nineteenth- and early twentieth-century American architecture is most apparent in the work of Louis Sullivan's protégé, the Rochester, New York–based architect Claude Bragdon. A devoted Theosophist, Bragdon attempted to create a new ornament for modern architecture using four-dimensional geometry, which he associated with human evolution to a higher plane of consciousness. On Bragdon see Linda Henderson, "Mysticism, Romanticism and the Fourth Dimension," in *The Spiritual in Art: Abstract Painting 1890–1985*, ed. Maurice Tuchman (Los Angeles: Los Angeles County Museum of Art, 1986), 219–38, and *The Fourth Dimension and Non-Euclidean Geometry in Modern Art* (Princeton, NJ: Princeton University Press, 1983), 186–95; and Jonathan Massey, "Architecture and Involution: Claude Bragdon's Progressive Ornament" (Ph.D. diss., Princeton University, 2001).

66. Both Burnham and Root were active in the New Church in Chicago. Burnham's parents sent him to a New Church school, and he was a committed member all his life. On the importance of Swedenborgianism to Burnham's life and work, see Frank Sewall, "Daniel Hudson Burnham," *The New Church Messenger* (July 3, 1912): 12–13. Irving D. Fisher describes Burnham's 1909 *Plan of Chicago* in relation to Emanuel Swedenborg's description of the heavenly city in "An Iconography of City Planning: The Chicago City Plan," in *Emanuel Swedenborg, A Continuing Vision: A Pictorial Biography and Anthology of Essays and Poetry*, ed. Robin Larsen, Stephen Larsen, James F. Lawrence, and William Ross Woofenden (New York: Swedenborg Foundation, Inc., 1988), 231–36, 245–62. Claiming that the early death of his first wife strengthened Root's faith, Harriet Monroe was convinced of the continued importance of Swedenborgianism throughout his life. Harriet Monroe, *A Poet's Life: Seventy Years in a Changing World* (New York: Macmillan, 1938), 110.

67. On Swedenborgianism in America, see Marguerite Beck Block, *The New Church in the New World: A Study of Swedenborgianism in America* (New York: Octagon Books, 1968).

68. John Root, "Faith and Reason," ca. 1876, quoted in Monroe, *John Wellborn Root*, 57.

69. On Inness's Swedenborgianism, see Sally M. Promey, "The Ribband of Faith: George Inness, Color Theory and the Swedenborgian Church," *The American Art Journal* 26, nos. 1 and 2 (1994): 45–65; Michael Quick, "George Inness: The Spiritual Dimension," in *George Inness: Presence of the Unseen* (Montclair, NJ: Montclair Museum, 1994), 29–33; and Eugene Taylor, "The Interior Landscape: George Inness and William James on Art from a Swedenborgian Point of View," *Archives of American Art Journal* 37, nos. 1 and 2 (1997): 2–10.

70. Root, "Art of Pure Color," 66. In opposition to these painters, he described the American Pre-Raphaelite painter William Richards as an artist of form and detail rather than color.

71. Root, "Broad Art Criticism."

72. Root, "Art of Pure Color," 82.

CHAPTER FOUR

1. Daniel Bluestone, "A City under One Roof: Skyscrapers 1880–95," in *Constructing Chicago*, 123–28.

2. "Chicago's Big Buildings," 25.

3. On the popularity of fraternal organizations in nineteenth-century America, see Wilson Carey McWilliams, *The Idea of Fraternity in America* (Berkeley and Los Angeles: University of California Press, 1973); Mark C. Carnes, *Secret Ritual and Manhood in Victorian America* (New Haven, CT: Yale University Press, 1989); Mary Anne Clawson, *Constructing Brotherhood: Class, Gender and Fraternalism* (Princeton: Princeton University Press, 1989); and Jason Kaufman, *For the Common Good? American Civic Life and the Golden Age of Fraternity* (New York: Oxford University Press, 2002). Mark A. Tabbert provides the official illustrated history of the American Freemasons in *American Freemasons: Three Centuries of Building Communities* (Lexington, MA: National Heritage Museum; New York: New York University Press, 2005). Lynn Dumenil describes the popularity of Freemasonry in late nineteenth-century and early twentieth-century America in *Freemasonry and American Culture 1880–1930* (Princeton, NJ: Princeton University Press, 1984). William D. Moore presents a comprehensive view of American Masonic architecture in *Masonic Temples: Freemasonry, Ritual, Architecture and Masculine Archetypes* (Knoxville: University of Tennessee Press, 2006).

4. Clawson, "Fraternal Orders in Nineteenth Century America," in *Constructing Brotherhood*, 111–44.

5. On late nineteenth-century American women's organizations, see Clawson, "The Rise of the Women's Auxiliary," ibid., 178–210. On the Women's Christian Temperance Union, see Helen E. Tyler, *Where Prayer and Purpose Meet: The Women's Christian Temperance Union Story* (Evanston IL: Signal Press, 1949); and Ruth Bordin, *Women and Temperance: The Quest for Power and Liberty, 1873–1900* (New Brunswick, NJ: Rutgers University Press, 1990). On the role of women's organizations in social and urban reform in the 1890s, see Mary Beard, *Women's Work in Municipalities* (New York: National Municipal League, 1915); Margaret Gibbs Wilson, *The American Woman in Transition: The Urban Influence, 1870–1920* (Westport, CA: Greenwood Press, 1979); Suellen M. Hoy, "'Municipal Housekeeping': The Role of Women in Improving Urban Sanitation Practices, 1880–1917," in *Pollution and Reform in American Cities, 1870–1930*, ed. Martin V. Melosi (Austin: University of Texas Press, 1980); Elizabeth Wilson, *The Sphinx in the City: Urban Life, the Control of Disorder, and Women* (Berkeley and Los Angeles: University of California Press, 1991); Daphne Spain, *How Women Saved the City* (Minneapolis: University of Minnesota Press, 2001); Maureen A. Flanagan, *Seeing with Their Hearts: Chicago Women and the Vision of the Good City, 1871–1933* (Princeton, NJ: Princeton University Press, 2002); and Alison Isenberg, chapter 1, "City Beautiful or Beautiful Mess? The Gendered Origins of a Civic Ideal," in *Downtown America: A History of the Place and the People Who Made It* (Chicago: University of Chicago Press, 2004), 13–41.

6. Spain, *How Women Saved the City*, 1–29. On settlement houses, see Allen F. Davis, *Spearheads for Reform: The Social Settlements and the Progressive Movement, 1890–1914* (New York: Oxford University Press, 1969).

7. The Pond brothers were considered experts in the design of settlement houses. See Allen B. Pond, "The Settlement House," *Brickbuilder* 1 (1902): 184–85; Guy Szuberla, "Three Chicago Settlements: Their Architectural Form and Social Meaning," *Journal of the Illinois State Historical Society* 70 (May 1977): 14–129; and Szuberla, "Irving Kane Pond."

8. On the Woman's Temple and the WCTU's goals for it, see Carrie V. Blewett, "Our House Beautiful," *Woman's Weekly* (Omaha, Nebraska) 8, no. 1 (February 1901); "The Temple as a Memorial

to Frances E. Willard," *Searchlight* vol. 6 no. 2 (February 1904), 2; Hoffman, *The Architecture of John Wellborn Root*, 193–94; Bordin, *Women and Temperance*, 140–48; Rachel E. Bohlmann, "Our 'House Beautiful': The Woman's Temple and the Women's Christian Temperance Union Effort to Establish Place and Identity in Downtown Chicago, 1887–98," *Journal of Women's History* 11, no. 2 (Summer 1999): 110–11; and Paula Lee, "The Temperance Temple and Architectural Patronage in Late-Nineteenth-Century Chicago," *Gender and History* 17, no. 3 (November 2005): 793–885.

9. Frances E. Willard, "President's Annual Address," *Report of the National Woman's Christian Temperance Union: Twenty-Second Annual Meeting Held in Music Hall, Baltimore, Maryland, October 18—23, 1895* (Chicago: Woman's Temperance Publication Association, 1895), 94. On Frances Willard, the founder of the WCTU, and her concept of "home protection," see Gwendolyn Wright, *Moralism and the Model Home: Domestic Architecture and Cultural Conflict in Chicago 1873–1913* (Chicago: University of Chicago Press, 1980), 105–19.

10. "Proposed Temperance Temple, Chicago: For the Woman's Christian Temperance Union," *Inland Architect and News Record* 12 (December 1888), unpaginated plate. Monroe, *John Wellborn Root*, 124–25.

11. Matilda B. Carse, "The Temperance Temple" and "History of the Temple Enterprise"; quoted in Hoffman, *Architecture of John Wellborn Root*, 93.

12. "In Their New Home," *Chicago Daily Tribune*, January 8, 1893, p. 12. This article contains a lengthy description of the interior design scheme for Willard Hall made by Burnham and Root's regular collaborator, the English decorator William Pretyman.

13. "Two Types of Office Building. Representations of the Original and Final Plans for a Downtown Structure," *Chicago Daily Tribune*, November 29, 1891, p. 28. Daniel Bluestone has commented on the frequency with which the typical tall office building was compared to a "dry goods box on end," in *Constructing Chicago*, 128.

14. Robert Craik McLean, "The Passing of the Woman's Temple," *Western Architect* 31, no. 1 (January 1922): 14.

15. On Burnham and Root's Masonic Temple, see "Secret and Benevolent Societies," in *Chicago of To-Day: The Metropolis of the West, the Nation's Choice for the World's Columbian Exposition* (Chicago: Acme Publishing and Engraving Co., 1891), 60; Alphonse Cerza, *A History of the Ancient and Accepted Scottish Rite in Illinois, 1846–1965* (Bloomington IN: Illinois Council of Deliberation, 1966), 59–61; Hoffman, *The Architecture of John Wellborn Root*, 196–202; and Moore, *Masonic Temples*, 81–82.

16. Norman T. Gassett, *History of the Apollo Commandery No. 1 Knights Templar of Chicago, State of Illinois* (Chicago, 1884), 31–32. The Lodge rooms of this building are illustrated in J. Carson Webster, "Richardson's American Express Building," *Journal of the Society of Architectural Historians* 9, nos. 1–2 (March–May 1950): 20–24, and in Moore, *Masonic Temples*, 81.

17. "A Mammoth Masonic Temple," *Chicago Daily Tribune*, January 15, 1890, p. 3.

18. *Graphic* (Chicago), November 15, 1890, p. 930. Gassette, a lawyer active in Chicago politics, did not live to see the building completed. He died in 1891.

19. "Grand Home for the Masons: The Temple to Be Built at State and Randolph Streets," *Chicago Daily Tribune*, April 6 1890, p. 26.

20. "Chicago's Masonic Temple," *New York Times*, March 21, 1890, p. 17; "Grand Home for the Masons". See also "Chicago's Great Masonic Temple; "The Masonic Temple," *Economist* 3 (June 21, 1890): 807; *Building Budget* 6, no. 6 (June 1890), vii; "Chicago: Buildings of Ten Stories or More Erected; The Windy City Passes into an Era of Very High Buildings," *New York Times*, March 9, 1891, p. 3.

21. "The Masonic Temple, Chicago," *Inland Architect and News Record* 16, no. 2 (September 1890), unpaginated plate; "An Architectural Marvel. An Outline of the Interior and Exterior of the Temple," *Chicago Daily Tribune*, November 7, 1890, p. 2. At twenty-two stories, the Masonic Temple remained the tallest building in Chicago until 1909, when the LaSalle and Blackstone hotels were built. Randall, *History of the Development of Building Construction in Chicago*, 18.

22. Masonic Fraternity Temple Association, *Masonic Temple Handbook* (Chicago: W. J. Jefferson Printing and Publishing Co., n.d. [ca. 1892]). Collection of the Chicago History Museum.

23. "Chicago," *American Architect* 30 (November 1890): 20; *Chicago Daily Tribune*, November 7, 1890, pp. 1–2; *Graphic* (Chicago) (November 15, 1890): 928–30.

24. Contemporary photographic views may be seen in *Chicago of To-Day*, 61; Flinn, *Chicago*, 137; and *The Rand McNally Souvenir Guide to Chicago* (Chicago: Rand McNally, 1927), 24, 63.

25. John C. Poppeliers, "The 1867 Philadelphia Masonic Temple Competition," *Journal of the Society of Architectural Historians* 26, no. 4 (December 1967): 278–84. On the design of Masonic Temples in the nineteenth century, see James Stevens Curl, *The Art and Architecture of Freemasonry: An Introductory Study* (London: Batsford, 1991), 221–29; and Moore, "An Order of Builders: Masonic Temples," in *Masonic Temples*, 119–47.

26. Moore, *Masonic Temples*, 125.

27. Ibid., 17–35.

28. Scottish Rite rituals were systematized in the United States in 1867. Ibid., 41–91.

29. Clawson, *Constructing Brotherhood*, 136–44.

30. On the class makeup of the Freemasons in this period, see Dumenil, "Brotherhood and Respectability," in *Freemasonry and American Culture 1880–1930*, 72–115; and Clawson, "Was the Lodge a Working Class Institution?" in *Constructing Brotherhood*, 87–110.

31. Dumenil, *Freemasonry and American Culture 1880–1930*, 12.

32. "Plumb, Level and Square. Cook County Masons Lay the Cornerstone of Their Temple," *Chicago Daily Tribune*, November 7, 1890, p. 1.

33. "Chicago's Great Masonic Temple."

34. Masonic Fraternity Temple Association, *Masonic Temple Handbook*, 5.

35. "It's Big Buildings—Chicago Not So Black As It's Painted," *Chicago Daily Tribune*, October 16, 1892, p. 35.

36. In 1924 the Masons issued $3 million worth of bonds to build a new headquarters, a twenty-two-story building on West Randolph Street known as the Oriental Theater Building. Designed by architects Rapp and Rapp, this new building was in an abstracted art-deco Gothic style. "Masonic Temple Bonds to Be Sold: Issue of $3,000,000 Secured by Mortgage on Chicago Structure Offered This Week," *New York Times*, September 22, 1924, p. 31.

37. Many civic, regional, and national events were held in the Masonic Temple rooms. For example, a National Federation of Catholic Women's Organizations was founded in the Masonic Temple in 1902. "Catholic Women Organize: National Federation of Their Clubs Is Launched at Chicago Meeting," *Washington Post*, April 7, 1902, p. 3.

38. Vanessa Schwartz refers to the rise of early mass culture in Paris in particular. Vanessa Schwartz, *Spectacular Realities: Early Mass Culture in Fin-de-Siècle Paris* (Berkeley and Los Angeles: University of California Press, 1998). Her work draws on the writing of the art historian T. J. Clarke, who has described the ways in which the social transformations brought about by the Hausmannization of Paris were reflected in contemporary painting. T. J. Clarke, *The Painting of Modern Life: Paris in the Art of Manet and His Followers* (Princeton, NJ: Princeton University Press, 1984). Both books depend on Guy Debord's concept of the "society of the spectacle," a place in which fantastic images blind citizens to the mechanisms of capital. Guy Debord, *La Société du spectacle* (Paris: Éditions Champ Libre, 1971). See also Rosalind Williams, *Dream Worlds: Mass Consumption in Late Nineteenth Century France* (Berkeley and Los Angeles: University of California Press, 1982). On the rise of consumer culture in America, see Richard Wightman Fox and T. J. Jackson Lears, eds., *The Culture of Consumption: Critical Essays in American History, 1880–1980* (New York: Pantheon Books, 1983).

39. "A City under One Roof—The Masonic Temple," *Scientific American* 70, no. 6 (February 10, 1894): 81–82.

40. "Features of Chicago Which Constitute the Seven Wonders of the City," *Chicago Daily Tribune*, December 5, 1897, p. 45.

41. The film featured "Cable cars and street traffic of all descriptions. Hundreds of shoppers. Fine perspective view looking north toward the Masonic Temple." It was advertised in the Edison films catalogue as part of the "Erie Railroad Series," which presented "novel and interesting views along the line of the Erie, such as do not always come within the observation of the general tourist." *Corner Madison and State Streets*, Chicago, Thomas A. Edison Inc.; producer, James

White (United States: Edison Manufacturing Co., 1897). Library of Congress Motion Picture, Broadcasting and Recorded Sound Division, Washington, DC.

42. "'Wise' Men Fall Victims to Old Swindling Games," *Chicago Daily Tribune*, October 6, 1901, p. 49.

43. On the tourist value of the tall office building, see Bluestone, *Constructing Chicago*, 104–51.

44. Julian Ralph, "The Highest of All Roof Gardens," *Harper's Weekly* 36 (September 3, 1892): 855.

45. Walter Benjamin famously described the Parisian arcade as one of the loci of modernity in "Paris, capitale du XIXe siecle" (1927–39). Republished in Walter Benjamin, *The Arcades Project*, ed. Roy Tiedemann, trans. Howard Eiland and Kevin McLaughlin (Cambridge, MA: Harvard University Press, 1999). Many scholars have described the department store, one of the first places where women could enter public life without chaperones, as the early site of modern consumer culture. See Gunther Barth, "The Department Store," in *City People: The Rise of Modern City Culture in Nineteenth-Century America* (New York: Oxford University Press, 1980); Michael Miller, *The Bon Marché: Bourgeois Culture and the Department Store, 1869–1920* (Princeton, NJ: Princeton University Press, 1981); Meredith Clausen, "The Department Store: Development of a Type," *Journal of Architectural Education* 39, no. 1 (Fall 1985): 20–27; Elaine S. Abelson, *When Ladies Go A-Thieving: Middle Class Shoplifters in the Victorian Department Store* (New York: Oxford University Press, 1989); Susan Porter Benson, *Counter Culture: Saleswomen, Managers and Customers in American Department Stores, 1890–1940* (Urbana: University of Illinois Press, 1988); and Rachel Bowlby, *Carried Away: The Invention of Modern Shopping* (New York: Columbia University Press, 2001). Bowlby discusses the role of the consumer landscape of Chicago in the late nineteenth-century novels of Theodore Dreiser in *Just Looking: Consumer Culture in Dreiser, Gissing, and Zola* (New York: Methuen, 1985).

46. George E. Moran, *Moran's Dictionary of Chicago and Its Vicinity* (Chicago: G. E. Moran, 1892), 159.

47. "The Chicago Masonic Temple Will Be the Largest on Earth," *Los Angeles Times*, December 7, 1890, p. 6.

48. "A City under One Roof—The Masonic Temple."

49. As Arnold Lewis has noted, European critics were particularly captivated by the elevator in American buildings. Lewis, *An Early Encounter With Tomorrow*, 147–48. On America as a glimpse into the future for European critics of the late-nineteenth and early-twentieth centuries, see Jean-Louis Cohen, *Scenes of the World to Come: European Architecture and the American Challenge 1893–1960* (Paris: Flammarion; Montreal: Canadian Center for Architecture, 1995).

50. "An 'L' Road Terminal Rumor. The Lake Street Line May Use a Portion of the Masonic Temple," *Chicago Daily Tribune*, April 23, 1891, p. 3.

51. Masonic Temple real estate advertising card, ca. 1893. Miscellaneous Pamphlets, collection of the Chicago History Museum.

52. Chicago was home to more than one panorama building, including the "Cyclorama." Opened in 1883, it displayed a 360-degree painting of the battle of Gettysburg. In 1884 the *Inland Architect* reported that interest in this original panorama building "has prompted the erection of another similar building by the American Panorama Company, on the corner of Hubbard and Wabash Avenues. The designs are by architect John M. Carrere of New York, to be superintended by architects Jenney and Otis . . . The painting will be the siege of Paris." "A New Panorama Building," *Inland Architect and Builder* 3, no. 2 (March 1884): 22. On the nineteenth-century panorama, see Evelyn Friutema and Paul Zoetmulder, eds., *The Panorama Phenomenon* (The Hague: Mesdag Panorama Foundation, 1981); Ralph Hyde, *Panoramania!* (London: Barbican Art Gallery, 1988); and Stephan Oettermann, *The Panorama: History of a Mass Medium*, trans. Deborah Lucas Schneider (New York: Zone Books; Cambridge, MA: MIT Press, 1997).

53. On the Astor House Hotel, see Margot and Carol Gayle, *Cast-Iron Architecture in America: The Significance of James Bogardus* (New York: W. W. Norton and Co., 1998), 117–19. On the Palace Hotel, see John Hoag, "Courtyard Hotels in the Wild West," *Architectural Review* (April 1969): 259.

54. Carol Willis explains the economic and programmatic reasons behind the evolution of this type in Chicago, as opposed to the higher buildings with smaller footprints that were built at the same time in New York City. Willis, *Form Follows Finance*, 19–79. On the atrium as a type, see Richard Saxon, *Atrium Buildings: Development and Design* (New York: Van Nostrand Reinhold and Co., 1983).

55. "Wind and Sleet Make the Masonic Temple Corner Difficult of Navigation," *Chicago Daily Tribune*, February 5, 1898, p. 3.

56. Meredith L. Clausen, "Paris of the 1880s and the Rookery," in *Chicago Architecture 1872–1922: Birth of a Metropolis*, ed. John Zukowsky (New York: Prestel, 1987), 157–71. Chicago's own department stores, including William Le Baron Jenney's the Fair (1890–91) and D. H. Burnham and Co.'s Marshall Field's (1902–14), were modeled on those in Paris. Neil Harris, "Shopping—Chicago Style," in Zukowsky, ed., *Chicago Architecture 1872–1922*, 137–56.

57. These effects were designed by two Englishmen, William Henry Burke and William Pretyman. Root had brought the English mosaic specialist Burke from London to lay the floor of the Rookery—a variegated yellow marble tile with brown and red borders to contrast with the white walls. Burke worked with Burnham and Root on the Monadnock, the Woman's Temple, the Masonic Temple, and the Mills Building in San Francisco, as well as on Adler and Sullivan's Auditorium, and Baumann and Huel's Chamber of Commerce, both in Chicago. William Henry Burke, "Marble Floor Mosaics," in *Industrial Chicago*, 2:541–55. The decorative painter William Pretyman worked with Burnham and Root on the interior murals and decorative painting of many of their buildings, including the Society for Savings Bank in Cleveland and the Woman's Temple. Pretyman prepared painted ceiling designs for Root's first version of the Reliance, but these were not carried out in the completed building. He was initially appointed "Chief of Color" for the World's Columbian Exposition, but resigned in 1892 after a dispute with Burnham after Root's death. On Pretyman's involvement with the fair, see C. Moore, *Daniel H. Burnham*, 1:50; Hoffman, *The Architecture of John Wellborn Root*, 98, 126, 180, 235; David F. Berg, *Chicago's White City of 1893* (Lexington: University of Kentucky Press, 1976), 98–99, 154; and Hines, *Burnham of Chicago*, 101–2.

58. This work may also be seen in *Collection of Photographs of Ornamental Iron Executed by Winslow Brothers*, (Chicago: Winslow Brothers, 1893).

59. "Wedded on Masonic Temple Roof. Dr. Dustin and Miss McKenzie Choose a Novel Place to Marry," *Chicago Daily Tribune*, July 5, 1895, 13. "By Climbing Stairs Cyclist Schinner's Unique Method of Training. Fit for a Day Race. Makes Trips by Foot to the Top of the Masonic Temple," *Chicago Daily Tribune*, November 13, 1898, p. 32. "Sure Catch: Juggler Bedini Impales Flying Turnip on Fork, and Louis Vetter Provides Italian Dinner," *Los Angeles Times*, July 4, 1902, p. A2. "Chief Three Miles in the Air: Head of Chicago Police Bars Airships from Overhead," *Washington Post*, September 4, 1905, p. 1. "Chicago to See First Airship. One to Fly over the City Daily Next Week," *Chicago Daily Tribune*, September 13, 1905, p. 6. "Flies Over Chicago: Knabenshue Makes Successful Airship Trip and Lands Safely," *New York Times*, September 28, 1905, p. 7. "Chicago's Aero Fair Settled," *Los Angeles Times*, May 23, 1907, p. 14.

60. These acts played at the Masonic Temple Roof Theater in the summers of 1898 and 1900. Masonic Temple Roof Theater Programs 1898–1903, collection of the Chicago History Museum.

61. "Is Crushed to Death. C. A. Chanter's Dreadful Fate at the Masonic Temple," *Chicago Daily Tribune*, December 12, 1892, p. 1. "Death from Long Fall in the Masonic Temple," *Chicago Daily Tribune*, July 26, 1901, p. 12. "Killed in Elevator Shaft. Chicago Man Falls 200 Feet and Meets Instant Death," *New York Times*, July 26, 1901, p. 8. "Fatally Hurt in Fall of Elevator," *Washington Post*, August 23, 1907, p. 3. "Masonic Temple Elevator Drops 18 Floors, 3 Hurt," *Chicago Daily Tribune*, September 2, 1911, 1. "Four Hurt in Fall of 18 Stories," *New York Times*, September 2, 1911, p. 3. "W. T. Clow Killed by 18 Story Fall in Masonic Temple," *Chicago Daily Tribune*, March 17, 1912, p. 1. "Falls 18 Floors to Death: Railroad Clerk Drops from Elevator in Masonic Temple Office Building," *Washington Post*, March 17, 1912, p. 16.

62. "Fire in Skyscraper: Panic among 4000 Occupants of the Masonic Temple. Elevator Men Were Heroic," *Washington Post*, January 24, 1904, p. 1. "Flames in Masonic Temple. Fire, Quickly Put under Control, Causes Panic among Dancers," *Chicago Daily Tribune*, October 25, 1907, p. 1.

63. Advertisements in Masonic Fraternity Temple Association, *Masonic Temple Handbook*. Collection of the Chicago History Museum.

64. "Leaps to His Death. Albert C. Greenleaf Plunges 16 Stories. Body Badly Crushed," *Chicago Daily Tribune*, January 16, 1898, 14. "Tragic Suicide in Chicago: A Despondent Man Jumps

from the 16th Floor of the Masonic Temple," *New York Times*, January 16, 1898, p. 10. "Jumps 14 Floors to Death. Anna Normoyle Crushed in Masonic Temple Rotunda. Suicide Due to Over-study," *Chicago Daily Tribune*, July 18, 1907, p. 1. "Jumps 250 Feet to Her Death: Girl Ends Her Life in Masonic Temple, Chicago," *New York Times*, July 18, 1907, p. 1. "Leaps 5 Floors to Death. G. A. Wright Takes Fatal Jump at Masonic Temple," *Chicago Daily Tribune*, July 4, 1911, p. 2. "Dives 19 Floors in Masonic Temple. Maniac Disrobes, Says He Is 'Going Swimming.' Plunges 225 Feet to His Death," *Chicago Daily Tribune*, December 13, 1911, p. 3. "Plunges from 19th Floor. Machinist's Body, in Falling, Strikes Man and Seriously Injures Him," *Washington Post*, December 13, 1911, p. 1. "Drops 14 Stories To Death: Suicide Evades Nets in Chicago's Masonic Temple by Jumping from Roof," *Washington Post*, September 19, 1912, p. 1. "Leap Lust Leads to Death Plunge? Swiss Mania May Explain C. R. Rasmussen's Fall from Masonic Temple," *Chicago Daily Tribune*, September 19, 1912, p. 3. "Dives off Top of Masonic Temple. Man Hurls Himself to Death in State Street from Capstone of Building," *Chicago Daily Tribune*, August 24, 1913, p. 1. "Jumps from 19 Story Roof: Painter Commits Suicide from Top of Chicago Masonic Temple," *Washington Post*, August 24, 1913, p. 3.

65. Konwinski was also known as Joseph Kelter. "Leaps to Death to Aid Science. Criminal Wills Body to Surgeons for Study of Robbery Life Causes," *Chicago Daily Tribune*, December 29, 1913, p. 3.

66. "Dies to Aid Surgeons: Suicide Wants Brain Examined for Criminal Trend. Plunges from 18th Floor," *Washington Post*, December 29, 1913, p. 1; "Ended Life to Aid Science: So Wrote Suicide in Willing His Body and Brain to Colleges," *New York Times*, December 29, 1913, p. 2.

67. Karl Marx famously defined *alienation* as the social result of capitalism. The sociologists Georg Simmel and Ferdinand Tonnies expanded on this concept in the context of modern social life in the early twentieth century. Bertell Ollman, *Alienation: Marx's Conception of Man in Capitalist Society* (Cambridge: Cambridge University Press, 1971). Anthony Vidler has discussed the effects of this societal change on urban and architectural form in *The Architectural Uncanny: Essays in the Modern Unhomely* (Cambridge, MA: MIT Press, 1992).

68. "Real Estate News," *Chicago Daily Tribune*, April 17, 1892, p. 27. "Giles Brothers and Company, Jewelers Failed," *Chicago Daily Tribune*, April 26, 1893, p. 3.

69. "Final Doom for Theater. Masonic Temple Roof Garden Hit by New Ordinance," *Chicago Daily Tribune*, November 18, 1904, p. 7. "Masonic Temple Is Hit. Judge Tuley Says It Must Obey Building Rules. Requires Owners to Rebuild Stairs at Cost of $50,000 or Close Halls on Upper Floors," *Chicago Daily Tribune*, March 1, 1905, p. 2.

70. "Riot 17 Floors Up, Wrecks Loop Hall. Shots Fired," *Chicago Daily Tribune*, February 24, 1921, p. 1.

71. Al Chase, "High Taxes Force Demolition of Many Historical Structures. Owners Learn That Wrecking Solves Problem, More Landmarks Slated for Early Removal," *Chicago Daily Tribune*, May 20, 1933, p. A10. Al Chase, "City's Buildings Wrecked in New Deal Depression: More Structures Torn Down than Erected," *Chicago Daily Tribune*, February 17, 1940, p. 4. Louther S. Horne, "In Chicago Skyline. Demolition of the 20 Story Capitol Building Gives Emphasis to Making Over of City," *New York Times*, July 2, 1940, p. E10.

72. Under the direction of architect Walter W. Ahlschlager, the atrium would be filled in with four-teen new elevators; the old ones, with their finely detailed metal cages exposed up the height of the building, would be demolished and replaced with office space. Al Chase, "Masonic Temple Sold (Actually) For $3,100,000," *Chicago Daily Tribune*, March 21, 1922, p. 27; "Masonic Temple Is Legitimately Sold: Famous Windy City Building Was Often 'Bought' by Unwary Tourists," *Los Angeles Times*, March 21, 1922, p. 122; "Chicago Masonic Temple Sold," *Wall Street Journal*, March 22, 1922, p. 5; "Capitol Building, Chicago," *Wall Street Journal*, June 19, 1922, p. 8.

73. The owners of the Capitol estimated the value of the building to be $750,000, and the cost of subway damage repair to be $100,000. "Capitol Building Asks $850,000 in Subway Damage," *Chicago Daily Tribune*, November 15, 1940, p. 7.

74. The Telenews, showing newsreels and cartoons, was one of eight theaters in the immediate area, including the Chicago Theater next door, built in 1921. In 1953 the Telenews became the Loop Theater, a picture palace, which closed in 1978. Though its original façade has been destroyed, the building stood until recently, home to a small theater group and a Walgreens drugstore.

75. "Monadnock Building to Be Restyled in City's Biggest Modernization Job," *Chicago Daily Tribune*, January 16, 1938, p. 12; "Chicago Remodels a Landmark, Gives Building a Cost Study. Progressive Styling Ups Occupancy 7% in Famed Monadnock," *Architectural Forum* (October 1938): 4.

76. Christmas card from Dorothy and Graham Aldis with an illustration of the Monadnock, ca. 1956. Monadnock Building, Miscellaneous Pamphlets, collection of the Chicago History Museum.

CHAPTER FIVE

1. Robert Bruegmann describes the development of State Street as Chicago's primary shopping street in the 1890s in *The Architects and the City*, 183–205.

2. In 1873 Hale and his brother George founded W. H. Hale and Co., later the Hale Elevator Co., to supply freight-bearing Otis hoists for commercial buildings in Chicago. In 1883 Hale bought out Otis, and expanded his business to New York, London, Paris, and Berlin. Ten years later he retired from the elevator business to concentrate on real estate development, investing in many syndicates that hired Daniel Burnham to design their buildings. On Hale, see Berger, *They Built Chicago*, 49–58. For a description of the complex process of design and construction of the Reliance Building, see Lewis H. Hill, *Report to the Commission on the Reliance Building* (Chicago: Commission on Chicago Landmarks, 1969); Donald Hoffman, "The Reliance Building, A Metamorphosis," in *The Architecture of John Wellborn Root*, 177–91; Commission on Chicago Historical and Architectural Landmarks, *Reliance Building* (Chicago: The Commission, 1979); and McClier Preservation Group, *The Reliance Building: Historic Structures Report*, 3 vols. (1994). The Reliance Building was named a National Historic Landmark in 1976.

3. On the reorganization of the firm after Root's death, see Peter B. Wight, "Daniel Hudson Burnham and His Associates," *Architectural Record* 38, no. 1 (July 1915): 3–7; Moore, *Daniel H. Burnham*, 1:82–86; and Hines, *Burnham of Chicago*, 268–69. Edward Clapp Shankland was Burnham's in-house engineer, and an expert in steel construction. He designed the giant roof trusses of the Manufacturers Building at the World's Columbian Exposition. Shankland described his working method in "Steel Skeleton Construction in Chicago," *Journal of the Institution of Civil Engineers* 128 (1896–97): 12–13. Atwood was educated in the Northeast at Harvard, and in the offices of William Ware, Henry Van Brunt, and Bruce Price. He left Burnham's employ in late 1895 and died very soon afterward. On Atwood see Daniel H. Burnham, "Charles Bowler Atwood," *Inland Architect and News Record* 26, no. 6 (January 1896): 56–57; and Ann Van Zanten, "The Marshall Field Annex and the New Urban Order of Daniel Burnham's Chicago," *Chicago History* 11, no. 3 (Fall and Winter 1982): 130–41.

4. "New Building Company Formed. Long Term Lease of the Hale Corner to Reliance Organization Recorded," *Chicago Daily Tribune*, July 23, 1893, p. 14.

5. On the George A. Fuller Company, see Raymond C. Daly, *75 Years of Construction Pioneering: George A. Fuller Company, 1882–1957* (New York: Newcomen Society in North America, 1957); and D. Van Zanten, "The Nineteenth Century," 42–45. The major works erected by the company in this time period are illustrated in *Fireproof Building Construction: Prominent Buildings Erected by the George A. Fuller Company* (New York: T. D. Rich and G. A. Fuller, 1904).

6. On the structure and construction of the Reliance, see "Springs Up by Magic," *Chicago Daily Tribune*, August 26, 1894, p. 34; William H. Birkmire, *Skeleton Construction in Buildings* (orig. pub. 1894; reprint, New Haven, CT: Research Publications, 1972); "The Reliance Building, Chicago," *Scientific American* (January 1895): 17; and Freitag, *Architectural Engineering*.

7. Hoffman, *The Architecture of John Wellborn Root*, 183–84.

8. Unfortunately, the claims made for terra-cotta in the 1890s were not borne out in reality. The terra-cotta used to clad Chicago skyscrapers in this period turned out to be less durable and resistant to water than initially imagined and often failed after a few years. The difference in expansion between the interior steel frame and the exterior terra-cotta tile often caused the tile to crack and fall off. Bruegmann, *The Architects and the City*, 200.

9. On the manufacture of plate glass in the Midwest and its use in tall office buildings in Chicago, see Thomas Leslie, "Glass and Light: The Influence of Interior Illumination on the Chicago School," *Journal of Architectural Education* 58, no. 1 (September 2004): 13–23; and Thomas Leslie, "'As Large as the Situation of the Columns Would Allow': Building Cladding and Plate Glass in the Chicago Skyscraper, 1885–1905," *Technology and Culture* 49, no. 2 (April 2008): 399–419.

10. "Old and New Chicago."

11. The history of the building's tenants may be traced through the real estate column in the *Chicago Daily Tribune*: "News of the Real Estate World," *Chicago Daily Tribune*, June 17, 1905, p. 14; Al Chase, "Pick Interests Pay $400,000 for Reliance. One of State Street's Oldest Skyscrapers Is Sold," *Chicago Daily Tribune*, December 24, 1919, p. 14; Al Chase, "Pick Interests Sell Reliance for $600,000," *Chicago Daily Tribune*, May 11, 1923, p. 24; Al Chase, "Walgreen Takes State Space of Warmington," *Chicago Daily Tribune*, May 8, 1928, p. 27; Al Chase, "Office Building in Loop Is Sold for $400,000. Accounting Firm Officials Head Buying Group," *Chicago Daily Tribune*, March 7, 1948, SWA.

12. "Informal Opening of 'The Reliance.' A Triumph of the Builder's Art—Unique Building Construction," *Chicago Daily Tribune*, March 16, 1895, p. 8. Despite these claims about the high moral tones of the tenants, in 1907 a twenty-six-year-old woman became seriously ill after a doctor performed an "illegal operation" on her, probably an abortion, in the Reliance. "Girl Seriously Ill. Mystery—Two Arrested Following Alleged Illegal Operation on Nellie E. Kilton. Both Deny," *Chicago Daily Tribune*, September 6, 1907, p. 3.

13. The decorative ironwork in the Reliance is described in "Reliance Building, Chicago, D. H. Burnham and Co., Architects, Ornamental Iron by the Winslow Brothers," *Ornamental Iron* 2, no. 4 (January 1895): 91–101.

14. B. F. Wheeler, "Women Office Assistants Paid for Being Pleasant," *Chicago Daily Tribune*, May 13, 1906, p. E1. This article describes a number of medical practices in Chicago office buildings.

15. "Technical Review: Fisher Building, Chicago—A Building without Walls," *Inland Architect and News Record*, Special Supplement 27, no. 4 (May 1896), n.p.

16. On the Venetian and the Champlain, see Bruegmann, *The Architects and the City*, 195–97, and *Holabird and Roche, Holabird and Root*, 1:141–42.

17. D. E. Waid, "Recent Brick and Terra-Cotta work in American Cities," *Brickbuilder* 4 (June 1895): 132.

18. Peter B. Wight, "Modern Architecture in Chicago," *Pall Mall Magazine* 18 (May–August 1899): 292–308; quotation is from p. 303.

19. John Wellborn Root, "A Great Architectural Problem," *Inland Architect and News Record* 5, no. 5 (June 1890): 67–71; Dankmar Adler, "Light in Tall Office Buildings," *Engineering Magazine* 4 (November 1892): 171–86; and Dankmar Adler, "The Influence of Steel Construction and Plate Glass upon Style," *Inland Architect and News Record* 28 (November 1896): 34–37.

20. Wolfgang Schivelbusch has described the aversion to sunlight in mid-nineteenth-century European bourgeois homes. Wolfgang Schivelbusch, *Disenchanted Night: The Industrialization of Light in the Nineteenth Century*, trans. Angela Davies (Berkeley and Los Angeles: University of California Press, 1988), 169–86.

21. Dietrich Neumann discusses efforts to promote the use of translucent glass tile in Chicago in "The Century's Triumph in Lighting: The Luxfer Prism Companies and Their Contribution to Early Modern Architecture," *Journal of the Society of Architectural Historians* 54, no. 1 (March 1995): 24–53.

22. "Old and New Chicago."

23. "Chicago," *American Architect and Building News* 47 (January 26, 1895): 43.

24. *Engineering Magazine* (London), no. 8 (October 1894–March 1895): 896.

25. Montgomery Schuyler, "Modern Architecture," *Architectural Record* 4 (July–September 1894): 1–13.

26. "Skyscraper Signs Scarce. Those on Higher Stories Can't Be Read from the Street," *Chicago Daily Tribune*, January 27, 1901, p. 36.

27. *Economist* 12 (August 25, 1894): 206.

28. Charles E. Jenkins, "A White Enameled Building," *Architectural Record*, vol. 4 (January–March 1895): 299–306; quotation is from p. 302.

29. Schuyler, "D. H. Burnham and Co.," 415.

30. "Sanitary Advice from Medical Men. Cook County Society Prepares a List of Recommendations," *Chicago Daily Tribune*, August 14, 1895, p. 3.

31. Platt, *Shock Cities*.

32. Flinn, *Chicago*, 39.

33. On the relationship between sanitation and city planning in nineteenth-century America, see Lloyd C. Taylor, *The Medical Profession and Social Reform, 1885–1945* (New York: St. Martin's Press, 1974); Jon A. Peterson, "The Impact of Sanitary Reform upon American Urban Planning, 1840–1890," *Journal of the Society of History* 13, no. 1 (Autumn 1979): 83–103; M. Christine Boyer, *Dreaming the Rational City: The Myth of American City Planning* (Cambridge, MA: MIT Press, 1983); John Duffy, *The Sanitarians: A History of American Public Health* (Urbana: University of Illinois Press, 1990); Martin V. Melosi, *The Sanitary City: Urban Infrastructure in America From Colonial Times to the Present* (Baltimore: Johns Hopkins University Press, 2000); and Bonj Szczygiel and Robert Hewitt, "Nineteenth Century Medical Landscapes: John H. Rauch, Frederick Law Olmsted and the Search for Salubrity," *Bulletin of the History of Medicine* 74 (2000): 708–34.

34. On these infrastructural changes aimed at improving public health, see Mayer and Wade, *Chicago*, 94–100, 274; William K. Beatty, "When Cholera Scourged Chicago," *Chicago History* 11, no. 1 (1982): 2–13; Daniel Bluestone, "'A Cordon of Verdure': Gardens, Parks and Cultivation 1830–1869," in *Constructing Chicago*, 7–35; and Platt, *Shock Cities*, 78–195.

35. The Chicago Board of Health was modeled on one founded in New York ten years earlier. See John Rauch, *The Sanitary Problems of Chicago, Past and Present* (Chicago, 1879). On Oscar De Wolf and the early days of the Chicago Department of Health, see Margaret Garb, "Health, Morality and Housing: The 'Tenement Problem' in Chicago," *American Journal of Public Health* 93, no. 9 (September 2003): 1420–30.

36. William Le Baron Jenney believed that control of sanitation was one of the architect's chief duties. Letter to the Regents of the University of Michigan, December 19, 1878; Chicago Historical Project, Microfilm Reel 11A, Scrapbook 2, Ryerson and Burnham Library, Art Institute of Chicago.

37. De Wolf particularly praised the factory town of Pullman, designed by Chicago architect S. S. Beman for the Pullman Railway Company, as a fine example of the harmonious meeting of architecture, urban planning, and public health. Oscar C. De Wolf, MD, Commissioner of Health for Chicago, "The Relation of State Medicine to the Profession of Architecture," *Inland Architect and Builder* 8, no. 8 (December 1886): 67–69.

38. Alex W. Murray, "The Sanitation of Cities," *Inland Architect and Builder* 3, no. 6 (July 1884): 75–76. On sewer gas, see William Paul Gerhard, "Recent Progress in House Drainage and Plumbing," *Inland Architect and Builder* 5, extra number (June 1885): 47. Gerhard criticized speculative house builders and plumbers for using fear of sewer gas to promote their products in magazines and advertisements.

39. Frederick Baumann, "Protection of Residences," *Inland Architect and News Record* 18, no. 4 (November 1891): 46–47. Baumann had earlier published "Sanitary Construction of Residences," *Building Budget* 3, no. 12 (December 1887): 163–65.

40. Charles N. Dowd, MD, "A Study of the Hygienic Conditions of Our Streets," *Inland Architect and News Record* 15, no. 6 (July 1890): 82–83. Reprinted from *Medical Record* (June 21, 1890).

41. Mary Douglas describes the social role of cleanliness taboos in her classic text, *Purity and Danger: An Analysis of the Concepts of Pollution and Taboo* (New York: Praeger, 1966).

42. Henry Blake Fuller, *The Cliff-Dwellers* (New York: Harper and Bros., 1893), 54.

43. *Industrial Chicago*, 1:212–13.

44. On Chicago public health initiatives implemented in response to this new way of understanding the spread of disease, see Harold L. Platt, "'Clever Microbes': Sanitation Science in Manchester and Chicago," in *Shock Cities*, 408–41.

45. Spain, *How Women Saved the City*, 6.

46. Adrian Forty, "Hygiene and Cleanliness," in *Objects of Desire: Design and Society Since 1750* (London: Thames and Hudson, 1986), 160.

47. De Wolf, "The Relation of State Medicine to the Profession of Architecture," 67.

48. Gwendolyn Wright describes the late nineteenth-century movement for domestic hygiene in *Moralism and the Model Home*, 117–28. See also Forty, *Objects of Desire*, 156–80; Suellen M. Hoy, *Chasing Dirt: The American Pursuit of Cleanliness* (New York: Oxford University Press, 1995); Annmarie Adams, *Architecture in the Family Way: Doctors, Houses, and Women, 1870–1900* (Montreal: McGill-Queen's University Press, 1996); and Nancy Tomes, *The Gospel of Germs: Men, Women and the Microbe in American Life* (Cambridge, MA: Harvard University Press, 1998). Mark Wigley has discussed the importance of the hygienic white wall as a form of "dress" for modern architecture in *White Walls, Designer Dresses: The Fashioning of Modern Architecture* (Cambridge, MA: MIT Press, 1996).

49. On the use of white porcelain tile as a hygienic surface in mid-nineteenth-century hospitals, see Robert Bruegmann, "Materials and Methods of Construction," in "Architecture of the Hospital 1770–1870: Design and Technology" (Ph.D. diss., University of Pennsylvania, 1976). Ellen Lupton and J. Abbott Miller describe the use of porcelain tile in the design of the modern kitchen and bathroom in *The Process of Elimination: The Kitchen, the Bathroom, and the Aesthetics of Waste* (New York: Princeton Architectural Press, 1992), 2–19.

50. Robert Edis, *Healthy Furniture and Decoration* (London: William Clowes and Sons Ltd., 1884), 17.

51. Daniel Burnham, "What Are Some of the Architectural Possibilities of Such Materials as Paper and Glass etc.?" *Inland Architect and Builder* 9 (June 1887): 89–90; *Building Budget* 3, no. 6 (June 1887): 83. Burnham was familiar with promoting glass: one of his first jobs was as a plate glass salesman. Moore, *Daniel H. Burnham*, 1:16.

52. The most famous of these is Orson Squire Fowler's proposal for an "Octagon House," which started a fad for octagonal buildings in the 1850s. With his design, Fowler, a phrenologist and amateur architect, intended to bring healthy and efficient living to all, including the "poorer classes." His Octagon House incorporated a number of technical innovations, including dumbwaiters, hot and cold running water, indoor water closets, centralized gas heating, and gas illumination and ventilation, as well as large areas of glass. Orson Squire Fowler, *The Octagon House: A Home For All*, with an introduction by Madeleine B. Stern (orig. pub. 1853; reprint, New York: Dover Publications, 1973). On Fowler see Walter Creese, "Fowler and the Domestic Octagon," *Art Bulletin* 28, no. 2 (June 1946): 89–102; John J. G. Blumenson, "'A Home for All': The Octagon in American Architecture," *Historic Preservation* 25 (July–September 1973): 30, 34; and Wayne Michael Charney, "The American Glass House: Its Conception and Realization, 1850–1950" (Ph.D. diss., Northwestern University, 1985).

53. Burnham, "What Are Some of the Architectural Possibilities of Such Materials as Paper and Glass etc.?" 89. While Burnham obviously admired this inventive design, he was rather more conservative in his own work. Burnham and Root designed two sanitariums, one in the Chicago suburb of Lincoln Park and one at Lake Geneva, a fashionable vacation retreat in Wisconsin. Sponsored by the *Chicago Daily News*, the Lincoln Park Sanitarium was built in 1887 for the care of poor children. It did not include glass screens or any kind of sophisticated technology. Instead, it was a simple wooden cabin built out over Lake Michigan on piers, open along all sides to allow healthy breezes to penetrate. Cynthia Mathews, "This Haven of Rest and Health: The Chicago Daily News Sanitarium," *Chicago History* 28, no. 3 (Spring 2000): 20–39.

54. Burnham, "What Are Some of the Architectural Possibilities of Such Materials as Paper and Glass etc.?" 89.

55. On attempts to reform the smoke problem in late nineteenth- and early twentieth-century Chicago, see *The Chicago Report on Smoke Abatement; A Landmark Survey of the Technology and History of Air Pollution Control* (orig. pub. 1915; reprint, Elmsford, NY: Maxwell Reprint, 1971); Christine Meisner Rosen, "Businessmen against Pollution in Late Nineteenth Century Chicago," *Business History Review*, no. 69 (Autumn 1995): 351–97; Harold L. Platt, "Smoke, Gender and the Reform of Environmental Policy in Chicago 1900–1920," *Planning Perspectives* 10, no. 11 (1995): 67–97; and, Platt, "Visible Smoke: Pollution and Gender Politics in Chicago," in *Shock Cities*, 468–91.

56. Root, "A Great Architectural Problem," 71.

57. Jenkins, "A White Enameled Building," 299–306; quotation is from p. 302.

58. "Chicago Is Enveloped in Smoke. Dirty, Black Clouds from Downtown Chimneys Hang over the City Like a Pall," *Chicago Daily Tribune*, December 2, 1898, p. 3. See also "Smoke Is Needless. This Is Shown by Buildings Using Improved Furnaces," *Chicago Daily Tribune*, July 30, 1892, p. 26.

59. Ferree, "Chicago," 10–11; quotation is from p. 11.

60. Wright, "The Art and Craft of the Machine," 68.

61. "Chicago's Climate," *Inland Architect and Builder* 3, no. 4 (May 1884): 51–52.

62. Editorial, *Inland Architect and Builder* 10, no. 3 (September 1887): 18.

63. William MacHarg, "Sanitary Engineering," *Building Budget* 4, no. 10 (August 1888): 120–21.

64. "Chicago Is Enveloped in Smoke."

65. *The Chicago Report on Smoke Abatement*, 82; "To Fight Chicago Smoke: A Society Incorporated for that Praiseworthy Purpose," *New York Times*, December 29, 1891, p. 5, col. 3.

66. "Rivals Old Vesuvius. Masonic Temple's Smoke Stacks Taken for a Volcano," *Chicago Daily Tribune*, July 25, 1892, p. 3. "Break Their Record for Smoke. Chicago's Most Obnoxious Chimneys Excel Their Former Efforts," *Chicago Daily Times*, July 29, 1892, p. 9.

67. Rosen, "Businessmen against Pollution in Late Nineteenth Century Chicago," 358. Owen F. Aldis arrived in Chicago from New England in 1871 with a degree in law, and became the Brookes' agent in 1879. He was extremely successful in real estate, managing an estimated 20 percent of Chicago office space by 1902. Berger, *They Built Chicago*. See also Owen F. Aldis and Peter C. Brooks, Narrative Summary of Correspondence, 1879–1920, Archives and Manuscript Department, Chicago History Museum).

68. Rosen, "Businessmen against Pollution in Late Nineteenth Century Chicago," 359.

CHAPTER SIX

1. On fictional American utopias from this period, see Vernon Louis Parrington, *American Dreams: A Study of American Utopias* (New York: Russell and Russell, 1964); W. H. G. Armytage, *Yesterday's Tomorrows: A Historical Survey of Future Societies* (Toronto: University of Toronto Press, 1968); Kenneth M. Roemer, *The Obsolete Necessity: America in Utopian Writings 1888–1900* (Ohio: Kent State University Press, 1976); Dolores Hayden, "Domestic Space in Fictional Socialist Cities," in *The Grand Domestic Revolution: A History of Feminist Designs for American Homes, Neighborhoods and Cities* (Cambridge, MA: MIT Press, 1981), 134–49; Thomas D. Clareson, *Science Fiction in America 1870s–1930s: An Annotated Bibliography of Primary Sources* (Westport, CA: Greenwood Press, 1984); and Donald E. Pitzer, ed., *America's Communal Utopias* (Chapel Hill: University of North Carolina Press, 1997).

2. The term *social condenser* comes from Soviet Constructivist architecture and is premised on the idea that architecture can influence social behavior. The goal of such buildings was to break down social hierarchy by bringing people together in cooperative living situations.

3. On the national debate over building height restrictions, see Robert Fogelson, "The Sacred Skyline: The Battle over Height Limits," in *Downtown*, 112–82.

4. On the 1893 Chicago height limit, see August Gatzert, *Limitation of Building Heights in the City of Chicago* (Chicago, 1913); Hoyt, *One Hundred Years of Land Values in Chicago*, 153; Willis, *Form Follows Finance*, 49–52; Martin, "Riveting," 194–245; and Fogelson, *Downtown*, 141–44.

5. "Question of High Buildings," *Inland Architect and Builder* 3, no. 2 (March 1884): 15. French building height restrictions were discussed in the same year. "Ordinance Limiting Height of Buildings," *Inland Architect and Builder* 4 (October 1884): 35–36.

6. "Height Is No Menace. Chicago's Office Big Buildings Safe as They Are Popular," *Chicago Daily Tribune*, February 19, 1894, p. 9. While the boosterish paper disagreed with such a pessimistic view, it did admit that the skyscraper posed a danger from two fronts, fire and smoke pollution. See also "Propositions to Limit the Height of Buildings," *Inland Architect and News Record* 27, no. 1 (February 1896): 2; "A Halt Call on 'Skyscrapers,'" *Scribner's Magazine* 19 (March 1896): 395–96; "Dust Nuisance for Those Who Inhabit High Buildings," *Inland Architect and News Record* 31 (February 1898): 9; and "A Supreme Court Sustains High Building Law," *Inland Architect and News Record* 34 (January 1899): 41.

7. Murray, "The Sanitation of Cities," 75.

8. *Industrial Chicago*, 1:199.

9. "High Building Construction Should Not Be Restricted," *Inland Architect and News Record* 39, no. 1 (February 1902): 1.

10. On the aesthetic and city planning side of the municipal reform movement in America, later named the City Beautiful movement, see Charles Mulford Robinson, *Modern Civic Art; or, The City Made Beautiful* (orig. pub. 1918; reprint, New York: Arno Press, 1970); Mel Scott, "The Spirit of Reform," in *American City Planning Since 1890* (Berkeley and Los Angeles: University of California Press, 1969), 6–17; William H. Wilson, *The City Beautiful Movement* (Baltimore: Johns Hopkins University Press, 1989); and M. Christine Boyer, "Would America Produce a Civilization of Cities? 1890–1909," in *Dreaming the Rational City*, 1–57. Jon A. Peterson discusses the smaller regional movements that contributed to the national one in "The City Beautiful Movement: Forgotten Origins and Lost Meanings," in *Introduction to Planning History in the United States*, ed. Donald A. Krueckeberg (New Brunswick, NJ: Center for Urban Policy Research, 1983), 40–56.

11. C. Howard Walker, "The Grouping of Public Buildings in a Great City," part 2, *Inland Architect and News Record* 37, no. 1 (February 1901): 3. As editor of the *Architectural Review*, Walker wrote extensively on the subject of city planning. He applied his knowledge to the design of the 1898 Great Exposition in Omaha and the 1904 Louisiana Purchase International Exposition in St. Louis.

12. Albert Kelsey, "Municipal Improvements," part 2, *Inland Architect and News Record* 46, no. 1 (August 1905): 6. See also part 1, vol. 45, no. 6 (July 1905): 63–64; part 3, vol. 46, no. 2 (September 1905): 17–18; part 4, vol. 46, no. 2 (November 1905): 11–13; part 5, vol. 49, no. 3 (March 1907): 44–45; part 6, vol. 49, no. 6 (June 1907): 78–79; part 7, vol. 50, no. 2 (August 1907): 20; and part 8, vol. 50, no. 4 (October 1907): 11.

13. Ralph Adams Cram, "Civic Development," part 1, *Inland Architect and News Record* 51, no. 3 (March 1908): 21.

14. Lucy Fitch Perkins, "The City Beautiful: A Study of the Artistic Possibilities of Chicago," *Inland Architect and News Record* 34, no. 2 (September 1899): 10–14; quotation is from p. 11. Perkins's husband, Dwight, later carried out some of these ideas as chair of the Special Park Commission. See Eleanor Ellis Perkins, *Eve Among the Puritans: A Biography of Lucy Fitch Perkins* (Boston: Houghton Mifflin, 1956).

15. "A New Era in Municipal Improvement," *Inland Architect and News Record* 43, no. 5 (June 1904): 25.

16. Albert Kelsey compared Ebenezer Howard's utopian scheme to Baron Georges-Eugène Haussmann's plan for Paris, arguing that both aimed at "countrifying the city." Kelsey, "Municipal Improvements," part 3, p. 17.

17. The *Inland Architect* frequently reported on the progress of plans for Washington, DC. See for example F. W. Fitzpatrick, "Beautifying the Nation's Capital," *Inland Architect and News Record* 35, no. 2 (March 1900): 10–14; "Permanent Plan for the City of Washington," *Inland Architect and News Record* 37, no. 1 (February 1901): 3–4; "Commission to Consider Improvements in the U.S. Capital," *Inland Architect and News Record* 37, no. 1 (February 1901): 7; "For Beautifying Washington," *Inland Architect and News Record* 38 (September 1901): 16; "Beautifying the Nation's Capital: Report of the Commissioners of the District of Columbia," *Inland Architect and News Record* 39, no. 1 (February 1902): 2–5; and "Architectural Measures Adopted at Washington," *Inland Architect and News Record* 45, no. 4 (May 1905): 33. On Burnham's involvement with this plan, see Thomas Hines, "The New Capital: The Washington Plan of 1902," in *Burnham of Chicago*, 139–57; and Kristen Schaffer, *Daniel H. Burnham: Visionary Architect and Planner* (New York: Rizzoli, 2003), 97–100, 107–20.

18. On the redevelopment of City Hall Park in New York City around the turn of the twentieth century, see Max Page, " Life-Thread of the City," in *The Creative Destruction of Manhattan 1900–1940* (Chicago: University of Chicago Press, 1999), 121–42.

19. William E. Curtis, "Beautiful Vienna," *Inland Architect and News Record* 38, no. 6 (January 1902): 43.

20. Kelsey, "Municipal Improvements," part 1, p. 63. C. Howard Walker, "Municipal Laws in Relation to Architecture," *Inland Architect and News Record* 34, no. 6 (January 1900): 42–43.

21. On the new science of city planning, see Scott, *American City Planning Since 1890*, 40–43.

22. Maureen A. Flanagan, *Charter Reform in Chicago* (Carbondale: Southern Illinois University Press, 1987).

23. John McGovern, "Chicago Is Not Yet Paris," *Building Budget* 3, no. 8 (August 1887): 101.

24. Perkins, "The City Beautiful," 11. Albert Kelsey described the lack of appeal in American lake and river fronts in "Municipal Improvements," part 1, pp. 63–64. On the reform of the lakefront, see Louis P. Cain, *Sanitation Strategy for a Lakefront Metropolis: The Case of Chicago* (DeKalb: Northern Illinois University Press, 1978).

25. While Ralph Adams Cram criticized the building of parks as only a partial solution, he still believed they were "the first step toward a civilized expression of civilization." Cram, "Civic Development," part 2, *Inland Architect and News Record* 5, no. 4 (April 1908): 32. The same point was made in a paper read before the Architectural League of America in Pittsburgh on April 17, 1905, where the author noted that parks were often employed in an effort to mitigate badly planned transit systems, instead of replacing those transit systems with more efficient ones. "The Grouping of Public Buildings," *Inland Architect and News Record* 45, no. 4 (May 1905): 40–41.

26. On the planning of these early Chicago parks, see Daniel Bluestone, "'A Cordon of Verdure': Gardens, Parks and Cultivation, 1830–1869" and "'A Different Style of Beauty: Park Designs, 1865–1880," in *Constructing Chicago*, 7–35, 36–61; Reuben M. Rainey, "William Le Baron Jenney and Chicago's West Parks: From Prairies to Pleasure-Grounds," in Waldheim and Ray, *Chicago Architecture*, 37–52; and Jane Wolff, "The Chicago Parks: Tableaus of Naturalization," in Waldheim and Ray, *Chicago Architecture*, 176–80. On the history of Grant Park, see Timothy J. Gilfoyle, *Millennium Park: Creating a Chicago Landmark* (Chicago: University of Chicago Press, 2006), 3–76.

27. Perkins, "The City Beautiful," 12.

28. Kelsey, "Municipal Improvements," part 2, *Inland Architect and News Record* 46, no. 1 (August 1905): 7. On the romantic garden suburb imagined as an antidote to the gridded city, see Kenneth T. Jackson, "Romantic Suburbs," in *Crabgrass Frontier*, 73–86.

29. Curtis, "Beautiful Vienna," 43.

30. Walker, "The Grouping of Public Buildings in a Great City," part 1, *Inland Architect and News Record* 36, no. 6 (January 1901): 42–43; part 2, vol. 37, no. 1 (February 1901): 3.

31. Kelsey, "Municipal Improvements," part 2, p. 6.

32. Perkins, "The City Beautiful," 11. In 1905 F. W. Fitzpatrick, the Washington correspondent for the *Inland Architect*, wrote a similarly glowing review of the artistic merit of Chicago's tall buildings as compared to those of New York. F. W. Fitzpatrick, "Chicago," *Inland Architect and News Record* 45, no. 5 (June 1905): 46–48.

33. On the World's Columbian Exposition, see Berg, *Chicago's White City of 1893*; Hines, "Legacies of the Fair 1893–1901," in *Burnham of Chicago*, 125–38; Donald L. Miller, *City of the Century: The Epic of Chicago and the Making of America* (New York: Simon and Schuster, 1996), 378–85, 488–504; Norm Bolotin, *The World's Columbian Exposition: The Chicago World's Fair of 1893* (Urbana: University of Illinois Press, 2002); and Schaffer, *Daniel H. Burnham*, 63–72. Donald Hoffman describes John Root's early plans for the fair in "The World's Columbian Exposition," in *The Architecture of John Wellborn Root*, 220–45.

34. On the relationship between Chicago and the White City, see Ross Miller, "Chicago Black and White: The Court, the University, the Midway and the Street," in *American Apocalypse: The Great Fire and the Myth of Chicago* (Chicago: University of Chicago Press, 1990), 195–250.

35. On these various proposals, see Robert Jay, "Taller Than Eiffel's Tower: The London and Chicago Tower Projects, 1889–1894," *Journal of the Society of Architectural Historians*, no. 46 (June 1987): 145–56.

36. "American High Buildings as Conceived by the French," *Inland Architect and News Record* 19 (May 1892): 48–49.

37. Daniel H. Burnham and Edward H. Bennett, *Plan of Chicago*, ed. Charles Moore (orig. pub. 1909; reprint, with an introduction by Kristen Schaffer Smith, New York: Princeton Architectural Press, 1993), 74–85. The text was written by Moore based on notes made by Burnham and Bennett. On the 1909 plan for Chicago, see Carl Condit, *Chicago 1910–29: Building, Planning and Urban Technology* (Chicago: University of Chicago Press, 1973), 59–85; Hines, "Beyond the White City: The Chicago Plan of 1909," in *Burnham of Chicago*, 312–45; Joan E. Draper, *Edward H. Bennett, Architect and City Planner, 1874–1954* (Chicago: Art Institute of Chicago, 1982); Fisher, "An Iconography of City Planning"; Schaffer, *Daniel H. Burnham*, 97–98; and Carl Smith, *The Plan of Chicago: Daniel Burnham and the Remaking of the American City* (Chicago: University of Chicago Press, 2006).

38. Burnham and Bennett, *Plan of Chicago*, 1.

39. Ibid., 116.

40. Walter Fisher, appendix, "Legal Aspects of the Plan of Chicago," in Burnham and Bennett, *Plan of Chicago*; quotation is from p. 141.

41. Carl Condit describes the partial implementation of the 1909 plan in *Chicago 1910–29*, 53, 80–81.

42. Burnham and Bennett paid particular attention to Michigan Avenue because, of all the ideas presented in the plan, it was the closest to being actually realized. The city had already taken up the problem of converting the Illinois Central rail yards along the shore of Lake Michigan just south of the Chicago River into Grant Park, widening and extending Michigan Avenue as a major boulevard adjacent to it. Burnham and Bennett, *Plan of Chicago*, 99–100.

43. On the transformation of Michigan Avenue during these years, see Condit, *Chicago 1910–29*, 75–100; Willis, *Form Follows Finance*, 49–65; John Stamper, *Chicago's North Michigan Avenue: Planning and Development, 1900–1930* (Chicago: University of Chicago Press, 1991); and Bruegmann, *The Architects and the City*.

44. Katherine Solomonson discusses the Chicago skyscrapers of this era, with special emphasis on the Tribune Tower, in *The Chicago Tribune Tower Competition: Skyscraper Design and Cultural Change in the 1920s* (Chicago: University of Chicago Press, 2001).

POSTSCRIPT

1. Rem Koolhaas, *Delirious New York: A Retroactive Manifesto for Manhattan* (orig. pub. 1978; reprint, New York: Monacelli Press, 1994), 9.

2. Arnold Lewis, *An Early Encounter with Tomorrow*.

3. *Chicago Daily News*, December 30, 1938; clipping in "Notes on the Monadnock" made by Aldis and Co., building managers, (October 1957). Archives and Manuscript Department, Chicago History Museum. Mies's admiration for the building was apparently so great that in his 1959 design for the adjacent Federal Building complex, he was careful not to expose the Monadnock to an open plaza, lest a developer be tempted to replace it with a new building befitting the new value of the site. Interview with Myron Goldsmith, "Chicago Oral History Project," p. 54. Ryerson Library, Art Institute of Chicago.

4. Jean-Louis Cohen presents a comprehensive analysis of the role America played in European constructions of modern architecture in "The Moderns Discover America: Mendelsohn, Neutra and Maiakovsky," in *Scenes of the World to Come*, 85–103. See also Thomas A. P. Van Leeuwen, "The Skyward Trend of Thought: Some Ideas on the History of the Methodology of the Skyscraper," in *American Architecture: Innovation and Tradition*, ed. David G. DeLong, Helen Searing, and Robert A. M. Stern (New York: Rizzoli, 1986), 57–81; and Robert Bruegmann, "The Myth of the Chicago School," in Waldheim and Ray, *Chicago Architecture*, 15–29.

5. Lewis and Cohen have noted the particular influence of the German critic Karl Hinkeldeyn in relaying information about Chicago architecture back to Germany. See Lewis, *An Early Encounter with Tomorrow*, 119; and Cohen, *Scenes of the World to Come*, 24.

6. Wilhelm Bode, "Moderne Kunst in den vereinigten Staaten von Amerika," *Kunstgewerbeblatt* 5 (1894): 118; quoted in Lewis, *An Early Encounter with Tomorrow*, 203. See also Paul Graef, *Neubauten in Nordamerika* (Berlin: Julius Becker, 1899).

7. Cohen provides a comprehensive bibliography of these publications in *Scenes of the World to Come*, 220–21. They include: Ludwig Hilberseimer, "Das Hochhaus," *Das Kunstblatt* 6 (December 1922): 525–31; Erich Mendelsohn, *Amerika: Builderbuch eines Architekten* (Berlin: Rudolf Mosse, 1926); Walter C. Behrendt, *Städtebau und Wohnungswesen in den Vereinigten Staaten: Bericht über eine Studienreise* (Berlin: Guido Hackebeil AG, 1926); Ludwig Hilberseimer, *Groszstadtarchitektur* (Stuttgart: Julius Hoffman, 1927); Richard Neutra, *Wie baut Amerika? Gegenwartige bauarbeit Amerikanischer kreis* (Stuttgart: Hoffmann, 1927); Bruno Taut, *Die neue Baukunst in Europa und Amerika* (Stuttgart: Verlag Julius Hoffmann, 1929); Bruno Taut, *Modern Architecture* (London: The Studio, 1929); and Richard Neutra, *Amerika: Die Stilbildung des neuen Bauens in der Vereinigten Staaten* (Vienna: Anton Schroll Verlag, 1930).

8. Adrian Forty describes the meaning of the term *sachlich* in early twentieth-century German architectural criticism in *Words and Buildings*, 180–84.

9. Hilberseimer, "Das Hochhaus," anonymous translation in Miscellaneous Pamphlets folder, Monadnock Building, Chicago History Museum.

10. Mendelsohn, *Amerika*, 64. This book was written in the wake of Mendelsohn's 1924 trip to New York, Buffalo, Detroit, and Chicago. Some of the images he used were taken by the Danish architect Knud Lonberg-Holm, who was teaching at the University of Michigan. On Mendelsohn's visit to the United States, see Cohen, *Scenes of the World to Come*, 86–92.

11. Hilberseimer, *Groszstadtarchitektur*, 65; Taut, *Die neue Baukunst in Europa und Amerika*, 35.

12. Although Taut credited Root in the caption to his photograph of the Monadnock, his knowledge of Root's work and of Chicago was vague. He described Root as the architect of the "very first of the skyscrapers, the lofty buildings of New York," and he dated the World's Columbian Exposition at 1900 instead of 1893. Taut, *Modern Architecture*, 65–68; quotation is from p. 66.

13. Neutra, *Amerika*, 104–5.

14. Walter C. Behrendt, *Modern Building: Its Nature, Problems and Forms* (New York: Harcourt and Brace, 1937), 120.

15. Walter C. Behrendt, *Der Sieg des neuen Baustils* (Stuttgart, 1927); Harry Francis Mallgrave has translated this book as *The Victory of the New Building Style*, with an introduction by Detlef Mertins (Los Angeles: J. Paul Getty Trust Publications, 2000), 121. On Behrendt's American connections, see M. David Samson, "'Unser New Yorker Mitarbeiter': Lewis Mumford, Walter Curt Behrendt, and the Modern Movement in Germany," *Journal of the Society of Architectural Historians* 55, no. 2 (June 1996): 126–39; and Mertins, introduction to *The Victory of the New Building Style*.

16. Al Chase, "Monadnock Building to be Restyled in City's Biggest Modernization Job," part 5, *Chicago Daily Tribune*, January 16, 1938, p. 12; "Custom Built Modernization Program," *The Economist*, March 26, 1938; and "Chicago Remodels a Landmark, Gives Building a Cost Study. Progressive Styling Ups Occupancy 7% in Famed Monadnock," *Architectural Forum* (October 1938). The original interiors were restored in the 1980s. Gary Washburn, "Tight Money a Parent of Renewal," *Chicago Tribune*, August 15, 1982; Jane Clark, "A Man and His Mountain: Restoring the Monadnock," *Inland Architect* 29, no. 1 (January–February 1985): 20–23; Michael L. Walsh, "Evolving Design," *Inland Architect* 31, no. 3 (May–June 1987): 50–53; Thomas G. Keohan, "Preserving Historic Office Building Corridors: The Monadnock Building, Chicago, Illinois," *Preservation Tech Notes* (July 1989): 1–8; and Steve Kersch, "Time Travel," *Chicago Tribune*, April 13, 1991, section 8, p. 17.

17. Root, "Broad Art Criticism."

18. Giedion, "The Chicago School," 310. On Giedion's architectural historiography, see Sokratis Georgiadis, *Sigfried Giedion: An Intellectual Biography*, trans. Colin Hall (Edinburgh: Edinburgh University Press, 1993); Detlef Mertins, "Transparencies Yet to Come: Sigfried Giedion and the Prehistory of Architectural Modernity" (Ph.D. diss., Princeton University, 1996); and Hilde Heynen, "Constructing the Modern Movement," in *Architecture and Modernity: A Critique* (Cambridge, MA: MIT Press, 1999), 26–70.

19. Giedion labeled the effect of transparency *Durchdringung*, meaning social as well as visual interpenetration. Heynen, *Architecture and Modernity*, 30–35; Forty, "Transparency," in *Words and Buildings*, 286–88.

20. Montgomery Schuyler, "D. H. Burnham and Co." (1896), in *"American Architecture," and Other Writings*, ed. William H. Jordy and Ralph Coe (Cambridge, MA: Harvard University Press, Belknap Press, 1961), 415. This essay was originally published as "Architecture in Chicago: D. H. Bunham and Co.," no. 2, part 2 of the Great American Architects series, *Architectural Record* 5 (February 1896): 49–72.

21. See for example Hitchcock, *Modern Architecture*; Mumford, *The Brown Decades*; Mumford, *Sticks and Stones*; and Hitchcock, *The Architecture of H. H. Richardson and His Times*.

22. Mumford, *The Brown Decades*, 57.

23. Museum of Modern Art, *Early Modern Architecture in Chicago 1870–1910: Catalogue of an Exhibition Held at the MoMA, New York January 18 to February 23 1933*, 2nd ed. (New York: Museum of Modern Art, 1940). See also Malcolm Vaughan, "Chicago Declared True Birthplace of Skyscrapers," *New York American*, January 21, 1933; and James Johnson Sweeney, "Architecture, Old and New," *Creative Art* (April 1933): 272–75. On Johnson's participation in this show, see Terence Riley, "Portrait of the Curator as a Young Man," in *Philip Johnson and the Museum of Modern Art: Studies in Modern Art no. 6* (New York: MoMA and Harry N. Abrams, 1998), 34–69.

24. Johnson used the Chicago skyscraper as a way to critique contemporary art-deco skyscrapers in New York as too ornamental and insufficiently structurally expressive. Philip Johnson, "The Skyscraper School of Modern Architecture," *The Arts* 17, no. 8 (May 1931): 569.

25. Thomas Tallmadge, ed., *The Origin of the Skyscraper* (Chicago: Alderbrink Press, 1931); Thomas Tallmadge, "Was the Home Insurance Building in Chicago the First Skyscraper of Skeleton Construction?" *Architectural Record* 76, no. 2 (August 1934): 113–18; and Thomas Tallmadge, *Architecture in Old Chicago* (Chicago: University of Chicago Press, 1941). While Tallmadge popularized this idea of the Home Insurance building's chronological primacy, this view was expressed as early as 1899 by the architect and critic Clarence H. Blackall, who called it the "first skeleton building" in "The Legitimate Design of the Architectural Casing for Steel Skeleton Structures."

26. Press release for the exhibition "Early Modern Architecture: Chicago 1870–1910," January 15, 1932. MoMA Archives.

27. Giedion, *Space Time and Architecture*, 368.

28. Randall, *History of the Development of Building Construction in Chicago*.

29. An earlier version was published as Carl Condit, "The Chicago School and the Modern Movement," *Art in America* (January 1948).

30. Carl Condit, *The Rise of the Skyscraper* (Chicago: University of Chicago Press, 1952), 19.

31. Condit, *The Chicago School of Architecture*, 110–11; quotation is from p. 110.

32. Colin Rowe, "Chicago Frame" (1956), in *"The Mathematics of the Ideal Villa" and Other Essays* (Cambridge, MA: MIT Press, 1976), 89–117.

SELECTED BIBLIOGRAPHY

The sources cited here include articles from professional trade journals as well as popular magazines and newspapers, all of which describe responses to the rapidly growing built environment of downtown Chicago in the 1880s and '90s. I also include early histories of modern architecture in which Chicago forms a central role, and later histories in which the complexities and contradictions of that world have been uncovered.

Abu-Lughod, Janet L. *New York, Chicago, Los Angeles: America's Global Cities.* Minneapolis: University of Minnesota Press, 1991.

Addams, Jane. *Hull House Maps and Papers.* Chicago, 1895.

Adler, Dankmar. "Architects and Trade Unions." *Inland Architect and News Record* 27 (May 1896): 32.

———. "The Influence of Steel Construction and Plate Glass upon Style." *Inland Architect and News Record* 28 (November 1896): 34–37.

———. "Light in Tall Office Buildings." *Engineering Magazine* 4 (November 1892): 171–86.

———. "Tall Buildings." *Inland Architect and News Record* 17, no. 5 (June 1891): 58.

"Anarchism." *Alarm: A Socialist Weekly* 1, no. 5, November 1, 1884, p. 1.

"Anarchy vs. Government," *Alarm: A Socialist Weekly* 2, no. 4, August 22, 1885, p. 1.

Andreas, Alfred T. *History of Chicago: From the Earliest Period to the Present Time.* 3 vols. Chicago, 1884–88.

Avrich, Paul. *The Haymarket Tragedy.* Princeton, NJ: Princeton University Press, 1984.

Barth, Gunther. *City People: The Rise of Modern City Culture in Nineteenth-Century America.* New York: Oxford University Press, 1980.

Baumann, Frederick. *The Art of Preparing Foundations for All Kinds of Buildings, with Particular Illustrations of the "Method of Isolated Piers" as Followed in Chicago.* Chicago: J. M. Wing, 1873.

———. "Thoughts on Style." *Inland Architect and News Record* 20, no. 4 (November 1892): 34–37.

———. "Two Questions Considered: First; Is Architecture an Art; Second; Can Architecture Again Become a Living Art? Preceded by a Historical Review of the Art." *Inland Architect and News Record* 29, no. 3 (April 1897): 23–26.

Beeks, James. *30,000 Locked Out! The Great Strike of the Building Trades in Chicago.* Chicago, 1887.

Behrendt, Walter C. *Modern Building: Its Nature, Problems and Forms.* New York: Harcourt and Brace, 1937.

———. *Städtebau und Wohnungswesen in den Vereinigten Staaten: Bericht über eine Studienreise.* Berlin: Guido Hackebeil AG, 1926.

———. *The Victory of the New Building Style* (1937). Translated by Harry Francis Mallgrave, introduction by Detlef Mertins. Los Angeles: J. Paul Getty Trust Publications, 2000.

Berg, David F. *Chicago's White City of 1893.* Lexington: University of Kentucky Press, 1976.

Berger, Miles L. *They Built Chicago: Entrepreneurs Who Shaped a Great City's Architecture.* Chicago: Bonus Books, 1992.

Blackall, Clarence H. "The Legitimate Design of the Architectural Casing for Steel Skeleton Structures." *American Architect and Building News* 66, no. 1249 (December 2, 1899): 78–80.

———. "Notes on Travel—Chicago." *American Architect and Building News* 22, no. 626 (December 24 and 31, 1887): 299–300, 313–14.

———. "On the Use of Colored Terracotta." *Brickbuilder* 1 (1892): 12.

Bletter, Rosemarie Haag. "The Invention of the Skyscraper: Notes on Its Diverse Histories." *Assemblage* 2 (1987): 110–17.

Block, Marguerite Beck. *The New Church in the New World: A Study of Swedenborgianism in America*. New York: Octagon Books, 1968.

Bluestone, Daniel. *Constructing Chicago*. New Haven, CT: Yale University Press, 1991.

———. "Sullivan's Chicago: From 'Shirt-Front' to Alley to All-Round Structures." Lecture given at "Sullivan at 150," Chicago History Museum, October 13–15, 2006.

Bogart, Ernest L. "The Chicago Building Trades Dispute I." *Political Science Quarterly* 16, no. 1 (March 1901): 114–41.

———. "The Chicago Building Trades Dispute II." *Political Science Quarterly* 16, no. 2 (June 1901): 222–47.

Bohlmann, Rachel E. "Our 'House Beautiful': The Woman's Temple and the Women's Christian Temperance Union Effort to Establish Place and Identity in Downtown Chicago, 1887–98." *Journal of Women's History* 11, no. 2 (Summer 1999): 110–11.

Bolotin, Norm. *The World's Columbian Exposition: The Chicago World's Fair of 1893*. Urbana: University of Illinois Press, 2002.

Bordin, Ruth. *Women and Temperance: The Quest for Power and Liberty, 1873–1900*. New Brunswick, NJ: Rutgers University Press, 1990.

Boyer, M. Christine. *Dreaming the Rational City: The Myth of American City Planning*. Cambridge, MA: MIT Press, 1983.

"Break Their Record for Smoke. Chicago's Most Obnoxious Chimneys Excel Their Former Efforts." *Chicago Daily Times*, July 29, 1892, p. 9.

Brooks, Michael W. "Ruskin's Influence in America." In *John Ruskin and Victorian Architecture*, 277–97. New Brunswick, NJ: Rutgers University Press, 1987.

Bruegmann, Robert. *The Architects and the City: Holabird and Roche of Chicago 1880–1918*. Chicago: University of Chicago Press, 1997.

———. *Holabird and Roche, Holabird and Root: An Illustrated Catalogue of Works, 1880–1940*. Vol. 1. New York: Garland, 1991.

———. "The Myth of the Chicago School." In Waldheim and Ray, *Chicago Architecture*, 15–29.

Burnham, Daniel H., and Edward H. Bennett. *Plan of Chicago*. Edited by Charles Moore. Orig. pub. 1909. Reprint, with an introduction by Kristen Schaffer Smith, New York: Princeton Architectural Press, 1993.

Cerza, Alphonse. *A History of the Ancient and Accepted Scottish Rite in Illinois, 1846–1965*. Bloomington, IN: Illinois Council of Deliberation, 1966.

"Chicago." *American Architect and Building News* 47 (January 26, 1895): 43.

"Chicago: Buildings of Ten Stories or More Erected; The Windy City Passes into an Era of Very High Buildings." *New York Times*, March 9, 1891, p. 3.

"Chicago Is Enveloped in Smoke. Dirty, Black Clouds from Downtown Chimneys Hang over the City Like a Pall." *Chicago Daily Tribune*, December 2, 1898, p. 3.

The Chicago Report on Smoke Abatement; A Landmark Survey of the Technology and History of Air Pollution Control. Orig. pub. 1915. Reprint; Elmsford, NY: Maxwell Reprint, 1971.

Chicago of To-Day: The Metropolis of the West, the Nation's Choice for the World's Columbian Exposition. Chicago: Acme Publishing and Engraving Co., 1891.

"Chicago's Big Buildings." *Chicago Daily Tribune*, September 13, 1891, p. 25.

"Chicago's Great Masonic Temple—The Structure Will Be the Highest Building in the World." *Chicago Daily Tribune*, June 18, 1890, p. 5.

"Chicago's New Office Buildings: Structure Commenced or Opened to the Public during the Current Month." *Chicago Daily Tribune*, May 8, 1892.

"A City under One Roof—The Masonic Temple." *Scientific American* 70, no. 6 (February 10, 1894): 81–82.

Ciucci, Giorgio, Francesco Dal Co, Mario Manieri-Elia, and Manfredo Tafuri, eds. *The American City: From the Civil War to the New Deal*. Translated by Barbara Luigia La Penta. Cambridge, MA: MIT Press, 1979.

Clausen, Meredith L. "Paris of the 1880s and the Rookery." In *Chicago Architecture 1872–1922: Birth of a Metropolis*, edited by John Zukowsky, 157–71. New York: Prestel, 1987.

Clawson, Mary Anne. *Constructing Brotherhood: Class, Gender and Fraternalism*. Princeton, NJ: Princeton University Press, 1989.

Cohen, Jean-Louis. *Scenes of the World to Come: European Architecture and the American Challenge 1893–1960*. Paris: Flammarion; Montreal: Canadian Center for Architecture, 1995.

Commission on Chicago Historical and Architectural Landmarks. *Monadnock Block*. Chicago: The Commission, 1976.

———. *Reliance Building*. Chicago: The Commission, 1979.

Condit, Carl. *Chicago 1910–29: Building, Planning and Urban Technology*. Chicago: University of Chicago Press, 1973.

———. *The Chicago School of Architecture: A History of Commercial and Public Buildings in the Chicago Area, 1875–1925*. Chicago: University of Chicago Press, 1964.

———. *The Rise of the Skyscraper*. Chicago: University of Chicago Press, 1952.

Cram, Ralph Adams. "Civic Development." Part 1. *Inland Architect and News Record* 51, no. 3 (March 1908): 21.

Cronon, William. *Nature's Metropolis: Chicago and the Great West*. New York: W. W. Norton and Co., 1991.

Currey, J. Seymour. *The Story of Old Fort Dearborn*. Chicago: A. C. McClurg and Co., 1912.

Daly, Raymond C. *75 Years of Construction Pioneering: George A. Fuller Company, 1882–1957*. New York: Newcomen Society in North America, 1957.

Darling, Sharon S. "Architectural Terra-Cotta." In *Chicago Ceramics and Glass: An Illustrated History from 1871 to 1933*, 161–98. Chicago: Chicago Historical Society, 1979.

David, Henry. *The History of the Haymarket Affair: A Study in American Social-Revolutionary and Labor Movements*. New York: Russell and Russell, 1936.

De Wolf, Oscar C., MD. "The Relation of State Medicine to the Profession of Architecture." *Inland Architect and Builder* 8, no. 8 (December 1886): 67–69.

Dowd, Charles N., MD. "A Study of the Hygienic Condition of Our Streets." *Inland Architect and News Record* 15, no. 6 (July 1890): 82–83.

Draper, Joan E. *Edward H. Bennett, Architect and City Planner, 1874–1954*. Chicago: Art Institute of Chicago, 1982.

Dreiser, Theodore. *Sister Carrie*. New York: Doubleday, Page and Co., 1900.

Duffy, John. *The Sanitarians: A History of American Public Health*. Urbana: University of Illinois Press, 1990.

Dumenil, Lynn. *Freemasonry and American Culture 1880–1930*. Princeton, NJ: Princeton University Press, 1984.

Egbert, Donald Drew. "The Idea of Organic Expression and American Architecture." In *Evolutionary Thought in America*, edited by Stow Persons, 336–96. New Haven, CT: Yale University Press, 1950.

Egbert, Donald Drew, and Paul Sprague. "In Search of John Edelmann." *AIA Journal* 45 (February 1966): 35–41.

Eidlitz, Leopold. *The Nature and Function of Art, More Especially of Architecture*. New York: A. C. Armstrong and Son, 1881.

Ericsson, Henry. *Sixty Years a Builder: The Autobiography of Henry Ericsson*. Chicago: A. Kroch and Sons, 1942.

"Features of Chicago Which Constitute the Seven Wonders of the City." *Chicago Daily Tribune*, December 5, 1897, p. 45.

Ferree, Barr. "Chicago." Part 1. *Architecture and Building* (January 2, 1892): 10–11.

———. "Chicago—The Buildings." Part 2. *Architecture and Building* (January 9, 1892): 17.

———. "Chicago—The Buildings—The Plans." Part 3. *Architecture and Building* (January 16, 1892): 27–28.

———. "The High Building and Its Art." *Scribner's Magazine* 15 (March 1894): 312.

———. "The Modern Office Building." *Inland Architect and News Record* 27 (February 1896): 4–5; 27 (March 1896): 12–14; 27 (April 1896): 23–25; 27 (June 1896): 45–47.

Fink, Leon. *Workingmen's Democracy: The Knights of Labor and American Politics*. Urbana: University of Illinois Press, 1983.

Fireproof Building Construction: Prominent Buildings Erected by the George A. Fuller Company. New York: T. D. Rich and G. A. Fuller, 1904.

Fisher, Irving D. "An Iconography of City Planning." In *Emanuel Swedenborg: A Continuing Vision; A Pictorial Biography and Anthology of Essays and Poetry.* New York: Swedenborg Foundation, Inc., 1988.

Flanagan, Maureen A. *Seeing with Their Hearts: Chicago Women and the Vision of the Good City, 1871–1933.* Princeton, NJ: Princeton University Press, 2002.

Flinn, John J. *Chicago: The Marvelous City of the West; A History, An Encyclopedia.* Chicago: Standard Guide Co., 1892.

———. *The Standard Guide of Chicago.* Chicago: Standard Guide Co., 1893.

Fogelson, Robert. *Downtown: Its Rise and Fall, 1880–1950.* New Haven, CT: Yale University Press, 2001.

Foner, Philip S., ed. *The Autobiographies of the Haymarket Martyrs.* New York: Humanities Press, 1969.

Forty, Adrian. *Words and Buildings: A Vocabulary of Modern Architecture.* London: Thames and Hudson, 2000.

Freitag, Joseph Kendall. *Architectural Engineering with Special Reference to High Building Construction including Many Examples of Chicago Office Buildings.* New York: J. Wiley and Sons, 1906.

———. *The Fireproofing of Steel Buildings.* New York: J. Wiley and Sons, 1899.

Friedman, Donald. *Historical Building Construction, Design and Materials.* New York: W. W. Norton, 1995.

Fuller, Henry Blake. *The Cliff-Dwellers.* New York: Harper and Bros., 1893.

———. "The Upward Movement in Chicago." *Atlantic Monthly* 80 (October 1897): 534–47.

Gage, John. *Color and Culture: Practice and Meaning from Antiquity to Abstraction.* Boston: Little, Brown and Co., 1993.

Gatzert, August. *Limitation of Building Heights in the City of Chicago.* Chicago, 1913.

George, Henry. *Progress and Poverty: An Inquiry into the Cause of Industrial Depressions and of Increase of Want with Increase of Wealth; The Remedy.* New York: D. Appleton and Company, 1881.

Geraniotis, Roula. "German Architects of Nineteenth Century Chicago." Ph.D. diss., University of Illinois, 1985.

———. "German Architectural Theory and Practice in Chicago, 1850–1900." *Winterthur Portfolio* 21 (Winter 1986): 293–306.

———. "The University of Illinois and German Architectural Education." *Journal of Architectural Education* 38, no. 4 (Summer 1985): 15–21.

Geraniotis, Roula, and Gerald R. Larson. "Toward a Better Understanding of the Iron Skeleton Frame in Chicago," *Journal of the Society of Architectural Historians* 46, no. 1 (March 1987): 39–48.

Gibbs, Kenneth Turney. *Business Architectural Imagery in America 1870–1930.* Ann Arbor: UMI Research Press, 1984.

Giedion, Sigfried. "The Chicago School." In *Space Time and Architecture, the Growth of a New Tradition*, 385–88. Orig. pub. 1941. Reprint; Cambridge, MA: Harvard University Press, 1974.

Gilbert, James. *Designing the Industrial State: The Intellectual Pursuit of Collectivism in America, 1880–1940.* Chicago: Quadrangle Books, 1972.

———. *Perfect Cities: Chicago's Utopias of 1893.* Chicago: University of Chicago Press, 1991.

Green, James. *Death in the Haymarket: A Story of Chicago, the First Labor Movement, and the Bombing That Divided America.* Rev. and expanded 2nd ed. New York: Pantheon, 2006.

Greenough, Horatio. "American Architecture (1843–52)." In *Form and Function: Remarks on Art, Design, and Architecture*, edited by Harold Small, 51–68. Berkeley and Los Angeles: University of California Press, 1947.

Hales, Peter Bacon. *Silver Cities: Photographing American Urbanization, 1839–1939.* Albuquerque: University of New Mexico Press, 2005.

"A Halt Call on 'Skyscrapers.'" *Scribner's Magazine* 19 (March 1896): 395–96.

Hammett, Edward S. "The Building and the Designing of the 'Skyscraper.'" *American Architect and Building News* (November 1905): 158–60.

"Height Is No Menace. Chicago's Big Office Buildings as Safe as They Are Popular." *Chicago Daily Tribune*, February 19, 1894, p. 9.

Hermant, Jacques. "L'architecture aux Etats-Unis et a l'exposition universelle de Chicago." *L'Architecture* 7 (October 20, 1894): 341–46.

Hilberseimer, Ludwig. *Groszstadtarchitektur*. Stuttgart: Julius Hoffman, 1927.

———. "Das Hochhaus." *Das Kunstblatt* 6, no. 2 (December 1922): 525–31.

Hill, Lewis H. *Report to the Commission on the Reliance Building*. Chicago: Commission on Chicago Landmarks, 1969.

Himmelwright, A. L. A. "High Buildings." *North American Review* 163 (November 1896): 580–86.

Hines, Thomas S. *Burnham of Chicago, Architect and Planner*. Chicago: University of Chicago Press, 1979.

Hirsch, Eric L. *Urban Revolt: Ethnic Politics in the Nineteenth-Century Chicago Labor Movement*. Berkeley and Los Angeles: University of California Press, 1998.

Hitchcock, Henry Russell. *The Architecture of H. H. Richardson and His Times*. New York: MoMA, 1936.

———. *Modern Architecture: Romanticism and Reintegration*. Orig. pub. 1929. Reprint; New York: Arno, 1972.

———. "Ruskin and American Architecture, or Regeneration Long Delayed." In *Concerning Architecture: Essays on Architectural Writers and Writing Presented to Nikolaus Pevsner*, ed. John Summerson, 166–206. London: Penguin Press, 1968.

Hoffman, Donald. *The Architecture of John Wellborn Root*. Chicago: University of Chicago Press, 1973.

———. "The Setback Skyscraper City of 1891: An Unknown Essay by Louis H. Sullivan." *Journal of the Society of Architectural Historians* 29, no. 2 (May 1970): 181–87.

Holland, Robert A. *Chicago in Maps 1612–2002*. New York: Rizzoli, 2005.

Horsman, Reginald. *Race and Manifest Destiny: The Origins of American Racial Anglo-Saxonism*. Cambridge, MA: Harvard University Press, 1981.

Hoyt, Homer. *One Hundred Years of Land Values in Chicago*. Chicago: University of Chicago Press, 1933.

Industrial Chicago. Vols. 1 and 2. Chicago: Goodspeed Publishing Co., 1891.

"Informal Opening of 'The Reliance.' A Triumph of the Builder's Art—Unique Building Construction." *Chicago Daily Tribune*, March 16, 1895, p. 8.

Isenberg, Alison. "City Beautiful or Beautiful Mess? The Gendered Origins of a Civic Ideal." In *Downtown America: A History of the Place and the People Who Made It*, 13–41. Chicago: University of Chicago Press, 2004.

"It's Big Buildings—Chicago Not So Black as It's Painted." *Chicago Daily Tribune*, October 16, 1892, p. 35.

Jackson, Kenneth T. *Crabgrass Frontier: The Suburbanization of the United States*. New York: Oxford University Press, 1985.

Jenkins, Charles E. "A White Enameled Building." *Architectural Record* 4 (January–March 1895): 299–306.

Jenney, William Le Baron. "A Few Practical Hints." Address delivered to the Chicago Architectural Sketch Club, January 1889. Excerpted in *Industrial Chicago*, vol. 2, *The Building Interests* (Chicago: Goodspeed Publishing Co., 1891), 609–21.

———. "An Age of Steel and Clay." *Inland Architect and News Record* 15, no. 7 (December 1890): 75–77.

———. "Architecture." *Inland Architect and Builder* 1 (March 1883): 18–20; (April 1883): 33–34; (May 1883): 48–50; (June 1883): 63 (July 1883), 76–78; 2 (September 1883): 105–6; (October 1883): 117; (November 1883): 130–32; (December 1883): 144–46; (January 1884): 158; and 3 (February 1884): 3.

———. "The Chicago Construction, or Tall Buildings on a Compressible Soil." *Inland Architect and News Record* 18 (November 1891): 41.

Jordy, William H. *Progressive and Academic Ideals at the Turn of the Twentieth Century*. Vol. 4 of *American Buildings and Their Architects*. New York: Oxford University Press, 1972.

———. "The Tall Buildings." In *Louis Sullivan: The Function of Ornament*, ed. Wim de Wit, 65–157. New York: W.W. Norton, 1986.

Junge, W. H. "Terra Cotta." *Inland Architect and Builder* 5, no. 4 (May 1885): 64–65.

Keil, Hartmut, and John B. Jentz, eds. *German Workers in Industrial Chicago, 1850–1910: A Comparative Portrait*. DeKalb: Northern Illinois University Press, 1983.

Kelsey, Albert. "Municipal Improvements." Part 1. *Inland Architect and News Record* 45, no. 6 (July 1905): 63–64.

———. "Municipal Improvements." Part 2. *Inland Architect and News Record* 46, no. 1 (August 1905): 6.

———. "Municipal Improvements." Part 3. *Inland Architect and News Record* 46, no. 2 (September 1905): 17–18.

———. "Municipal Improvements." Part 4. *Inland Architect and News Record* 46, no. 2 (November 1905): 11–13.

———. "Municipal Improvements." Part 5. *Inland Architect and News Record* 49, no. 3 (March 1907): 44–45.

———. "Municipal Improvements." Part 6. *Inland Architect and News Record* 49, no. 6 (June 1907): 78–79.

———. "Municipal Improvements." Part 7. *Inland Architect and News Record* 50, no. 2 (August 1907): 20.

———. "Municipal Improvements." Part 8. *Inland Architect and News Record* 50. 50, no. 4 (October 1907): 11.

Kirkland, Joseph. *The Story of Chicago*. Chicago: Dibble Publishing Co., 1892.

Laing, Alan K. *Nathan Clifford Ricker 1843–1924: Pioneer in American Architectural Education*. Urbana: University of Illinois Press, 1973.

Landau, Sarah Bradford. *P. B. Wight, Architect, Contractor, and Critic, 1838–1925*. Chicago: Art Institute of Chicago, 1981.

Lane, M. A. "High Buildings of Chicago." *Harper's Weekly* 35 (October 31, 1891): 853–54, 856–57.

Larson, Paul Clifford, and Susan M. Brown, eds. *The Spirit of H. H. Richardson on the Midland Prairies*. Ames: Iowa State University Press, 1988.

Lears, T. J. Jackson. *No Place of Grace: Antimodernism and the Transformation of American Culture 1880–1920*. New York: Pantheon Books, 1981.

Lee, Paula. "The Temperance Temple and Architectural Patronage in Late-Nineteenth-Century Chicago." *Gender and History* 17, no. 3 (November 2005): 793–885.

Leslie, Thomas. "'As Large as the Situation of the Columns Would Allow': Building Cladding and Plate Glass in the Chicago Skyscraper, 1885–1905." *Technology and Culture* 49, no. 2 (2008): 399–419.

———. "Glass and Light: The Influence of Interior Illumination on the Chicago School." *Journal of Architectural Education* 58, no. 1 (September 2004): 13–23.

Lewis, Arnold. *An Early Encounter with Tomorrow: Europeans, Chicago's Loop, and the World's Columbian Exposition*. Urbana: University of Illinois Press, 1997.

"Like a City of Steel. How Chicago's Big Buildings Are Being Constructed." *Chicago Daily Tribune*, June 25, 1891, p. 8.

Lindholm, S. V. "Analysis of the Building-Trades Conflict in Chicago, from the Trades-Union Stand-Point." *Journal of Political Economy* 8, no. 3 (June 1900): 327–46.

McGovern, John. "Chicago Is Not Yet Paris." *Building Budget* 3, no. 8 (August 1887): 101.

Mack, Robert C. "The Manufacture and Use of Architectural Terra-Cotta in the United States." In *The Technology of Historic American Buildings*, ed. H. Ward Jandel, 117–50. Washington DC: Foundation for Preservation Technology, 1983.

Maher, George W. "Originality in American Architecture." *Inland Architect* 10, no. 4 (October 1887): 34–35.

Mallgrave, Harry Francis. *Gottfried Semper, Architect of the Nineteenth Century: A Personal and Intellectual Biography*. New Haven, CT: Yale University Press, 1996.

———. "Semper, Klemm and Ethnography." *Lotus International*, no. 109 (2001): 118–31.

Martin, Carlos Eduardo. "Riveting: Steel Technology, Building Codes and the Production of Modern Places." Ph.D. diss., Stanford University, 1999.

Marx, Leo. *The Machine in the Garden: Technology and the Pastoral Ideal in America*. Orig. pub. 1964. Reprint, London: Oxford University Press, 1967.

Masonic Fraternity Temple Association. *Masonic Temple Handbook*. Chicago: W. J. Jefferson Printing and Publishing Co., n.d. (ca. 1892).

Matthiessen, F. O. *American Renaissance: Art and Expression in the Age of Emerson and Whitman*. London: Oxford University Press, 1941.

Mayer, Harold M., and Richard C. Wade. *Chicago: Growth of a Metropolis*. Chicago: University of Chicago Press, 1969.

Melosi, Martin V., ed. *Pollution and Reform in American Cities, 1870–1930*. Austin: University of Texas Press, 1980.

Mendelsohn, Erich. *Amerika: Builderbuch eines Architekten*. Berlin: Rudolf Mosse, 1926.

Menocal, Narciso. *Architecture as Nature: The Transcendentalist Idea of Louis Sullivan*. Madison: University of Wisconsin Press, 1981.

Metzger, Charles Reid. *Emerson and Greenough: Transcendental Pioneers of an American Aesthetic*. Berkeley and Los Angeles: University of California Press, 1954.

Miller, Donald L. *City of the Century: The Epic of Chicago and the Making of America*. New York: Simon and Schuster, 1996.

Miller, Ross. *American Apocalypse: The Great Fire and the Myth of Chicago*. Chicago: University of Chicago Press, 1990.

Monroe, Harriet. *John Wellborn Root: A Study of His Life and Art*. Orig. pub. Boston: Houghton, Mifflin and Co., 1896; reprint, Park Forest, IL: Prairie School Press, 1966.

Montgomery, Royal E. *Industrial Relations in the Chicago Building Trades*. Chicago: University of Chicago Press, 1927.

Moore, Charles. *Daniel H. Burnham: Architect, Planner of Cities*. Orig. pub. 1921. Reprint, New York: Da Capo Press, 1968.

Moore, William D. *Masonic Temples: Freemasonry, Ritual, Architecture and Masculine Archetypes*. Knoxville: University of Tennessee Press, 2006.

Moran, George E. *Moran's Dictionary of Chicago and Its Vicinity*. Chicago: G. E. Moran, 1892.

Morris, Frank M. *Morris' Dictionary of Chicago*. Chicago: Frank M. Morris, 1891.

Morrison, Hugh. *Louis Sullivan: Prophet of Modern Architecture*. Orig. pub. 1935; reprint, New York: W. W. Norton, 1998.

Moses, John. *History of Chicago*. Chicago: Munsell and Co., 1895.

Moudry, Roberta, ed. *The American Skyscraper: Cultural Histories*. Cambridge: Cambridge University Press, 2005.

Mumford, Lewis. *The Brown Decades: A Study of the Arts in America, 1865–1895*. New York: Harcourt, Brace and Company, 1931.

———. *Sticks and Stones: A Study of American Architecture and Civilization*. New York: W. W. Norton and Company, 1934.

Murray, Alex W. "The Sanitation of Cities." *Inland Architect and Builder* 3, no. 6 (July 1884): 75–76.

Museum of Modern Art. *Early Modern Architecture in Chicago 1870–1910: Catalogue of an Exhibition Held at the MoMA, New York January 18 to February 23 1933*. 2nd. ed. New York: Museum of Modern Art, 1940.

Nash, Roderick. *Wilderness and the American Mind*. Orig. pub. 1967. Reprint, New Haven, CT: Yale University Press, 1982.

Neutra, Richard. *Amerika: Die Stilbildung des neuen Bauens in der Vereinigten Staaten*. Vienna: Anton Schroll Verlag, 1930.

———. *Wie baut Amerika? Gegenwartige bauarbeit Amerikanischer kreis*. Stuttgart: Hoffmann, 1927.

"New Business Buildings of Chicago." *Builder* 63, no. 2579 (July 9, 1892): 23-25.

O'Gorman, James F. "The Marshall Field Wholesale Store: Materials toward a Monograph." *Journal of the Society of Architectural Historians* (October 1978): 175–94.

———. *Three American Architects: Richardson, Sullivan, and Wright, 1865–1915*. Chicago: University of Chicago Press, 1991.

"Old and New Chicago. Vast Changes That Have Taken Place in Architecture." *Chicago Daily Tribune*, May 24, 1896, p. 43.

Palladino, Grace. "Skyscrapers, Building Trades Councils, and the Rise of the Structural Building Trades Alliance." In *Skilled Hands, Strong Spirits: A Century of Building Trades History*, 13–26. Ithaca, NY: Cornell University Press, 2005.

SELECTED BIBLIOGRAPHY

Parsons, Lucy, ed. *The Life of Albert R. Parsons*. Chicago, 1889.

———. "Our Civilization. Is It Worth Saving?" *Alarm: A Socialist Weekly* 1, no. 28, August 8, 1885, p. 3.

———. "Word to Tramps." *Alarm: A Socialist Weekly* 1, no. 1, October 4, 1884, p. 1.

Perkins, Lucy Fitch. "The City Beautiful: A Study of the Artistic Possibilities of Chicago." *Inland Architect and News Record* 34, no. 2 (September 1899): 10–14.

Peterson, Jon A. "The Impact of Sanitary Reform upon American Urban Planning, 1840–1890." *Journal of the Society of History* 13, no. 1 (Autumn 1979): 83–103.

Philpott, Thomas Lee. *The Slum and the Ghetto: Immigrants, Blacks and Reformers in Chicago, 1880–1930*. Orig. pub. 1978. Reprint, Belmont, CA: Wadsworth, 1991.

Platt, Harold L. "Jane Addams and the Ward Boss Revisited: Class, Politics and Public Health in Chicago 1890–1938." *Environmental History* 5, no. 2 (2000): 194–222.

———. *Shock Cities: The Environmental Transformation and Reform of Manchester and Chicago*. Chicago: University of Chicago Press, 2005.

———. "Smoke, Gender and the Reform of Environmental Policy in Chicago 1900–1920." *Planning Perspectives* 10, no. 11 (1995): 67–97.

Pommer, Richard, and Barry Bergdoll. "American Architecture and the German Connection." *Kunstchronik* 42, no. 10 (October 1989): 570–74.

Pond, Allen B. "The Evolution of an American Style." *Inland Architect and News Record* 10, no. 9 (January 1888): 98.

Prestiano, Robert. *The Inland Architect: Chicago's Major Architectural Journal 1883–1908*. Ann Arbor, MI: UMI Research Press, 1973.

Rainey, Reuben M. "William Le Baron Jenney and Chicago's West Parks: From Prairies to Pleasure-Grounds." In Waldheim and Ray, *Chicago Architecture*, 37–52.

Ralph, Julian. "Chicago—The Main Exhibit." *Harper's Monthly Magazine* 84 (February 1892): 425–36.

———. "The Highest of All Roof Gardens." *Harper's Weekly* 36 (September 3, 1892): 855.

Rand McNally. *Bird's-Eye Views and Guide to Chicago*. Chicago: Rand McNally, 1898.

Randall, Frank A. *History of the Development of Building Construction in Chicago*. Urbana: University of Illinois Press, 1949.

Rauch, John. *The Sanitary Problems of Chicago, Past and Present*. Chicago, 1879.

Rebori, A. N. "The Work of Burnham and Root, D. H. Burnham and Co., and Graham, Burnham and Co." *Architectural Record* 38, no. 1 (July 1915): 32–168.

"The Reliance Building." *Engineering Magazine* (London), no. 8 (October 1894–March 1895): 896.

"Reliance Building, Chicago, D. H. Burnham and Co., Architects, Ornamental Iron by the Winslow Brothers." *Ornamental Iron* 2, no. 4 (January 1895): 91–101.

Reps, John. *Town Planning in Frontier America*. Princeton, NJ: Princeton University Press, 1969.

Ricker, Nathan Clifford. "Possibilities for American Architecture." *Inland Architect and Builder* 6, no. 5 (November 1885): 62–63.

Rieff, Daniel D. "Viollet-le-Duc and American Nineteenth Century Architecture." *Journal of Architectural Education* 42, no. 1 (Fall 1988): 32–47.

Robinson, Charles Mulford. *Modern Civic Art; or, The City Made Beautiful*. Orig. pub. 1918. Reprint, New York: Arno Press, 1970.

Rodgers, Daniel T. *The Work Ethic in Industrial America, 1850–1920*. Chicago: University of Chicago Press, 1974.

Roediger, David R. *The Wages of Whiteness: Race and the Making of the American Working Class*. London: Verso, 1991.

Roediger, David R., and Philip S. Foner. *Our Own Time: A History of American Labor and the Working Day*. New York: Greenwood Press, 1989.

Roessel, Annemarie van. *Daniel H. Burnham and Chicago's Loop District*. Chicago: Art Institute of Chicago, 1996.

Root, John Wellborn. "Architects of Chicago." *Inland Architect and News Record* 16, no. 8 (January 1891): 91–92.

———. "Architectural Ornamentation." *Inland Architect and Builder* 5 (April 1885): 54–55.

———. "Art of Pure Color." *Inland Architect and Builder* 1, no. 5 (June 1883): 66–67; 1, no. 6 (July 1883): 80, 82; 2, no. 1 (August 1883): 89; 2, no. 2 (September 1883); 106.

———. "Broad Art Criticism." *Inland Architect and News Record* 11 (February 1888): 3–5.

———. "A Great Architectural Problem." *Inland Architect and News Record* 15, no. 5 (June 1890): 67–71.

———. *John Wellborn Root: The Meanings of Architecture; Buildings and Writings*. Edited by Donald Hoffman. New York: Horizon Press, 1967.

———. "Style." *Inland Architect and Builder* 13, no. 10 (January 1887): 99–101.

———. "The Value of Type in Art." *Inland Architect and Builder* 2, no. 4 (November 1883): 132.

Rosen, Christine Meisner. "Businessmen against Pollution in Late Nineteenth Century Chicago." *Business History Review*, no. 69 (Autumn 1995): 351–97.

Rowe, Colin. "Chicago Frame" (1956). In *"The Mathematics of the Ideal Villa" and Other Essays*, 89–117. Cambridge, MA: MIT Press, 1976.

Ruskin, John. *The Stones of Venice*. 3 vols. Orig. pub. 1851–53. Reprint, New York: Garland Publishing, 1979.

Sawislak, Karen. *Smoldering City: Chicagoans and the Great Fire, 1871–74*. Chicago: University of Chicago Press, 1995.

Saxton, Alexander. *The Rise and Fall of the White Republic: Class Politics and Mass Culture in Nineteenth-Century America*. London: Verso, 1990.

Schaack, Michael J. *Anarchy and Anarchists: A History of the Red Terror and the Social Revolution in America and Europe; Communism, Socialism and Nihilism in Doctrine and Deed; The Chicago Haymarket Conspiracy and the Detection and Trial of the Conspirators*. Chicago: F. J. Shulte and Co., 1889.

Schaffer, Kristen. *Daniel H. Burnham: Visionary Architect and Planner*. New York: Rizzoli, 2003.

Schilling, George A. "A History of the Labor Movement in Chicago." In *The Life of Albert R. Parsons with Brief History of the Labor Movement in America*, edited by Lucy Parsons. Chicago: Lucy E. Parsons, 1903.

Schneirov, Richard. *Labor and Urban Politics: Class Conflict and the Origins of Modern Liberalism in Chicago, 1864–97*. Urbana: University of Illinois Press, 1998.

———. *Union Brotherhood, Union Town: The History of the Carpenter's Union of Chicago, 1863–1987*. Carbondale: Southern Illinois University Press, 1988.

Schuyler, Montgomery. *"American Architecture," and Other Writings*. Edited by William Jordy and Ralph Coe. Cambridge, MA: Harvard University Press, Belknap Press, 1961.

———. "Architecture in Chicago: D. H. Burnham and Co." *Architectural Record* 5 (February 1896): 49–72.

———. "Glimpses of Western Architecture: Chicago." *Harper's New Monthly Magazine* 83, no. 495 (August 1891): 395–406.

———. "Modern Architecture." *Architectural Record* 4 (July–September 1894): 1–13.

Schwartz, Vanessa. *Spectacular Realities: Early Mass Culture in Fin-de-Siècle Paris*. Berkeley and Los Angeles: University of California Press, 1998.

Scully, Vincent. *The Shingle Style and the Stick Style*. Orig. pub. 1955; reprint, New Haven, CT: Yale University Press, 1971.

Semper, Gottfried. "Development of Architectural Style," translated by John W. Root and Fritz Wagner. Part 1. *Inland Architect and News Record* 14, no. 7 (December 1889): 76, 78.

———. "Development of Architectural Style," translated by John W. Root and Fritz Wagner. Part 2. *Inland Architect and News Record* 12, no. 8 (January 1890): 92–94.

———. "Development of Architectural Style," translated by John W. Root and Fritz Wagner. Part 3. *Inland Architect and News Record* 15, no. 1 (February 1890): 5–6.

———. "Development of Architectural Style," translated by John W. Root and Fritz Wagner. Part 4. *Inland Architect and News Record* 15, no. 2 (March 1890), 32–33.

———. *"The Four Elements of Architecture" and Other Writings* [1851]. Translated by Harry Francis Mallgrave and Wolfgang Herrmann. Cambridge: Cambridge University Press, 1989.

Shankland, Edward Clapp. "Steel Skeleton Construction in Chicago." *Journal of the Institution of Civil Engineers* 128 (1896–97): 12–13.

Shore, Elliott, Ken Fones, and James P. Darby. *The German-American Radical Press: The Shaping of a Left Political Culture, 1850–1940*. Chicago: University of Illinois Press, 1992.

Siry, Joseph. *Carson Pirie Scott: Louis Sullivan and the Chicago Department Store*. Chicago: University of Chicago Press, 1988.

———. *The Chicago Auditorium Building: Adler and Sullivan's Architecture and the City*. Chicago: University of Chicago Press, 2002.

Slotkin, Richard. *The Fatal Environment: The Myth of the Frontier in the Age of Industrialization 1800–1890*. New York: Atheneum, 1985.

Smith, Carl. *The Plan of Chicago: Daniel Burnham and the Remaking of the American City*. Chicago: University of Chicago Press, 2006.

———. *Urban Disorder and the Shape of Belief: The Great Chicago Fire, the Haymarket Bomb and the Model Town of Pullman*. Chicago: University of Chicago Press, 1995.

Smith, Henry Nash. *Virgin Land: The American West as Symbol and Myth*. Orig. pub. 1950. Reprint, Cambridge, MA: Harvard University Press, 1978.

Solomonson, Katherine. *The Chicago Tribune Tower Competition: Skyscraper Design and Cultural Change in the 1920s*. Chicago: University of Chicago Press, 2001.

Spain, Daphne. *How Women Saved the City*. Minneapolis: University of Minnesota Press, 2001.

Spencer, Herbert. "The Sources of Architectural Types" (1852). In *Essays: Scientific, Political and Speculative*, 2:371–80. New York: D. Appleton and Co., 1910.

Starrett, Theodore. "John Wellborn Root." *Architecture and Building* 44, no. 11 (November 1912): 429–31.

Starrett, W. A. *Skyscrapers and the Men Who Built Them*. New York: Charles Scribner and Sons, 1928.

Steadman, Philip. *The Evolution of Designs: Biological Analogy in Architecture and the Applied Arts*. New York: Cambridge University Press, 1979.

Stein, Roger B. *John Ruskin and Aesthetic Thought in America, 1840–1900*. Cambridge, MA: Harvard University Press, 1967.

Stratton, Michael. *The Terra Cotta Revival: Building Innovation and the Industrial City in Britain and North America*. London: Victor Gollancz, 1993.

Sudduth, H. T. "La Salle St. Chicago." *Harper's Weekly* 34 (May 31, 1890): 346–47.

Sullivan, Louis. *Autobiography of an Idea*. Orig. pub. 1924. Reprint, New York: Dover Publications, 1956.

———. "Characteristics and Tendencies of American Architecture." *Inland Architect and Builder* 6 (November 1885): 58–59.

———. *Democracy: A Man Search* (1905–8). Introduction by Elaine Hedges. Detroit: Wayne State University Press, 1961.

———. "The High Building Question." *Graphic* 5 (December 19, 1891): 405.

———. *"Kindergarten Chats" and Other Writings*. Orig. pub. 1918. Reprint, New York: Dover, 1979.

———. *Louis Sullivan: The Public Papers*. Edited by Robert Twombley. Chicago: University of Chicago Press, 1988.

———. "The Tall Office Building Artistically Considered." *Inland Architect and News Record* 27 (February 1896): 32.

———. "What Is the Just Subordination, in Architectural Design, of Details to Mass?" *Inland Architect and Builder* 9, no. 5 (April 1887): 51–54.

Swenarton, Mark. *Artisans and Architects: The Ruskinian Tradition in Architectural Thought*. London: Macmillan Press, 1989.

Szczygiel, Bonj, and Robert Hewitt. "Nineteenth Century Medical Landscapes: John H. Rauch, Frederick Law Olmsted and the Search for Salubrity." *Bulletin of the History of Medicine* 74, no. 4 (2000): 708–34.

Szuberla, Guy. "Irving Kane Pond: A Michigan Architect in Chicago." *Old Northwest* 5, no. 2 (Summer 1979): 109–40.

Tafuri, Manfredo, and Francesco Dal Co. *Modern Architecture*. New York: Harry N. Abrams, Inc., 1977.

"Tale of a Skyscraper. Curious Statistics about the Monadnock Building." *Chicago Daily Tribune*, February 24, 1896, p. 3.

Tallmadge, Thomas. *Architecture in Old Chicago*. Chicago: University of Chicago Press, 1941.

———. ed. *The Origin of the Skyscraper*. Chicago: Alderbrink Press, 1931.

Taut, Bruno. *Modern Architecture*. London: The Studio, 1929.

———. *Die neue Baukunst in Europa und Amerika*. Stuttgart: Verlag Julius Hoffmann, 1929.

"To the Workingmen of America." *Alarm: A Socialist Weekly* 1, no. 5, November 1, 1884, p. 1.

"To What Extent Is It Necessary in Design to Emphasize the Essentially Structural Elements of a Building?" *Inland Architect and News Record* 9, no. 6 (May 1887): 59–62.

Trachtenberg, Alan. *The Incorporation of America: Culture and Society in the Gilded Age*. New York: Hill and Wang, 1982.

Tunnick, Susan. *Terra-Cotta Skyline: New York's Architectural Ornament*. New York: Princeton Architectural Press, 1997.

Turak, Theodore. "The Ecole Centrale and Modern Architecture: The Education of William Le Baron Jenney." *Journal of the Society of Architectural Historians* 29, no. 1 (March 1970): 40–47.

———. "William Le Baron Jenney, Teacher." *Threshold: Journal of the University of Illinois at Chicago School of Architecture* (Fall 1991): 61–82.

Turner, Frederick Jackson. *The Significance of the Frontier in American History*. Orig. pub. 1893. Reprint, New York: Henry Holt and Co., 1920.

Twombly, Robert. "Cuds and Snipes: Labor at Chicago's Auditorium Building, 1887–89." *Journal of American Studies* 31 (1997): 79–101.

———. *Louis Sullivan: His Life and Work*. New York: Viking Penguin, 1986.

Twose, George M. R. "Steel and Terra Cotta Buildings in Chicago." *Brickbuilder* 3 (1894): 1–5.

———. "The Use of Terra-Cotta in Modern Buildings." *Engineering Magazine* 8 (October 1894–March 1895): 203–19.

Tyler, Helen E. *Where Prayer and Purpose Meet: The Women's Christian Temperance Union Story*. Evanston, IL: Signal Press, 1949.

Van Brunt, Henry. *Architecture and Society: Selected Essays of Henry Van Brunt*. Edited by William A. Coles. Cambridge, MA: Harvard University Press, Belknap Press, 1969.

———. "Architecture in the West." *Inland Architect and News Record* 14, no. 7 (December 1889): 78–80.

———. "John Wellborn Root." *Inland Architect and News Record* 16, no. 8 (January 1891): 85–88.

———. "On the Present Condition and Prospects of Architecture." *Atlantic Monthly* 57 (January–June 1886): 374.

Van Eck, Caroline. *Organicism in Nineteenth-Century Architecture: An Inquiry into Its Theoretical and Philosophical Roots*. Amsterdam: Architectura and Natura Press, 1994.

Van Leeuwen, Thomas A. P. "The Skyward Trend of Thought: Some Ideas on the History of the Methodology of the Skyscraper." In *American Architecture: Innovation and Tradition*, ed. David G. DeLong, Helen Searing, and Robert A. M. Stern, 57–81. New York: Rizzoli, 1986.

Van Zanten, David. "Architectural Polychromy: Life in Architecture." In *The Beaux-Arts and Nineteenth-Century French Architecture*, ed. Robin Middleton, 196–215. Cambridge, MA: MIT Press, 1982.

———. "The Centrality of the Columbian Exposition in the History of Chicago Architecture." In Waldheim and Ray, *Chicago Architecture*, 30–36.

———. "The Nineteenth Century: The Projecting of Chicago as a Commercial City and the Rationalization of Design and Construction." In *Chicago and New York: Architectural Interactions*, 30–49. Chicago: Art Institute of Chicago, 1984.

———. "Sullivan to 1890." In *Louis Sullivan: The Function of Ornament*, ed. Wim de Wit, 13–64. New York: W.W. Norton, 1986.

———. *Sullivan's City: The Meaning of Ornament for Louis Sullivan*. New York: W. W. Norton, 2000.

Vickers, R. H. "Development of American Architecture." *Inland Architect and Builder* 3, no. 4 (May 1884): 50.

Vidler, Anthony. *The Architectural Uncanny: Essays in the Modern Unhomely*. Cambridge, MA: MIT Press, 1992.

———. *Warped Space: Art, Architecture, and Anxiety in Modern Culture*. Cambridge, MA: MIT Press, 2000.

Viollet-le-Duc, Eugène-Emmanuel. *Discourse on Architecture*. Translated by Henry Van Brunt. Boston: James R. Osgood and Co., 1875.

———. *Habitations of Man in All Ages*. Translated by Benjamin Bucknall. London: Sampson Low, Marston, Searle, and Rivington, 1876.

Waid, D. E. "Recent Brick and Terra-Cotta Work in American Cities." *Brickbuilder* 4 (June 1895): 132.

———. "Terra-Cotta Work in Skeleton Construction." *Brickbuilder* 3 (October 1894): 216.

Waldheim, Charles, and Katerina Ruedi Ray, eds. *Chicago Architecture: Histories, Revisions, Alternatives*. Chicago: University of Chicago Press, 2005.

Walker, C. Howard. "The Grouping of Public Buildings in a Great City." Part 2. *Inland Architect and News Record* 37, no. 1 (February 1901): 3.

———. "Municipal Laws in Relation to Architecture." *Inland Architect and News Record* 34, no. 6 (January 1900): 42–43.

Ward, David. *Cities and Immigrants: A Geography of Change in Nineteenth-Century America*. New York: Oxford University Press, 1971.

———. *Poverty, Ethnicity and the American City 1840–1925*. New York: Cambridge University Press, 1989.

Weingarden, Lauren S. "The Colors of Nature: Louis Sullivan's Architectural Polychromy and Nineteenth-Century Color Theory." *Winterthur Portfolio* 20, no. 4 (Winter 1985): 243–60.

———. "Naturalized Nationalism: A Ruskinian Discourse on the Search for an American Style of Architecture." *Winterthur Portfolio* 24, no. 1 (Spring 1989): 43–68.

Wermiel, Sara E. *The Fireproof Building: Technology and Public Safety in the Nineteenth-Century American City*. Baltimore: Johns Hopkins University Press, 2000.

"What Are the Present Tendencies of Architectural Design in America?" *Inland Architect and News Record* 9, no. 3 (March 1887): 23–26.

"What Are Some of the Architectural Possibilities of Such Materials as Paper and Glass etc.?" *Inland Architect and News Record* 10 (June 1887): 88–90.

"What Is the Just Subordination in Architectural Design of Detail to Mass?" *Inland Architect and News Record* 9, no. 5 (April 1887): 51–54.

Wight, Peter B. "Daniel Hudson Burnham and His Associates." *Architectural Record* 38, no. 1 (July 1915): 3–7.

———. "The Development of New Phases of the Fine Arts in America." *Inland Architect and Builder* 4, no. 4 (November 1884): 51–53; 4, no. 5 (December 1884): 63–65.

———. "Modern Architecture in Chicago." *Pall Mall* 18 (July 1899): 299.

Wigley, Mark. *White Walls, Designer Dresses: The Fashioning of Modern Architecture*. Cambridge, MA: MIT Press, 1996.

Willis, Carol. *Form Follows Finance: Skyscrapers and Skylines in New York and Chicago*. New York: Princeton Architectural Press, 1995.

Wilson, Elizabeth. *The Sphinx in the City: Urban Life, the Control of Disorder, and Women*. Berkeley and Los Angeles: University of California Press, 1991.

Wilson, William H. *The City Beautiful Movement*. Baltimore: Johns Hopkins University Press, 1989.

Winslow Brothers Co. *Collection of Photographs of Ornamental Iron Executed by the Winslow Brothers Co.* Chicago: Winslow Brothers, 1893.

Wolff, Jane. "The Chicago Parks: Tableaus of Naturalization." In Waldheim and Ray, *Chicago Architecture*, 176–80.

Woods, Mary N. "The First American Architectural Journals: The Profession's Voice." *Journal of the Society of Architectural Historians* 48 (June 1989): 117–38.

———. *From Craft to Profession: The Practice of Architecture in the Nineteenth Century*. Berkeley and Los Angeles: University of California Press, 1999.

Wright, Frank Lloyd. "The Art and Craft of the Machine" (1901). In *Frank Lloyd Wright Collected Writings*, vol. 1, *1894–1930*, edited by Bruce Brooks Pfeiffer, 58–69. New York: Rizzoli, 1992.

Wright, Gwendolyn. *Moralism and the Model Home: Domestic Architecture and Cultural Conflict in Chicago 1873–1913*. Chicago: University of Chicago Press, 1980.

Zukowsky, John, ed. *Chicago Architecture 1872–1922: Birth of a Metropolis*. New York: Prestel, 1987.

INDEX

Note: Italicized page numbers indicate illustrations.